'Peter Fiennes really can see the wood for the trees – he blends mythology, natural history and a sense of righteous anger to produce a paean of praise to our ancient woodlands and modern forests, and the life support system they provide.'

Stephen Moss, author of *Wild Kingdom*

'A tender hymn to the trees, a manifesto for a woodland society, a contemporary gazette of ideas and attitudes radiating into the future like annual rings from the original pith … In this lyrical, informative, unashamedly arboreal propaganda, one man's walk in the woods can inspire a generation.'

Paul Evans, author of *Field Notes from the Edge*

'Fiennes is the best of guides, gently, eloquently and with a fierce humour telling a sad story – relating chapters of fascinating detail to brighten his tale and quoting the poets as he goes.'

John Wright, author of *A Natural History of the Hedgerow*

Footnotes

A Journey Round Britain
in the Company of Great Writers

Peter Fiennes

ONEWORLD

A Oneworld Book

First published by Oneworld Publications, 2019

Copyright © Peter Fiennes 2019

The moral right of Peter Fiennes to be identified as the Author of this work has been asserted by him in accordance with the Copyright, Designs, and Patents Act 1988

ISBN 978-1-78607-629-8
eISBN 978-1-78607-630-4

Typeset by Tetragon, London
Printed and bound in Great Britain by Clays Ltd, Elcograf S.p.A.

Illustrations © Alice Carter

Oneworld Publications
10 Bloomsbury Street
London WC1B 3SR
England

Stay up to date with the latest books,
special offers, and exclusive content from
Oneworld with our newsletter

Sign up on our website
oneworld-publications.com

MIX
Paper from
responsible sources
FSC® C018072

'He's gone: but you can see
his tracks still, in the snow of the world.'

NORMAN MACCAIG, 'PRAISE OF A MAN'

1. ENID BLYTON

2. WILKIE COLLINS

3. WILKIE COLLINS & ITHELL COLQUHOUN

4. CELIA FIENNES

5. GERALD OF WALES

6. EDITH SOMERVILLE & VIOLET 'MARTIN' ROSS

7. BERYL BAINBRIDGE & J. B. PRIESTLEY

8. CHARLES DICKENS & WILKIE COLLINS

9. SAMUEL JOHNSON & JAMES BOSWELL

10. BERYL BAINBRIDGE & J. B. PRIESTLEY

11. *IN THE PUB...*

12. CHARLES DICKENS

THE ISLE OF SKYE
DUNVEGAN
PORTREE
URQUHART CASTLE
LOCH NESS

EDINBURGH

CARLISLE   ⑩   NEWCASTLE

⑧   BRADFORD
MANCHESTER
LIVERPOOL   ⑨   DONCASTER
CHESTER
LINCOLN

SNOWDON
⑥
WELSHPOOL

STRATA FLORIDA   PRESTEIGNE   ⑦   BIRMINGHAM
⑤   BOURNVILLE
ST DAVID'S
HEREFORD
CARDIFF   GLOUCESTER   LONDON
MANORBIER
BRISTOL   BATH   WESTMINSTER   GAD'S HILL
GLASTONBURY   ABBEY   ⑫
TAUNTON   ②
LAUNCESTON   ④   WAREHAM
EXETER   ①   SWANAGE
PLYMOUTH
LAND'S END
LAMORNA COVE   ③   LIZARD

Contents

*Footnotes**

Preface

'But once in my life ... I did have a feeling that the
world was a phantom. That was when I was in England.'

NIRAD C. CHAUDHURI, *A PASSAGE TO ENGLAND*

The premise of this book is simple, or that is what it seemed
when I started. I was going to travel around Britain in the footsteps of a succession of (mostly) famous writers, without leaving
any gaps, and without straying from their recorded paths, passing
from one to the next like a baton in a relay, or a snowball swelling
as it rolls, picking up people and debris along the way. I was keen
to take in as much of the country as I could, but I also decided,
for no good reason, that the journey should unspool in one continuous loop.

My first idea was to organize the route chronologically. The
earliest journey made here is by Gerald of Wales (1188) and the
most recent is by Beryl Bainbridge, who smoked her way around
England almost eight hundred years later. But then I thought it
would be more interesting to move from childhood (Enid Blyton in
the Isle of Purbeck) to death (Charles Dickens, whose corpse was
shunted by train from his home in Gad's Hill, Kent, to Westminster
Abbey). The ghost of that second idea remains, faint traces of the
Seven Ages of Man (there's even a mid-life crisis), although we all
know that the best journeys never go entirely to plan.

I was pleased I started with Enid Blyton. Her influence runs
deep in all of us, I came to believe – or at least her idea of what

Britain should be has proved surprisingly tenacious. I nosed around her life and *Footnotes* became an attempt to understand her, and the other writers, by looking at the places they had travelled through and written about. Enid is the only one who doesn't actually go anywhere. That seems appropriate, but I was also happy to discover that she is a much more interesting person than we have been led to believe.

Footnotes also started as a rather grandiose attempt to bring modern Britain into focus by peering through the lens of past writers. I steeped myself in what they had seen and witnessed, tried to adapt to the different ways they thought, absorbed what mattered to them and the tenor of their times … and then stepped into the present. Sometimes it can take a shock, like getting off a train in a foreign land, to open our eyes and ears. Of course it was hopeless. 'The diversity', Orwell wrote, 'the chaos!' But one of the connecting threads of this book is an examination of what conservationists call 'shifting baseline syndrome', the disorientating idea that as every generation passes, our understanding of what is 'normal' moves, without us even realizing it. We can no longer remember, or we have no direct experience of what it was like, to live in a different world. In short, how do we know whether life is getting better, or worse? And not just for humanity. Especially not that. Because surely by now we have all got the message that our lives are not separate from everything that connects and supports us. We urgently need to lift our eyes and take the long view.

Anyway, I should quickly add that I also managed to have a lot of fun, following this opinionated band of writers around Britain. We live in a beautiful land. I indulged a lifetime's obsession with old guidebooks. There is so much to enjoy, from the wilds of Skye and Snowdon to the big night out in Birmingham. And the people. They are so friendly and open. Until, just occasionally, they are not. Of course it is ludicrous to generalize, but even so I did find myself succumbing to a sneaking desire to say something about identity. Who are we? What do we want? They seemed like good questions to ask, in the company of some of our greatest writers, given these restless times.

PETER FIENNES, LONDON, 2019

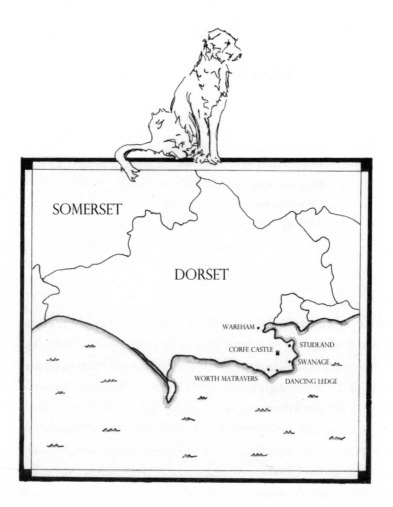

Enid Blyton,
Swanage and the Isle of Purbeck, 1940–1960s

ONE

'I Am Your Storyteller'

'Oh voice of Spring of Youth
Heart's mad delight,
Sing on, sing on, and when the sun is gone
I'll warm me with your echoes
Through the night.'

ENID BLYTON, *SUNDAY TIMES*, 1951

It is April in the Dorset seaside resort of Swanage and the town is struggling to emerge from a long and grisly winter. Not ice-bound, exactly, but the last few months have been dank and chill and unremittingly dreary. Only last week, the 'Beast from the East' had lashed the peninsula's narrow lanes and calcareous hills with a clogging, heavy snow; now it has returned (a 'mini-beast' the papers are calling it), but this time with a supercharged wind, gusting up the Channel, flailing a couple of panicking teenagers on the esplanade and shepherding the town's elderly smokers into the uneasy sanctuary of the bus shelter. Everything, everywhere, is being clawed and rummaged by a foul sleet and the streets are slick with last season's grime. It is, I am certain, the kind of day that Enid Blyton would have described as 'lovely'.

Enid Blyton had no time for bad weather. There really is no such thing if you are wearing the right clothing. And perhaps that is why she always spent her holidays in Swanage and almost never visited sunnier lands. There may have been other reasons, but anyway she was ambivalent about America, disliked Walt

Disney and – while we are at it – was perpetually disappointed in the BBC. Nor did she much care for children who had no interests other than the cinema; nor spoiled, selfish and conceited children; nor mothers who left their homes and their husbands to pursue careers (although this is undeniably odd given her own hard-fought success). As soon as she could, she avoided her brothers and cut her mother dead. She disapproved of divorce, and first husbands (the heavy-drinking type), and the sour opinions of grown-ups, and said she loathed lies and deceit. She was desperately unhappy if she couldn't write, but hated sitting still. And when she was writing, she feared (but used) her subconscious and avoided convoluted plots. She found other people's illnesses alarming or tiresome, along with people with 'inferiority complexes', or anyone who gives up; and she preferred children who are 'ordinary' or 'normal' (although where did that leave her own two daughters?); and she disapproved of cruel, sad tales (Grimm in particular), and girls who think of nothing but boys ('disgusting'), and things that are frightening, and cruelty to animals and birds (especially that: 'I think both those boys should have been well and truly whipped, don't you?'); and interruptions to her work; and silence.

So, it is complicated. And I am sure it would be just as easy for any of us to draw up a list of the things that rile and enrage us – but it is good to remember that there was as much (and more) that Enid Blyton loved. Practical jokes, for example, and laughter. Birdsong. Cherry blossom. The sight and feel of cut flowers. The sea. Summer holidays in the Isle of Purbeck, when she would put aside her typewriter and swim around the pier and play tennis, and finish the prize crossword, and read Agatha Christie novels, and take long walks across the moors, and play with her children, Gillian and Imogen, and transfuse her love of nature straight into their eager young hearts. A round of golf (or sometimes three) in the afternoon. Country lanes. A game of bridge (especially winning). The sunshine of the woods and commons. Her dogs, gardens and husbands. Writing. Writing. Writing. But above all she bathed in the love of the millions of children who devoured her books, and clamoured for her attention, and came to her readings, and joined her clubs, and pursued her with gifts and letters, and visited her at Green Hedges, the large, mock-Tudor home she named and nurtured in Beaconsfield (although, we still have to ask: where did that leave her own two daughters?).

Enid Blyton adored Swanage. Once she'd discovered the place (in the spring of 1931, on a day trip from Bournemouth where she was holidaying with Hugh Pollock, her first husband, and pregnant with her first child, Gillian), she came again and again, often three times a year, sometimes staying for weeks at a time. On that first trip, as she told the 'Dear Boys & Girls' in a letter to *Teachers' World*, she came soaring over the hills on the road from Wareham, driving her 'little car', and saw 'the ruin of an old, old castle' on 'a rounded hill'. It is hard to shake the idea (it's the way she writes) that here is Noddy, rattling into Toyland with grumpy old Big Ears in the passenger seat, rather than Enid crying with delight at her first glimpse of Corfe Castle (and Hugh, hands tight on the wheel, his mind already drifting towards the first strong drink of the day in the lounge bar of the Castle Inn).

The castle hasn't changed much since. Excitingly, the jackdaws that Enid wrote about are still here, dozens of them, puffing up their grey-black feathers and asserting noisy ownership over the ruined battlements. On the day I visit, and sit where Enid once sat, on the soft grass that now covers the old moat, I find their bright, blank gaze disturbing. They stand too close, watching all the time, and seem to be choosing which part of my flesh they'd like to snag with their sharp beaks. But Enid loved them. "'Chack!" they cried, "Chack, chack!"' as she wrote in her letter to the young readers of *Teachers' World*; and then, in the very first of the Famous Five books, *Five on a Treasure Island*, here they are again, swarming all over the ruined castle on Kirrin Island, 'Chack, chack, chack!' – with Timmy the dog leaping into the air and snapping at their cowardly hides.

Everyone is convinced that Corfe Castle was the model for Kirrin Castle, but Enid would never say, and when I ask the taxi driver if it is true (he's a local man, brought up in Corfe, speeding me through the village on the road from Wareham Station to Swanage), his answer is a succinct and scornful 'No'. It is possible he just doesn't want to talk about Enid Blyton. If you only have the output of the BBC to go on, or the memoirs of her second daughter, Imogen, then you are going to be under the impression that Enid was a dysfunctional narcissist, a cold-hearted snob, a racist and the worst of mothers who preferred the company of children she'd never met to the grating shrieks and demands of her own. Perhaps the people of Corfe have had enough of the association. Until recently there was a Blyton-themed shop in the village, called Ginger Pop, but the owner closed it down because the guardians of Enid Blyton's copyright were traducing her memory with a load of overpriced spin-offs and politically correct rewrites. At least, that's how she saw it. She was also irritated by tight-fisted browsers who told her what a lovely shop she was running, but then wandered out without buying anything. There was also, apparently, a spot of bother about some golliwogs in the window.

Anyway, my taxi driver is much more interested in talking about the second homes that are sucking the life out of the village. Enid Blyton never owned a house here, although in 1956 she did buy a farmhouse in north Dorset. She didn't live there – it was rented and used as a working farm – but she did set her eight-eenth Famous Five book, *Five on Finniston Farm*, in its ancient and mysterious passageways. In 1940 Enid had decided to take a room with her two young girls at the Old Ship Inn in Swanage. The place was hit by a Luftwaffe bomb later in the war, after which she tried the Marine Villas on the front and then, as her fame and fortune blossomed, she moved on to the Grosvenor Hotel (since demolished, mercifully; it looked as ugly as a burst spleen). When she tired of the Grosvenor's pretensions, she tried the Grand on the east side of town, which is where I'm heading.

The taxi driver has moved on to the topic of crime. He says there is none (or nothing worth mentioning), and that the people of Purbeck just step out of their homes leaving their front doors unlocked without a backward glance. This is also just about the first thing the late-night barman tells me when I arrive at the Grand ('I moved here from Kilburn and it's nothing like that; it's more like you're living in the 1950s or '60s. No one ever locks their doors'). And again with the two other taxi drivers I meet on the Isle of Purbeck ('Leicester'; '1960s'; 'Huddersfield'; '1950s'; 'never lock my front door, ever'). I can only hope that there are no burglars reading this (living in the here and now, finding it hard to make ends meet among the well-locked doors of London or Liverpool). They'd fill their boots.

Still, this is clearly something that draws people to the Isle of Purbeck. The hope that they can sidestep everything that has gone wrong elsewhere: splintered communities, broken homes, soaring crime rates, metrification. It's a backwater wrapped in a time warp. And although the Isle of Purbeck is not a real island (it's a peninsula, in the shape of an upside-down goat's head, bounded by the River Frome to the north and a small stream near East Lulworth to the west), I suspect this desire to seal herself off is what brought Enid here too. Even in 1942, when Vera Lynn's latest hit, 'The White Cliffs of Dover', was playing from every gramophone in the land, Swanage must have felt like a place out of time and cut off from the rest of Britain.

There are mixed messages about Swanage in the guidebooks of Enid's day. In 1935 Paul Nash denounced the place in the *Shell Guide to Dorset* as 'perhaps the most beautiful natural site on the South Coast, ruined by two generations of "development" prosecuted without discrimination or scruple'. The *Penguin Guide to Wilts and Dorset* (1949) is more forgiving, and I prefer to think Enid had this one on her hotel bedside table. 'Swanage', the writer purrs, 'is an outstanding example of the little fishing village grown up into something better.'

Today, the brutal wind is making it hard to get a fix on Swanage. A mucky brown scurf has gathered in foamy clumps where the sea meets the shore. It is especially thick at the groynes, where occasionally it is whipped up and flung onto the esplanade, scattering into tiny flecks that fly through the air before fizzling out on the windscreens of neatly parked cars. Inflatable beach toys are bucking against each other in the shop fronts, shaking off sprays of sleet and squeaking in plastic distress. Damp bunting is pressed against the awnings. The shops and streets are almost deserted. It's cold outside, but inside the Ship, where Enid (aged forty-two) stayed with Gillian (eight) and Imogen (five) in 1940, they are showing a Premier League football match on the wall-filling TV and there's the close, happy atmosphere that all good pubs have when the afternoon is young, the weather is wild, a fire is burning, and everyone has decided that they might as well stay for another. A man leaning heavily on the bar tells me that the local Purbeck beer is good, but he draws a blank when I ask him about Enid Blyton. He moved here recently from somewhere in the North (Preston, was it?), and (gesturing vaguely) lives just up the road. I ask if he has locked his front door and he gives me a sharp look.

In mid-1940 Enid had been married to Captain Hugh Alexander Pollock for fifteen years, although Hugh was not on

holiday with his family this time. He was probably at home at
Green Hedges, helping organize the local Home Guard, which
he'd joined a few months earlier. Hugh was a veteran of the First
World War, too old to fight in this latest conflagration (he was
fifty-one), but desperate to do something. He'd first enlisted in
1912 – he was an army regular by the time the First World War
started – and for four years he'd seen almost continuous service in
Gallipoli, Palestine and France. After the war ended, he'd stayed
on as a temporary captain in the Indian Army, before becoming
an editor at the London publishing company George Newnes. It
was here, almost as soon as his feet were under the desk, that he
had written to Enid Blyton, an inordinately ambitious, but so far
only moderately successful, children's author, and suggested that
they collaborate on a book about zoos. He met her for the first
time, briefly, in his offices on 1 February 1924, an event marked
by Enid in her diary:

> Met Phil [a female friend] at 2.45 & we went & had
> coffee together till 3.30. Then I went to see Pollock. He
> wanted to know if I'd do a child's book of the Zoo! He
> asked me to meet him at Victoria tomorrow to go to the
> zoo. I said I would. Home at 5.

Now, I don't know how much of what follows was commonplace
in the world of publishing in the 1920s, but Hugh clearly had
more on his mind than books and zoos. His transparently cunning
suggestion was that he and Enid should meet at Victoria station
(she would travel up from Surbiton, taking time off from her work
as a nursery governess), before proceeding to Regent's Park and
London Zoo, where they could discuss the possible book. In the
event, things moved bewilderingly fast, as Enid noted in her diary
entry for 2 February, the very next day:

> Met Hugh at two. Went to the Zoo and looked around.
> Taxied to Piccadilly Restaurant and had tea and talked
> till six! He was very nice. We're going to try and be real
> friends and not fall in love! – not yet at any rate. We are
> going to meet again tomorrow.

And so they did. The next day they were discussing 'the zoo book' over a long walk in the park followed by tea in the Piccadilly restaurant. Enid was dazzled by this trim, authoritative, older, military man (he was thirty-five to her twenty-six). And when Hugh (after just two days) tried to suggest to the ferociously focused Enid that their friendship should be 'platonic for 3 months' and (in a letter written on 5 February) that he was 'fond' of her in 'a big brotherly sort of way', Enid raged in her diary: 'I'll small sister him.' The next day (just four days after they had met for the first time), Enid wrote:

> Wrote a long letter to Hugh till 9 telling him exactly
> what I think. Guess he won't like it much, but he's
> going to fall in love if he hasn't already. I want him
> for mine.

And that was that. If Enid ever wanted something, she tended to get it. Sure, there were some hurdles along the way, but the end was never in doubt. For one thing, Hugh had to let his first, estranged wife know that he wanted a divorce. He'd married Marion Atkinson in 1913 and they'd had two boys (the elder, William, dying in 1916). Marion had left Hugh for another man when he was away fighting – and I'm sure this rejection explains another part of the appeal of Enid for Hugh. In most ways she really was very young for her years, and Hugh craved unwavering commitment.

Progress, as mapped out in Enid's diary, was breathless. On 21 February she had 'a glorious love letter from Hugh this morning. Such a lovely, lovely one. He is a lovely lover.'

On 23 February 'We had taxied to Victoria and Hugh took me in his strong arms & kissed my hair ever so for the first time. We had dinner at Victoria & I caught the 10.30 train. It was a lovely, lovely day. I do love dear, lovely Hugh.'

On 29 February they went to their first dance together ('I loved it & loved it'), and through March they dined at Rules in Covent Garden and strolled in Embankment Gardens and the Tivoli. By the end of the month they were shopping for signet rings together. In mid-April they were on holiday in Seaford ('We went for a walk to Hope Gap, & sat on the downs, & Hugh was a darling lover'); she missed him horribly when he went back to London. In early June Hugh presented Enid with a ring ('it's a LOVELY one'). July found them flat-hunting in Chelsea. And on 28 August 1924 they were married at Bromley Register Office. It was a small affair – with no room for her mother.

If Hugh was looking for uninhibited innocence, someone to soothe his wartime nerves with love and fill his days with chatter and japes, then Enid (who'd hardly been to a dance, or dated a man, but who was burning with pent-up desire for a husband, and her own children, and kittens, and a fox terrier, and a cottage with roses and honeysuckle clambering at the door and her very own garden, heaving with hollyhocks, pixies and frogs), then Enid was manna from heaven. And perhaps what Enid didn't notice, or understand, was quite how deeply Hugh had been scarred by the war. Even in their first weeks they would 'row ferociously'. They argued over who would be 'master' in their marriage and after a miserable day Enid was glad to tell Hugh that it would be him. Enid gave her ring back at least once. She discovered that Hugh could draw from a bottomless well of possessive jealousy – he even managed to be suspicious of an unknown man who was coming to stay in their boarding home when he and Enid were taking a short (chaperoned) holiday. On 7 May she had written in her diary: 'But oh I do so wish he would get over his jealousy. It makes me afraid of marrying him.' And perhaps, also, Enid didn't grasp the significance of Hugh's frequent 'flus and food poisonings and occasional absences and dark moods. He had surely been drinking hard since the war, and despite Enid's hopes that she had found someone 'masterful', she (with her unwavering certainty and bright clear path to the future) was in truth a lifeline flung to a floundering man.

And they loved one another – wholeheartedly and thrillingly. It's too easy to poke around someone's diary (especially, let's face it, Enid Blyton's) and find things to snigger at. Her language is limited (just how 'lovely' can everything be?) and at times jarringly old-fashioned. She buys a 'ripping new attaché case'. They go to see Jackie Coogan in *Long Live the King* and 'it was topping'. She misses Hugh when he's not there and 'it's BEASTLY'. His 'eyes were as blue as the water' she confides, or sometimes 'the sky', and on 22 March, on Hugh's first visit to her home, 'We stayed in the drawing room by ourselves and Hugh loved me tremendously.' But not like that! Because before you start imagining a scene that never unfolded (or at least not yet), it turns out that on this occasion Enid was simply sitting at Hugh's knee while he read Kipling at her.

It is hard to believe that there really was a time when millions of people talked as though they were stopping off for tea and a restrained and unconsummated affair at a station café in Carnforth. Clipped and constipated. Ripping and topping. But there they all were (it wasn't just something they put on for the films and the newsreels) – and (to state the bleeding obvious) their emotions and actions were just the same as ours. To take one tiny example, here is an entry in Enid's daughter Gillian's diary from July 1946: 'Today I got 7 for French. We swam in gym. It was wizard.' And indeed I grew up in a household where my mother (born 1922) was always asking me to 'go and make love to' my aunt or the elderly next-door neighbour, and all she expected (I presume) was for me to ask them nicely to lend us some sugar or help with the hoovering. Perhaps what needs saying is that the language Enid Blyton uses in her books may have dated, but it was undeniably authentic.

Anyway, enough of that. The weather hasn't improved when I finally drag myself away from the public bar of the Ship Inn, but I am eager to get on the trail of Enid Blyton. She knew these Swanage streets well – she used to sign books at Hill & Churchill's bookshop (now closed) and take long daily swims from the beach (a horrible thought on this bitter day). And it was here, in 1940 (with the beach closed and littered with tank traps and the town alert to the possibility of spies and fifth columnists), that she came up with the idea of the Famous Five books, a series of rollicking adventures starring four gloriously unsupervised children and a monomaniacally heroic rescue dog.

Swanage would have been smaller in Enid's day: more compact and Victorian. But it's still an easy, fun-loving place (I can see that much through the driving sleet), and its essence is surely unchanged: a fishing village turned pleasure beach, with big wide skies looping over a great scoop of a bay, flanked by low, treeless hills. There's a jaunty pier, in front of which are the Georgian Marine Villas, where Enid and the children stayed in the summer of 1941. It seems strange to think of Enid ploughing ahead with her summer holidays as the war raged, the children under strict orders to avoid the beach and the freshly poured concrete pillboxes, but instead heading inland to the moors, or east along the coast towards Old Harry Rocks.

That said, Enid had a talent for avoiding inconvenient or distressing developments and even a world war couldn't disrupt her routine for long, or staunch the flow of words. In 1941 she published twelve books, despite paper shortages; in 1942 there were twenty-six, including *Five on a Treasure Island*. This ability (or desire) to ignore or blank what she didn't want to see is not that unusual, of course, and the war years were a time of huge creative ferment for Enid, although it is also incredible to think that she only really achieved her final, world-conquering momentum in the 1950s. Barbara Stoney, in her biography of Enid Blyton, lists an eye-bleeding seventy (seventy!) books published in 1955, including – but most certainly not limited to – countless Bible and New Testament stories, *Mr Tumpy in the Land of Boys and Girls*, what seems like a dozen Noddy books, another Famous Five outing (the fourteenth), *Clicky the Clockwork Clown*, a Secret Seven book (the seventh), more adventures from Bobs, her long-dead fox terrier, *Robin Hood*, *Neddy the Little Donkey*, *Enid Blyton's Foxglove Story Book*, *Bimbo and Blackie Go Camping*, something to do with golliwogs, *Mr Pink-Whistle's Party* (good grief) – and on and on and on.

As I battle my way through the wind and the rain along the fringes of Swanage's empty esplanade, I come across the Mowlem Swanage Rep Theatre, a squat, square, post-Enid building, heavy with glass and concrete, today showing *Peter Rabbit*. The very young and the elderly are well catered for in Swanage – you can see it in the many benches and greens and places selling sticky treats – and so indeed are dairy lovers. Parked out front of the theatre is a dark 'Swanage Dairy' van, on its side a nicely etched pledge, written large, to fulfil 'all your dairy supplies'. I remember when my eldest daughter was young how much she loved her Noddy videos, in particular one called, I think, *Noddy Helps Out* (doesn't he just), in which Toyland's milkman is feeling droopily depressed about something. I have no idea what his problem was – I'm certainly not going to watch the damn thing again – but the tape played on an eternal loop, grimly soundtracked by the milkman's plaintive cries: 'Milk-O! Milk-O!' and little Noddy's insufferable laughter. 'Milk-O! Milk-O-o-o!' I have been haunted by his misery ever since. If you think about it, every single one of Enid Blyton's stories is concerned with resolving someone's unhappiness – the bullied are rescued, wrongdoers are punished and redeemed, the righteous are rewarded – although she was always adamant that the story was what mattered. The message ('all the Christian teaching I had … has coloured every book I have written for you') had to be smuggled in, 'because I am a storyteller, not a preacher'.

Enid Blyton also said that the ideas for her stories, and the people and places she put in them, did not come from real life but from her prodigious imagination (no giggling at the back, not until *you've* become the world's bestselling children's author). She said that once she had enough to get started (perhaps the setting, the main characters and a hazy outline of the beginnings of the first scene) she only had to sit at her typewriter, empty her mind and everything (the people, the fairies, the teddy bears, dogs and dolls, the plot and the dialogue) would all just unspool onto the page. As she put it in a series of letters to the psychologist Peter McKellar, she lowered herself into a sort of trance – think of Homer and his Muse – and the words flowed. So if, say, she had decided to write about a girl's boarding school, and she wanted the main character to be exceptionally naughty, she would close her eyes and a girl called Elizabeth and her friends and the scenes would appear. All she had to do was write them down. Conversations, jokes, names of characters … she said she didn't even know where most of this stuff came from. It just billowed out of her.

In her early years she tended to write in the morning, or in the cracks in the day, but later, when she was a full-time author, she would carry on till sundown, working to a rigid routine, breaking

at set times for lunch, letter-writing, the crossword, a spot of gar-
dening, tea with the children and supper with her husband. If she
wrote 6,000 words in a day that was generally enough to merit
a mention in her diary. Over 10,000 were cause for celebration.
A Famous Five book could be written in a couple of weeks. She
wrote in her autobiography, *The Story of My Life*: 'If you could
lock me up into a room for two, three or four days, with just my
typewriter and paper, some food and a bed to sleep in when I was
tired, I could come out from that room with a book finished and
complete, a book of, say, sixty thousand words.'

In all she wrote a staggering 750 books, but no one (not even
Enid) could be quite sure about the exact number. She had them
all lined up in her library at Green Hedges, but there was always
a nagging feeling that there was something missing. And it wasn't
just the books. There was the poetry, the plays and pantomimes,
the magazine articles (she edited and wrote most of *Enid Blyton's
Magazine* and *Sunny Stories* and poured out articles for *Teachers'
World*), the hundreds of thousands of letters to her young fans,
the household she ran, the tennis and golf and gardens, and the
adult play (never produced nor seen again after its rejection – it
was, said her daughter Imogen, with damning relish, 'shallow and
trivial' and 'never reached the stage and would not have run for
a week if it had'). There were the illustrations to organize and
approve (she had an immaculate eye for what would work: just
look at Eileen Soper's exquisitely evocative Famous Five draw-
ings; or the pin-perfect artwork by the Dutch artist Harmsen van
der Beek for Noddy, who seems to have worked himself to death
trying to keep up with Enid's industrial output). And there were
the printers to oversee, proofs to approve, publishing contracts
to negotiate (she enjoyed that, and spread herself across several
different companies), the interviews, the talks to children (and oh
how she loved those talks). And her *clubs*! And the charities, her

own and others; she was quietly generous with her time and her burgeoning fortune.

In short, Enid's days were laden with work. She went to bed early, armed with one small medicinal sherry, got up early and got busy. She was heartbroken when, in the 1950s, people started to suggest that one person couldn't possibly be solely responsible for this extraordinary deluge of print. She worked so hard, driven by ambition, of course, but also an absolute dedication to her reading public and a desire to get her message across, a message that as the years went by was deliberately posed as a riposte to all that money-mad stuff coming out of America and Disney. And then to hear the rumours that it wasn't even *her* creating these lovingly crafted stories, but some kind of Blyton factory, staffed with bored typists, tapping away all day, slipping in the word 'lovely' every now and then, after all, how hard could this tosh be, right? It was agonizing. She was so upset that in 1955 she even sued some hapless young South African librarian, who had dared to suggest that 'Enid Blyton' was a fraud. Enid won the case, the librarian was forced to apologize, but it didn't settle the rumours. And also: what kind of paranoid ingrate takes a *librarian* to court? What, people wondered, not for the first time, does Enid Blyton have to hide? For an author whose public persona was so intimately entwined with her works, this rosy-cheeked, country-dwelling, dog-loving, flower-gathering, pie-baking, laughing, hugging, storytelling *mother* of two adoring *children* – any whiff of some alternative reality was potentially devastating.

We can't say that Enid Blyton invented the author-as-brand (that was probably Charles Dickens). In fact she wasn't even the first children's author to package up her life and her books into one appetizing and marketable story (I guess that would be Beatrix Potter), but it is hard to think of any other author, before or since, who worked so relentlessly on cultivating her own success and burnishing her public image. Once she had decided, as a young child, to become an author (and a children's author at that), she was extraordinarily consistent in how she appeared to the world. She ploughed through every obstacle. She happily admitted to having received dozens (hundreds?) of rejection slips. We praise the resilience of others (think of J. K. Rowling writing in that Edinburgh café, shivering as she fumbled open yet another envelope of bad news), but with Enid Blyton her blinkered refusal to give in and go away is seen by some as rather sinister. Publishers who tried to reject her early stories and poems about flower fairies and thistledown were simply treated to more of the same. In the end most of them succumbed – particularly when they got a whiff of the sales.

Enid understood better than anyone the importance of tending her brand. She ensured her wartime divorce (and swift remarriage) was kept secret from the world by swapping husbands (and her married name) while everyone's attention was elsewhere. After the war was over she carried on as though nothing had changed, except the children's 'daddy' was no longer a man in uniform, he was a doctor called Kenneth. Gillian and Imogen are still there in the family photos, stroking kittens and riding horses, but it was now Enid and twinkly Dr Kenneth Darrell Waters who were looking on fondly. The change of name didn't matter, because Enid was never Mrs Pollock or Mrs Darrell Waters anyway – not to the world and its children. She was 'Miss Blyton'. And throughout a life of hectic industry Enid kept her famous signature, marking every book with its comfortingly rounded initial 'E', its soft but perky pen-work and the firm double underline a binding promise of extra helpings of adventure and fun.

Enid Blyton may have said that her stories and their settings emerged from her subconscious, but Swanage, the Isle of Purbeck and its fields and moors, farmhouses, beaches, coves and caves are what fed her imagination. I am slipping and skidding along the coastal path that leads from Swanage to the village of Studland, battered by the ferocious wind, scoured by sleet, hood up, head down, wondering what would happen if I just keeled over into a ditch – and how long it would take before I was found. I am the only fool on the path. The way is narrow and glutinous with a cold, deep, clutching mud. In places, especially where the path is steep, clumps of blackthorn are crowding close, the early blossom clinging in misery to the branches, but at least the bushes provide a veneer of shelter. Once I reach the top, the wind rages over the open fields and I have to fight my way to the headland and the view of Old Harry Rocks – three collapsed chalky arches rising from the sea. There are a couple of people here, whooping into the gale, and then, emerging out of the snow (the temperature is dropping) a party of teenagers comes into view, one bouncing a football, some on their phones, laughing and sauntering along as if they were on Oxford Street.

It is exhilarating here, at Britain's southern edge, leaning into the wind at the top of the giddy cliffs, watching the waves heave and thrash against Old Harry Rocks. A seagull comes screaming up from the sea and is flung inland. Everything – the deadly waves, the torn trees, the shrieking people – feels wild and unfettered. Unhinged even. Do not imagine for a second that Enid, for all her mimsy, would not have revelled in this mayhem. She loved a good thunderstorm. And even though Gillian thought her mother was essentially a shy person, she lived her life with passion and a whirling energy. Gillian's sister Imogen, in her troubling 'fragment' of autobiography *A Childhood at Green Hedges*, published twenty years after her mother's death, quotes her friend Diana Biggs:

> Your parents came over for a drink and I remember
> walking into our drawing-room. Enid Blyton was sitting

in that settee. It is over forty years ago, but … none of
that has dimmed my first impression. She was incredibly
vibrant, an absolutely vital person. Everyone else in the
room sort of faded. It was just this incredible personality
sitting on the settee …

So. Enid had energy and fire and immense creativity (measured
by volume, at the very least). But what she did not have, it turns
out, is the ability to bring specific landscapes to life. She is not,
in that portentous phrase, 'a writer of place' – looking to portray
with fine detail a well-loved meadow or clifftop walk – or indeed
to take that meadow and transform it through her art into something that sparks with its own unique essence and fire. The simple
fact is that Enid writes in archetypes (another word would be
clichés). She had no interest in writing with evocative precision
about specific places. It is certainly very hard to pin them down
in her writings. I am criss-crossing the south-eastern tip of the
Isle of Purbeck, from Swanage to Studland, via Old Harry Rocks
and the Agglestone Rock, taking in Agglestone Cottage and the
views from the moor over to Brownsea Island, and although
I *know* (because I've been told) that Hill Cottage near the golf
course (bought by Enid's second husband Kenneth for £1 in
1951) is the model for Agglestone Cottage, and that George found
Timmy (found him!) on the moor above Kirrin Cottage, and that
Brownsea Island was transformed into Whispering (or Wailing)
Island in *Five Have a Mystery to Solve*, there really is almost no clue
in most of her books. What you will find is an 'old' farmhouse
and a 'blue' sea and a 'lovely' bay.

The path from Old Harry Rocks heads north and east along the
clifftop, following the coast, through stretches of flowering gorse
and scraps of woodland, and into the village of Studland. Enid
and Kenneth started taking their holidays here from 1960 onwards,

abandoning the Grand in Swanage in favour of the Knoll House Hotel. It's possible that Enid wanted to be more secluded (she was very famous by now), or that she wanted to be near Kenneth's golf course (she learned late, but could whip through three rounds in a day). The price wouldn't have bothered her. Kenneth, said Enid's daughter Imogen, was not slow to take advantage of his and Enid's joint account, and 'once he had acquired the taste for spending money, he began to spend a great deal'. But only on the big things (jewellery and a chauffeur for Enid, a Rolls-Royce and a Bentley); he would also hoard paperclips and hand-deliver any letter he could. Enid didn't care either way. She found it funny. Anyway, people seem to agree that Kenneth was a good husband for Enid: an old-school doctor, devoted, somewhat rigid, energetic, enjoyed a simple joke, conservative, busy and serious, rather deaf (which didn't help his temper, although Enid's perfect diction was a boon), and resolutely middle-brow in his cultural tastes. At one time there was talk of Enid becoming a professional musician (or at least her father had hoped so) and she was also a talented artist, but all of that seems to have faded away in the Kenneth years.

The Knoll House Hotel is low, friendly and soothing – and I can see why Enid was drawn to it. By 1960 she was already suffering from the Alzheimer's that led to her death in November 1968, aged just seventy-one. Certainly her output was dropping: she wrote the last Famous Five book in 1963, published three books in 1964, and then fell uneasily silent. As Barbara Stoney writes in her biography, 'as time went by she found it increasingly difficult to concentrate long enough to write coherently or to stop her fantasy world from spinning over into the reality of her day-to-day life'. She had always had a fear of losing control – of what might be lurking in her memories, or in the depths of her subconscious – and these years must have been terrifying.

But I like to think she found pleasure at the Knoll. She used to sit in the dining room watching the children. There are gorgeous views from some of the public rooms (and her preferred bedroom at the back), over Scots pines and a weather-worn tennis court down to the sparkling bay. There's a brass bust of Enid in an alcove at the hotel (they are very proud of the connection) as well as one of Winston Churchill. I wonder if the Churchill bust was here when Enid was staying. Her first husband, Hugh Pollock, oversaw the production of Churchill's monumental *The World Crisis* (later *The Great War*) in the 1930s, the two of them spending long days locked away at Chartwell, editing and rewriting, tucking into the brandy and cigars. It must have been a thrilling experience for Hugh (he revered Churchill), but another turbo-boost to his alcoholism. He drank heavily for most of his and Enid's marriage, although he tried to hide it from her. And she was eager to be deceived, even if her diaries are full of his illnesses and indispositions. When he fell seriously ill in 1938 Enid found a great cache of empty bottles in their cellar – his secret hoard, brooding under their home, like a long-forgotten treasure trove in an ancient dungeon, just waiting to be discovered. Enid had plenty of secrets of her own, but she hated other people's.

It is troubling to think of Enid in these later years, her mind skimming between the daily routine and her 'fantasy world'. She had always dreaded what might be waiting for her, once her defences were down. It's no wonder there are so many caves and secret passageways and hidden tunnels in her books. It's right there in *Five on a Treasure Island*, after the enormous storm has upended everything: 'There was something else out on the sea by the rocks beside the waves – something dark, something big, something that seemed to lurch out of the waves and settle down again.'

Once, everything flowed so easily for Enid; the boundary connecting her 'under-mind', as she called it, was porous and thin; and she only had to peek inside, hold the door ajar, and her stories (her safe, jolly stories) would slip out and arrange themselves on the page. But now the doors were wide open and dark things were stirring. I don't think she was hiding anything genuinely horrifying (or even criminal) from herself. I think it is more likely that she was agonized by the gap between the way she wanted to be, the way, in fact, the best characters in her story books always behaved – Christian, kind, loving, open, generous – and the way she had been in her life. Or maybe she found it hard to reconcile what she thought and felt and *wanted* (her ferocious drive, her self-absorbed writing life) with the way she imagined she should behave. Perhaps she was tormented by how far she had fallen short of her own absurd and impossibly perfect brand.

Enid preferred to write her books, and live her life, on the surface. And to keep things vague. But even if it is hard to locate specific places, here in the Isle of Purbeck, the truth is that *everything* inside an Enid Blyton book is instantly recognizable. She takes the world and makes it less confusing, kneading her ingredients into something manageable, safe, tidy and above all familiar. Even when she is leading us up a Faraway Tree to a land of saucepan men and irritated polar bears, all of these things have their untroubling place – and the children are free to go home once the fun is over. Perhaps, on second thoughts, Enid really did manage to capture the essence of the Isle of Purbeck. And all those people who have moved here, looking for a lost land of unlocked front doors, well-tended hedgerows and a steam train panting in a siding at the heart of an English village – perhaps it is Enid Blyton who has drawn them here. Just how deep does her influence run? There was a time, not so long ago, when it would have been hard to find a single child in Britain who had not read (or been read) at least one Blyton book, and suckled themselves to sleep on her warm, tender, infinitely reassuring

words. We are all, as she so often said, her children. And she is
our storyteller.

Here's Julian (the oldest of the four children) in *Five Have a
Mystery to Solve*: 'I somehow feel more English for having seen
those Dorset fields, surrounded by hedges, basking in the sun.'
To be clear, Enid Blyton didn't *invent* that particular image of
Englishness – you might as well credit P. G. Wodehouse or John
Constable or the Acts of Enclosure – but she certainly spread
it far and wide. And although I am sure it is true, as Enid's
daughter Gillian said, that 'every nationality enjoyed them [her
books] just as much as the English children did', that only goes
to show that it is not just the English who are in thrall to the
vision – that wistful English vision, polished over the years – of
pure, unsullied village life, of George Orwell's 'old maids biking
to Holy Communion through the mists of the autumn mornings'.
Orwell wrote much more than that, of course, in his attempt to
define Englishness ('the diversity of it, the chaos!'), and even in
the same paragraph there is plenty about 'clogs in the Lancashire
mill towns' and 'queues outside the Labour exchanges'. But it is
the misty mornings that linger. Perhaps they get to us all in the
end. And the fact is, these things really do exist – ancient water
meadows, thistledown drifting in country lanes, cheery publicans,
apple-choked orchards and the soft silence of village greens fading
into the twilight – and even now they are here, right here, in the
Isle of Purbeck. However much the frozen wind may howl. And
whether or not you are all of a sudden shaken by an irresistible
urge (a spasm of fury from the world outside this muffling cocoon)
to rage and stamp all over someone's immaculate front lawn. It
is here – and everything else will pass. Softly now. Just come on
in. It's all lovely. Quite, quite lovely.

When I throw open the curtains in my top-floor room at the Grand the next morning, I am met by a searing blaze of sunshine. The wind has gone. The sky is a tentative, early morning blue, rinsed and in recovery from yesterday's storms. The sea is flat, tense even (and also, as Enid could tell us, undeniably blue). There's a ginger cat sitting on the sleek green lawn just below my window, where Enid once walked (the world is full of colour this fine day), and as I watch it stretches and strolls with its tail high towards the steps that lead to the Grand's private beach. It is a day to be up and doing. Adventures are around the corner. My wife, Anna, has arrived and I turn, the curtains still in my hands, and half-shout, 'Look at this weather. It's LOVELY!' Ah, the salty tang of the fresh Swanage air.

Enid moved her Swanage base from the Grosvenor Hotel to the Grand in 1952 and kept on coming until she discovered Studland's Knoll House Hotel in 1960. The holidays of her most prolific years were spent here in the Grand, swimming and playing golf with Dr Kenneth now that her children had left for their universities. In essence, the place probably hasn't changed much since. The great central staircase, now quietly suffocating under the weight of its own dusky blue carpet, was presumably here; the pictures, of sailing ships and sunny seas and storms, look ageless; the views from the back, over the sea, are of course the same (if you squint and wear blinkers to block out some more recent developments); but I'm not so sure about the insinuatingly bland background music that chases us from bedroom to breakfast. It wouldn't have bothered Kenneth (if he listened to music at all he liked it simple and LOUD), but I can imagine Enid telling someone sharply to turn it off.

I feel sure that Enid enjoyed her journey along Britain's social scale. She was often accused of being class-obsessed (or rather, for unthinkingly writing about families with cooks and gardeners

and tuck boxes), but I'm not convinced she was any more preoccupied with class than other writers of her time, whatever their
background. That's just the way it was – and is. In fact, there was
an awful lot of snobbery *about* Enid Blyton. Sure, she lived in a
large house in the country and wore tweeds, she kept a chauffeur
and spoke with a honeyed, nursery nanny accent, and she took
her holidays at the Grand in Swanage (although don't get your
hopes up, it's not *that* grand ...), but everyone knew, or at least
those awful English people who care so much about such things
knew, and they made sure that everyone else knew, that she had
been born in a small two-bedroom flat above a shop in south-east
London (No. 354 Lordship Lane, East Dulwich, if you'd like to
go and pay homage) and she wasn't the blue-blooded *grande dame*
of Beaconsfield that she was never even pretending to be. You
see, Enid got it in the neck from every kind of snob: intellectual,
literary, high culture, inverted, Oxbridge, working class, the middle
don't-get-above-yourself class, anti-women snobs, anti-success
snobs, and all the other dreary, run-of-the-mill, 'where-do-you-
come-from?' snob snobs.

She didn't seem to care. Of course it grieved her that the BBC
had a secret policy to keep her from their programmes. She also
found it easier, as the years went by, to define herself as solely
a children's writer (although she had always wanted more and
hoped one day to write for adults, even if, as seems likely, she had
no talent for the task). But she was buoyed by Hugh and then
Kenneth and found infinite reassurance in her clubs and readers
and her all-conquering book sales.

And then there were the joys of Swanage, which we are keen to
see on this extraordinary, unexpectedly bright day. More than that,
it would be a relief to get away from the Grand's busy conservatory
breakfast room, which is in danger of being overwhelmed by an
awkward, infectious silence, a familiar English embarrassment that

fills and agitates the tense air (and even now is no doubt stifling hotel and B&B breakfast rooms across the land). I'm as susceptible to it as anyone. Knives scrape on plates; feet shuffle towards the buffet and back; uneasy, secretive whispers escape from the tables ('full English?'; 'looks like a nice day'; '*did you bring the suncream?*'; 'more tea?'); and all the while the morning *Mail*'s crisp new pages crackle and softly fall, to the 'tut' and snort of its readers and even, just once, a plaintive moan of despair.

We leave in a hurry and head westwards along the coastal path from Swanage. We pass the Wellington Clock Tower, which once stood by London Bridge before it was dismantled and brought here, along with any number of London iron bollards and the actual façade of Swanage's town hall (which came from a building in Cheapside). Nothing is quite what it seems. We skirt the lifeboat station (well supported by Enid in her day) and Peveril Point, site of many shipwrecks (and a naval battle between King Alfred and the Danes). The path runs through green fields, with the cliffs and the sea on our left. Banks of dark, bare thorn bushes keep us from the edge. Young teasels nod and bob in a slight breeze. There are larks overhead and when we stop to lie on a grassy bank a blackbird hops close and inspects us with an eager eye. I would be even happier if I could find some heather (you will remember that no Enid Blyton camping trip is complete without a bed of heather, gathered in armfuls and arranged under sleeping bags into soft, springy mattresses), but all I can see is yellow gorse and empty fields, cropped close by sheep.

There's a mist gathering far out to sea, but no cloud in the sky. Below us, just over the thorns, the sea is whumping into the caves at the foot of the cliffs, the waves sucking and slapping at the rocks. When Celia Fiennes came here in the 1680s on one of her horseback tours around Britain, she – like Enid – became obsessed with the craggy shoreline and its caves:

At a place called Sea Cume [Seacombe] the rockes
are so craggy and the creekes of land so many that the
sea is very turbulent, there I pick'd shells and it being a
spring-tide I saw the sea beat upon the rockes at least 20
yards with such a foame or froth, and at another place
the rockes had so large a cavity and hollow that when
the sea flowed in it runne almost round, and sounded
like some hall or high arch.

None of this has changed, although the abundant glut of 'very
large and sweet' 'lobsters and crabs and shrimps' that Celia
noted (and devoured, 'boyled in the sea water and scarce cold')
has taken a battering over the last three hyperactive centuries of
unchecked consumption.

There are very few people about on this early spring day. We
pass the occasional middle-aged couple and greet them with a
wave of cheery recognition. A climber is letting himself slowly
down the cliff, shouting to someone far below. A rescue helicopter
appears noisily over the horizon and hovers, before disappearing
back the way it came. We walk on, and at Dancing Ledge (an
artificial swimming pool created in a cove when a schoolmas-
ter dynamited the rocks so his pupils could enjoy a safer swim)
we meet a man who runs 'adventures': climbing, sea kayaking,
caving … Imagine living in a time when gunpowder was freely
available – and anyone who wanted to rearrange the coastline
could just crack on. It's only 100 years ago. Enid came here often
with Gillian and Imogen, and the place emerged straight onto
the pages of *First Term at Malory Towers* (1946):

[It] had been hollowed out of a stretch of rocks, so that
it had a nice, rocky, uneven bottom. Seaweed grew at
the sides, and sometimes the rocky bed of the pool felt

a little slimy. But the sea swept into the big, natural pool each day, filled it, and made lovely waves all across it.

Yes, it's here all right. The 'adventure man' is urging us huskily to join him in climbing the cliffs today or, failing that, to come back tomorrow and get involved in some sea-caving. He seems especially keen to convince my wife. Apparently it's quite hard work, but well worth it. And not at all dangerous. Oh no.

I am sure Enid would have tried it. She had a love of nature and adventure instilled in her by her father, she always said, and it was partly his restless influence (as well as a horror of turning into her mother, a bored, bereft housewife) that drove her on. Her father, Thomas, was a cutlery salesman from Sheffield when he married Theresa Mary Harrison. Enid, their first child, was born in 1897. Two boys followed rapidly – Hanly and Carey – by which time the family was living in a semi-detached house with a sizeable garden in Beckenham, Kent. Enid said that her father gave her a small patch of this garden and, as she told her young readers in *The Story of My Life*:

> Nobody knew how much I loved it. Well, *you* might know, perhaps, because some of you feel exactly the same about such things as I felt. You don't tell anyone at all, you just think about them and hug them to yourself.

Enid was a lonely, secretive child, most likely. She didn't get on with her mother and blamed her when Thomas went to live with another woman, leaving Theresa to bring up the three children. Her mother, she wrote later, 'was not very fond of animals', the sure-fire signifier in Enid's fiction that someone was a wrong 'un. Enid was twelve when her father left home for good. On the night before he left, as he and Theresa screamed and raged at each other,

Enid tried to drown out the noise by telling stories to little Hanly and Carey. And that, as any amateur psychologist could tell you, was what she continued to do for the rest of her life. Drown out the noise with her stories.

This is not to say that she had a miserable childhood. She had friends. She was offensively successful at school (head girl for her final two years; tennis champion; captain of the lacrosse team; recipient of endless academic prizes). But it is also true that none of her friends knew that her father had left home, and when Enid herself was given the chance to leave (in 1916, aged nineteen, to work on a farm and then at a kindergarten, launching herself on a career of teaching), she hardly ever saw her family again. She was twenty-three when her father died of a stroke at his new home (and not out boating on the Thames, as she was told, to spare her hearing about his new lover). Although she had seen a bit of him over the years, she didn't go to his funeral.

So maybe now is the moment to take a longer look at the elephant in the room (or drag Jumbo out of the toy cupboard). There is a popular view of Enid Blyton, entirely at odds with her own carefully tended self-image, that she was an unpleasant, cold-hearted, cruel woman and a neglectful, spiteful mother. As her daughter Imogen put it on the very first page of her 'fragment' of autobiography: 'Which of us was the more emotionally crippled I cannot tell.'

But it goes deeper. There are plenty of people who are consumed with a visceral loathing of Enid Blyton – the author, the person – and all her works. This includes many librarians (whose lives have been devoted to the joys of reading), who would like to build a funeral pyre of every last book that Enid ever wrote, hose it down with petrol and toss on the flaming match. She has been denounced by fellow writers, clerics, critics, parents and politicians. Her plotlines are all the same, they say. The characters are wooden. The language is lumpen. Everything she ever created is suffused with a ghastly middle-class morality, a small-minded insularity, a twee, limping, class-ridden, racist, sexist, smug, sanctimonious sentimentality. Her stories are vicious, bullying, shallow, preposterous, predictable, unfunny, patronizing. They are lost in a never-never land of happy families, boarding school tuck shops, forelock-tugging, cap-doffing retainers and creepy elves. Goddammit, they're *childish*.

Here's the critic Colin Welch writing in *Encounter* magazine in 1958, in an article called 'This Insipid Doll', thrashing about in impotent rage because his children loved Noddy and would accept nothing else for their bedtime story:

> If Noddy is 'like the children themselves' [Enid's stated aim], 'it is the most unpleasant child that he most resembles. He is querulous, irritable, and humourless. In this witless, spiritless, snivelling, sneaking doll the children of England are expected to find themselves reflected.

Almost as much of Colin Welch's fury seemed to be aimed at the author, Enid Blyton, as it was at her creation, little Noddy. What especially enraged him (apart from having to read Noddy books to his children every night) was that he thought Enid Blyton was writing *down* to her audience: 'by putting everything within the reach of the child's mind, they cripple it ... Enid Blyton is the first successful writer of children's books to write beneath her audience'. He writes longingly of the Winnie the Pooh books, *Alice in Wonderland* and Edward Lear, books he could enjoy reading (stretching, wondrous, magical books) as much as his children would enjoy hearing them. But he misses the point, because Enid's books were written for children. She was quite clear on this point, especially as the grown-up criticism grew: she couldn't care less what adults thought. They could go whistle, taking their harsh and confusing adult world with them. It is probably why Enid set up so many clubs. Just for her and 'her' children. There must have been hundreds of thousands of children in the Famous Five Club: collecting silver foil to raise money for charity, writing to Enid, sharing their hopes and dreams.

Are the works of Enid Blyton a gateway drug, luring young children into the joys of reading, before guiding them on to better and brighter things? Or is there a danger that the youthful Blyton aficionado will get trapped in her two-dimensional world, main-lining monosyllables and addicted to easy thrills? Thirty years later you'll find them slumped and drooling on a sofa, watching *Friends* on an eternal Netflix loop.

Enid herself set out to write for every age group. You could grow up with Blyton, she proclaimed, from Mister Twiddle to the Famous Five via Noddy and St Clare's. But surely even in her headier moments she didn't expect children to read *only* her works? I certainly had my fill of Noddy growing up (and not just the books, but the jigsaw puzzles and clockwork cars and pert pink toothpaste). And I remember the Bible stories and dipping into the Secret Seven. But it was the Famous Five books that obsessed me – *Mystery Moor, Smuggler's Top, Finniston Farm* – right up to the day I arrived at my new school, aged eight, clutching my absolute favourite, *Five Go Adventuring Again* (you know, the one with the secret passage and the bearded tutor, Mr Roland, whom Timmy bites on the ankle, because he knows, doesn't he, that Roland's a bad 'un – he has a beard, for God's sake! – and is plotting to steal Uncle Quentin's inventions), and I was sneered at by one of the older boys. 'What a baby – reading Enid Blyton,' he scoffed. 'Everyone's a critic,' I must have sobbed, as I stuffed the book back down deep into my bag, never to be opened again. Or not until I read it to my own children. Ha! Take that, school bully.

But was my emotional and mental development stunted by my love of Blyton? The BBC was quite clear that it would have been – and seems to have carried out a policy of no-platforming from the very earliest days. In 1938 Enid's first husband, Hugh Pollock, even wrote to the head of the BBC, John Reith (whom he knew slightly) asking if he could put in a good word for Enid. It didn't work. An internal BBC memo from 1940 was brutal in its reasons for rejecting one of her submissions, 'The Monkey and the Barrel Organ': 'This not really good enough. Very little happens and the dialogue is so stilted and long-winded … It really is odd to think that this woman is a best-seller. It is all such very small beer.'

In 1949 a BBC producer called Lionel Gamlin wrote to Enid Blyton asking if she would be happy to be interviewed for one of his programmes. He must have been startled by the reply:

Dear Mr Gamlin

Thank you for your nice letter. It all sounds very interesting – but I ought to warn you of something you obviously don't know, but which has been well-known in the literary and publishing world for some time – I and my stories are completely banned by the B.B.C. as far as children are concerned – not one story has ever been broadcast, and, so it is said, not one ever will be.

She suggested that Lionel Gamlin seek confirmation from his bosses, which he must have done because in his next letter to Enid he glosses over his invitation and says he regrets that she felt unable to contribute to the programme. Enid set him straight: 'I think, if you don't mind, I must just put it on record that I did not refuse to appear in your Autograph Album series, but, on the contrary, would have been delighted to do so.'

But the ban continued. In November 1954, with Enid at the height of her fame, the BBC show *Woman's Hour* came under immense pressure from its listeners to include an interview with Blyton, or at least broadcast some of her stories. The editor, Janet Quigley, wrote to Jean Sutcliffe of the Schools Department, asking for her help in beating back the BBC producers who thought that 'we are being rather stuffy and dictatorial in not allowing listeners to hear somebody whose name is a household word'.

Jean Sutcliffe's reply is a masterclass in old-school elitism. She says that if the invitation to Enid Blyton is 'simply to meet her' and ask her to give her views on 'Horror comics or Hats ... then no harm could be done'. But if she is 'allowed to lay down the law on ... writing for children – unchallenged ... the BBC becomes just another victim of the amazing advertising campaign which has raised this competent and tenacious second-rater to such astronomical heights of success'. She goes on: 'It is because of all this that I think people in positions like ours have every right to exercise our judgement in deciding who shall utter unchallenged on certain subjects.'

In other words, Enid could come on to the BBC to talk about hats and horror comics, but under no circumstances would she be allowed to discuss her own writing 'unchallenged'. And nor would the BBC be dramatizing any of her stories. These days we'd say that Enid Blyton was the victim of a culture war. Or maybe standards have slipped. It wasn't until the 1990s that the BBC finally relented with the release of the Noddy videos ('Milk-o-o-o').

Even after her death, the BBC hadn't finished with Enid. They'd banned her books; now they trashed her character. In *Enid*, a 2009 dramatization of her life, they had Helena Bonham Carter play her in full-on Bellatrix Lestrange mode: an ice-cold witch who'd rather hug a fox terrier than pick up her own crying baby; who threatens to dismiss her chauffeur for coughing and then goes back to gloating over another bundle of fan mail; who drives her sweet and loving husband Hugh to drink (it's Matthew Macfadyen playing Hugh, his whipped-spaniel eyes milking every vicious slight from his wife); and who warmly (falsely!) welcomes the children who've won the chance to meet her by ushering them into her study for home-made cakes and stories (while her own two little girls, whom she hardly ever talks to, look on in misery through the bars of the banisters).

As Hugh slurs at one point: 'the only reason your fans adore you is because they don't actually know you'. And then he goes to bury Bobs the terrier in the garden while she stares at him with cold contempt from her study window before rattling out another cloying story on her infernal typewriter about how happy 'Bobs' is with his daddy and mummy in their sham of a rural idyll.

You can see why the film-makers did it. It's a lip-smacking story: iconic children's author, twee moralist and the epitome of old-school England turns out to be a hypocritical bastard. And it has helped shape what most of us think we know about Enid Blyton. The main source was presumably Imogen's book, *A Childhood at Green Hedges: A Fragment of Autobiography by Enid Blyton's Daughter*, although Barbara Stoney's more measured biography certainly includes some juicy plums, and if you want to delve deeper there's also *Starlight* by Ida Pollock, Hugh's heroic second wife (also a prolific writer, but of romantic fiction).

Anyway, it's time to lift the stone. Yes, she really did beat her children, usually with the back of a hairbrush. She even beat Imogen once for laughing too much with one of the nannies. You could say that child-beating was not unusual in those days, but Enid was also accused by Imogen of emotional neglect: 'Every week without fail, throughout my whole boarding-school career, my mother wrote to me, short friendly letters, much the same as the ones she wrote to her fans.'

Enid loved her fan clubs and was nourished by the hundreds
of thousands of letters she received. But she also loved her own
children, I'm sure of that. The awful truth is that she may have
found Gillian easier than Imogen. Certainly that's what Imogen
thought: 'my sister's more generous and outgoing personality has
always been an easier one to relate to than my suspicious, defensive
and often downright rude one.'

Barbara Stoney and others have decided that Enid was essentially a child herself, hence her astounding facility for getting into
children's minds. Stoney wrote that when Enid was finding it
hard to conceive a child, her doctor found she had the ovaries of
a twelve-year-old. This rather creepy theorizing has led many to
decide that Enid was emotionally frozen at the moment when her
father left her mother. She certainly loved practical jokes, because
this is how she passed the time on 17 January 1926: 'Hugh and
I threw snowballs at people walking below. It was such fun. Sewed
till bed.' But, no, she did not have the mind of a twelve-year-old.

We are also told that she never took in any child refugees during
the war, and even when her friend, Dorothy Richards, asked her
to put up some people who had been bombed out of London, she
gave them shelter for a week and then threw them out because
they were getting in the way of her writing. I think we can agree
she was no Angela Lansbury in *Bedknobs and Broomsticks*, although
she did take in a young maid fleeing Austria in 1939, and they
became firm friends. She also ditched most of her friends when
she became famous, ignored her brothers as much as she could,
and cut off her mother (refusing to send her money and missing
her funeral). Years later, as Enid slipped into pre-senile dementia,
and even though her mother had been dead for years, she tried,
painfully and repeatedly, to go and see her.

So, yes, she lied to others (and to herself) and there were parts
of her life that she worked hard to forget. She could be arrogant

(although which writer isn't, living at the nexus of fantasy and self-doubt?). She had at least one affair, not that it should matter to anyone other than Hugh – but this is squeaky-clean Enid Blyton we are talking about, so of course there's a prurient interest.

But that was just the warm-up, because here is a Top Ten of Enid Blyton Accusations (with a bonus at the end):

1. SHE REALLY WAS A TERRIBLE MOTHER

Here's Imogen:

> On Saturday mornings, my sister and I would go down to the lounge to collect our pocket money … It was on one of these occasions … that I came upon a new piece of knowledge. Something made me realize that this woman with dark curly hair and brown eyes … who paid me just as she paid the staff … was also my mother. By this time I had met mothers in stories that were read to me, Enid Blyton stories included, and I knew that a mother bore a special relationship to her child, from which others were excluded. In my case the pieces of the puzzle failed to fit together. There was no special relationship. There was scarcely a relationship at all.

There was a time when British middle-class parents were quite capable of neglecting their children. Seeing them just once a day to bid them goodnight. Sending them to boarding schools. I imagine Enid hoped for more – except she was also just so busy. She seems to have wanted to cram all her mothering moments into her Swanage holidays and the brief hour before dinner. It's worth knowing that Gillian said that she talked with Enid 'freely from early childhood'.

2. BUT SHE PRETENDED TO BE THE PERFECT MOTHER

Imogen: 'There is a well-established myth that my mother read frequently to my sister and myself, trying out her stories on us, her own small critics. This is quite untrue. I can only remember her reading one book to me …'

And Enid: 'Gillian and Imogen read every book I write, usually before it goes to my publishers. Their favourites have always been your favourites.'

And Gillian: 'I used to read chapters of her latest book hot from the typewriter after school, impatient for the next day's instalment.'

3. SHE WAS VICIOUS

Enid asked Hugh to take the blame for the breakdown of their marriage because she thought news of a divorce would be disastrous for her reputation. In return, she promised Hugh full access to their children, Gillian and Imogen. She broke this promise and Hugh never saw his children again.

We don't know what was agreed, but this sounds right. It's true that poor Hugh (alcoholic, paranoid and adrift) seems at one point to have decided that his children were better off without him. Time drifted. Also, there's something undeniably absent about Hugh. Ida describes how when Alistair, Hugh's son from his first marriage, wrote to let him know he was getting married and ask him to the wedding, Hugh contrived not to go – and possibly never even contacted him.

4. AND SHE WAS SPITEFUL

Here's Imogen: 'I remember one remark she made before a meal in the dining-room to my stepfather. "I do dislike people with

inferiority complexes. Don't you, Kenneth?" When he had made
the required affirmative answer, she continued with her superb
timing. "Don't you think that Imogen has a dreadful inferiority
complex?"'

Imogen's book is a howl of pain. She writes with scrupulous
honesty about her feelings and memories – and a strange air
of judicious detachment ('I read many Enid Blyton books ...').
Or maybe she's just numb. But it is painful to read; and con-
trasts starkly with Gillian's bland, amiable memories. In her
afterword to Imogen's book, Gillian writes: 'It is strange to see
one's childhood through the eyes of a sister: people, events,
emotions charged with a different significance; reinterpreted.'
And she finishes: 'I and my children are very happy to have
this record of a part of our family history and I think that my
mother would have been delighted that it had been written by
her daughter, Imogen.' Which is an extraordinarily diplomatic
response to Imogen's raging memoirs. Her mother would have
been 'delighted'? Really? It sounds to me like she's handling
Imogen with kid gloves.

5. AND SHE WAS VINDICTIVE

After the war, when Hugh tried to find employment at his old
firm, George Newnes, Enid is said to have blocked him. As his
boss said: 'In the end, Enid is more important to us than you are.'
Many other publishers closed their doors to Hugh.

Here's Ida Pollock: 'It soon became clear that the Blyton
"camp" had started to set in motion a serious smear campaign.
Hugh Pollock, the story went, was an adulterous alcoholic who
had shamelessly betrayed, then cold-bloodedly abandoned his
brilliant and long-suffering wife.'

Was this Enid herself at work? Possibly, but publishers are

an unsentimental bunch. Not to mention the most appalling gossips.

6. BUT IT GETS WORSE

Hugh and Ida's daughter, Rosemary (Ba) suffered from terrifying asthma attacks, sometimes only surviving on 'a cocktail of drugs'. Hugh and Ida were bankrupt (he couldn't get any work ...), so Ida's friend Dora (an actress, who relished a scene) went to see Enid at Green Hedges to ask if she would include Ba in the Trust that Hugh had set up for Gillian and Imogen – so they could afford to buy Ba some medicine.

Here's Ida:

> Told this woman on the doorstep was a relation of mine Enid may have felt a degree of curiosity, or perhaps she was drawn by the tenuous link with Hugh. Anyway, Dora was admitted. To begin with, I think, she was polite and conciliatory. Surely, she suggested, it should be possible to open up the Trust – after all, Hugh had established it for the security of his children. And his little girl, Rosemary, was very unwell.
>
> 'Definitely not', said Enid – or words to that effect. The Trust had been set up for Gillian and Imogen, and she had their interests to consider. But now, Dora pointed out, Hugh had another daughter. Everyone was worried about Rosemary – alias Ba – and surely ...
>
> 'I don't care', said Enid Blyton, 'if the child dies.'

According to Ida, Enid regretted what she had said and 'eventually' opened the Trust. But, still ... what kind of person says *that*? Assuming that is what she said.

7. HER STORIES ARE UNBEARABLY SEXIST

What with Anne always doing the dishes and making the sandwiches and waving Dick and Julian (and George, on sufferance) off on their adventures. The mothers stay at home and smile a lot. The fathers go out to work. Yes, these books are sexist.

It's a small thing, but there's always George, everyone's favourite character, the girl who'd rather be a boy. Reinforcing stereotypes, sure, but she has such fierce honesty. She is based on Enid herself.

8. HER STORIES ARE UNDENIABLY RACIST

Exhibit 'A': *Here Comes Noddy Again*, written in 1951. In which our little hero gives a lift to an ill-mannered golliwog, who leads him to the dark woods and 'three black faces suddenly appeared in the light of the car's lamps' and Noddy is mugged, his clothes and car stolen. Enid insisted that there were more bad teddy bears in her stories than bad golliwogs – and that they're 'merely lovable black toys, not Negroes [*sic*]'.

Some years after Enid's death, the golliwogs in her books were all replaced by goblins – and it's certainly easier to excuse Enid than it is anyone who agitates, today, for their reinstatement.

9. HER STORIES ARE MADDENINGLY MIDDLE-CLASS

Indeed they are. All the villains in the Famous Five stories have rough voices and beards, the foreigners are wrong 'uns to a man, and the circus folk and gypsies are, at best, a mixed bunch. Meanwhile, the cooks are all apple-cheeked and smiling, the gardeners tip their caps and tell the young scamps to run along, and the police protect the property interests of the privileged.

Maybe it's best to read Enid Blyton's books as science fiction. Or even pause and wonder why the (much worse, but also of-its-time) sexism and xenophobia on show in the *Biggles* books or John Buchan are more often brushed aside with an indulgent chuckle.

10. AND SHE COULDN'T BLOODY WRITE

She may have written too much too fast, but don't pretend that her stories aren't some of the most accessible, immersive, utterly thrilling works that have ever been created. *For children.* I have reread dozens of her books recently and although they follow a grimly predictable (reassuring) pattern, and her incessant use of the words 'lovely' and 'blue' is irritating, I also quietly wept (yes, I did) when Elizabeth, *The Naughtiest Girl in the School*, is redeemed and her best instincts are coaxed into life. More often than not, Enid Blyton writes with addictive verve and JOY – and she knew exactly how to grip her audience.

11. SHE THREATENED TO FIRE A CHAUFFEUR FOR COUGHING ...

... while staring at him with breathtaking malignancy.

Really though, did she? As they write with *Fargo*-esque candour at the beginning of the BBC's *Enid*: 'The following drama is based on the lives of real people. Some scenes have been invented and some events conflated for the purposes of the narrative.'

It is worth asking how well any of us would fare under this detail of scrutiny. And why Enid Blyton was (and is) on the kicking end of so much virulent criticism. It couldn't be because she's a woman, could it? A wildly successful businesswoman, who dragged herself up from modest beginnings to become the world's best-selling children's author. Negotiating her own, highly favourable author deals. Planning and executing the roll-out of innumerable brands. This should have made her a hero to many, but she was also culturally and politically conservative and, crucially – as the new century took hold – a prominent symbol of the 'nanny knows best' Britain, with her hectoring morality lessons and smothering, Edwardian aspirations. As the country changed around her, most people moved on from Enid. But there were also plenty of others who wondered if there wasn't more to her story than the one she was so keen to tell about herself. They were undeniably gratified to learn that there was.

When I was studying English literature at university in the 1980s, we were asked to read Kingsley Amis's *Jake's Thing*, a book about a middle-aged man who's worried about his non-functioning penis (his 'thing', you see). One of my fellow students walked out within five minutes of the start of the first lecture, because she found the views of Kingsley Amis (the man, not the author) obnoxious and didn't want to hear what he might have put into his (probably obnoxious) book. Enid would have been the first to agree that there was an indissoluble connection between a writer's life and character and their work:

> As you can imagine, we are a happy little family. I could not possibly write a single good book for children if I were not happy with my family, or if I didn't put them first and foremost. How could I write good books for children if I didn't care about my own? You wouldn't like my books, if I were that kind of mother!

And – flipping it over: 'You cannot help knowing, too, whether you would *like* the writer or not, once you have read two or three of his books.'

But we were being told that there was *no link* between the biographical details of an author and what she puts into her work. It doesn't matter that Coleridge consumed opium by the jar or that Ezra Pound was a fascist – just look at what they wrote and ignore their lives. Their words should stand on their own.

I seem to remember that the philosophical foundation for this was a book by a man called Stanley Fish, and our lecturer excitedly pointed out that in chapter two of *Jake's Thing*, Jake gets a sum wrong when counting out some change in a shop: *so Jake cannot possibly be Kingsley Amis*. And anything that Jake says (however crude and unpleasant – and there was plenty) is not the view of the author, Kingsley Amis, but only of his character, Jake. What I wanted to ask (but didn't dare) was that if Jake's pustular outpourings were not the same as Kingsley Amis's, then how come you could read more or less the same stuff in Amis's gleefully inflammatory journalism? And anyway, Kingsley Amis was a notorious drunk, so he was bound to have got his sums wrong. (Incidentally, Kingsley Amis's suggested cure for the very worst of hangovers was a 'brisk fuck' – and I can easily imagine that waking up with a sore head to find a sour-breathed Kingsley humping and puffing on top of you would be enough to get anyone out of bed in double quick time and running for the shower, although it seems optimistic of Kingsley to think that he could have offered this service to everyone.)

We all know that not every (or any) character in an author's books necessarily reflects her own views, but I think Enid's deeper point is also true: we can't help knowing if we'd like an author after reading a couple of her books – and it makes me realize that I *do* like Enid Blyton. Kingsley too (and his jokes are better), but neither of them makes it especially easy.

If you walk inland from the Dancing Ledge, across fields lush
with early grasses, through stands of elder, alder and ash, and
skirt the hedgerows with the blackthorn blossoming, and climb
the bare hills that circle the village of Worth Matravers, you will
eventually reach the Square & Compass pub. I am sitting here
with Anna, outside in the drowsy afternoon sunshine, and there
is a robin preening itself at the far end of our wooden table. If
Enid were ever reincarnated, she would definitely come back as
a robin: eager, busy, bright-eyed, interfering and occasionally
vicious. The pub (or so it seems on this limpid afternoon) is probably the best pub in the world. There are home-made pies and
own-brewed cider being served indoors, a warren of old, dark,
secret rooms (yes!) and blazing fires. I have already tried rapping
on the panels, looking for a hidden passageway. Our view takes in
a steep country lane, ancient trees tipped with fresh spring leaves,
and a patchwork of fields unfurling to the blue horizon. It's like
Enid said, writing home in 1930 to the young readers of *Teachers'
World* from her cruise ship docked at Lisbon:

> but I hadn't seen any countryside anywhere that
> I thought was lovelier than England's. I had seen no
> animals nicer than ours, and no children that I liked
> better than English children … and I know that, no
> matter where I go or what I see in other countries, I shall
> always love England best.

If you are of a certain age, your mind will once have been filled
with this stuff. It hasn't gone away. Enid understood – just look at
the easy way she conjured her stories and teased at our childish
longings. How warm and safe she made us feel. The promise of
a green hill far away, and a land, right here, that could be better,
cleaner, kinder and happier. How we yearn for it. The pleasant

pastures and the clouded hills. The sweet peas and roses rising in perfumed abundance from busy front gardens. The unhurried village streets. But we've lingered too long and it's time to move on. There are places to see and other people to meet. So it's goodbye, Enid! Goodbye, Imogen and Hugh and Gillian! Goodbye, Dr Kenneth! Goodbye! We'll meet again, I feel sure. There's a train waiting, and we're not going to hide here any longer.

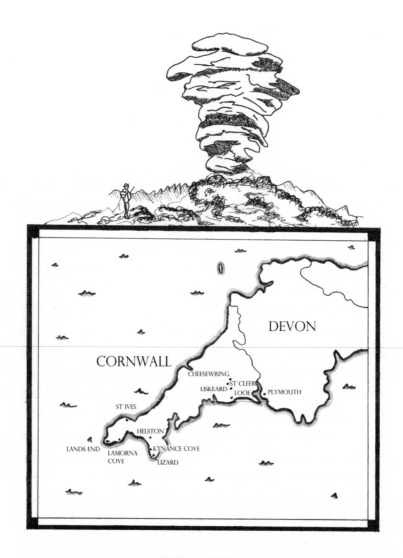

Wilkie Collins,
Plymouth to Lamorna Cove, July and August 1850

TWO

'Walk, and Be Merry'

'Never scramble your toes about, where toes have no business to be.'

WILKIE COLLINS, 1850

In July 1850 the twenty-six-year-old Wilkie Collins was travelling west from London to Plymouth, ensconced in one of the well-groomed carriages of the Great Western Railway (I'm guessing it was first class – Wilkie liked to live it large), on his way to Cornwall with a friend, the artist Henry Charles Brandling, to write a book about 'a part of your own country which is too rarely visited and too little known'. *Rambles Beyond Railways* was the descriptive title, and the plan was to 'wander hither and thither, in a zig-zag course', out of reach of railways, highways, stagecoaches, timetables and guidebooks, taking note with sketchbook and pen of the local characters and scenery. In 1850 Plymouth was literally the end of the line; in fact, according to Wilkie, the only other place left on earth that wasn't yet inundated with travel books was 'Kamtschatka' – and for practical reasons (he said 'patriotic'), Wilkie had chosen to set his own travel book in Cornwall. 'Even the railway stops short at Plymouth, and shrinks from penetrating to the savage regions beyond!' he trumpeted, in a manner calculated to send shivers down the spine of any modern-day marketing department. There was nothing anyone could ever tell Wilkie about how to promote his own books.

Things were looking up for Wilkie in the summer of 1850. His first published novel had appeared in February – *Antonina*, a spicy Gothic tale of feuding brothers set in the last days of Rome – and he was basking in the afterglow of a slew of positive reviews. (Better, he wrote in the introduction to the 1861 edition, than anything he had experienced since.) Also in February, his first play, *A Court Duel*, had been staged at a small theatre in Dean Street, with Wilkie awarding himself the minor part of a courtier. He had by now definitively abandoned a half-hearted plan (more his anxious father's than his own) to become a lawyer or indeed (his father's earlier plan) a clerk in the tea trade, and the trip to Cornwall was Wilkie's way of announcing, to himself and others, that he was determined to make his living as a writer. A travel book must have seemed like a canny next step: a modest way of sliding into the literary scene, in a genre that had predictably solid sales. With Henry Brandling providing the illustrations, they hoped to knock together a guide to a little-known part of Britain and, with luck, have it on the shelves in time for Christmas.

The railways were relatively new to Britain, but by 1850 about 6,000 miles of track had already been laid; that is, a staggering 5,900 more than had been there just twenty years earlier. Despite complaints about the noise and dirt, people were adapting fast to the presence of this transformative technology. Of course, progress was patchy and not all the track was actually connected to the network. Some of the railway companies were even using different gauges and, right up to the 1850s, different *times* (the GWR, where Wilkie rattled and lolled, used an ultra-wide gauge; and most cities ran to a local time that could be several minutes behind or ahead of London). But the railways had opened up Britain, connecting villages and valleys to the towns and cities with a timetabled ease that would have been inconceivable a generation earlier. People and goods were on the move and the country was shifting and shrinking in the minds of its inhabitants. In fact, the roll-out of the railways was so rapid in mid-nineteenth-century Britain that if you fast-forward 100 years, to a time when Enid, Gillian and Imogen were travelling home by train to Beaconsfield from their holiday in Swanage, the network they used was essentially the same one that Wilkie explored 100 years earlier. They could have intersected at Bath, Reading or even Didcot, all stations that were up and running in the year 1850.

Wilkie was never a fan of the discomfort of railways. Indeed, despite the persona he would adopt in *Rambles Beyond Railways*, he probably didn't much care for the outdoors either. Here he is describing the countryside in a letter written to his friend Charles Ward just three months earlier:

> cursed confused chirping of birds – an unnecessarily large supply of fresh air – and a d–d absence of cabs, omnibuses, circulating libraries, public houses, newspaper offices, pastry cooks shops, and other articles of civilisation.

Or maybe Wilkie is showing off, a young man feeding lines to a sophisticated older friend. But he was always a Londoner at heart, more so than any other Victorian novelist, even his friend Charles Dickens, who moved to London as a child and split his time between the capital and Kent in middle age. Wilkie had London baked into his *bones*. He was born in Cavendish Street, Marylebone and he died at home in Wimpole Street, aged sixty-five, just a short stroll (or anguished, morphine-clouded, gout-ridden hobble) from his place of birth. He always liked to travel, though (to Paris and the English coast, especially), and it was probably this trip to Cornwall that sparked his lifelong love of the sea.

Wilkie and Henry were heading to Plymouth, where the train line ended, because they planned to take a boat from there to St Germans, over the River Tamar (there was no useful bridge at that time – and even now you'll find the ferry helpful), and then walk to Land's End and back. Both men had brought knapsacks and walking sticks and we can also assume that Wilkie was dressed with bohemian eccentricity. He was a small man (short even by Victorian standards), with the tiniest little hands and feet. Once, when he was staying with friends in the country, his shoes fell apart and the only replacement pair that could be found in the house belonged to an even tinier great-aunt. Not that Wilkie cared: he knew he was odd-looking, but he had an eager, sweet temperament and he enjoyed the sparkle of attention and conversation that flowed from his unusual appearance and calculatedly contrary opinions.

There's a picture of Wilkie hanging in the National Portrait Gallery, painted in 1850 by his friend the pre-Raphaelite John Everett Millais, the year of the trip to Cornwall. Wilkie is seated, gazing thoughtfully into the distance, his little ring-clad fingers pressed together at the tips (although thanks to Millais they're not *that* little), small round glasses (he was short-sighted), and wearing a sober dark jacket (but with a gold-seamed cravat, watch chain and shirt studs). There's not much sign of the large bump that rose from his high forehead, the result, it was said, of his own difficult birth. He looks unusually neat – and serious. Young, of course. Maybe even rather depressed (although perhaps that's how Millais rendered 'thoughtful intellectual'). What the portrait gives no sign of is Wilkie's extreme restlessness. By every other account, he was sharp, hungry and a notorious fidget, brimful of ideas and passions, interested in everything and everyone, courteous to others, certainly, but also sure enough of himself to fill the railway carriage with chatter and schemes and urgent talk. Perhaps Henry Brandling was pleased to find that the train was at last pulling into Plymouth, after its long, lurching journey from London.

The two friends headed for Devonport and there they found William Dawle, a boatman who could row them to St Germans, although he insisted they first stop at a tavern in Saltash, just across the Tamar, while they waited for the tide to turn. This suited Wilkie – he was eager to go with the flow – and for the next couple of hours they poured beer into Dawle, and themselves, and even Dawle's friend (an immense but catatonically drunk 'shrimper' who was meant to be helping row the boat, or at the very least entertain them with a song, even though very early in the long evening he lost the ability to move or speak). The place, says Wilkie, was the only light in the surrounding darkness (just think, for a moment, how *dark* that Cornish night was) and, like all good taverns surely were in those days, it was in 'festive uproar', the entire population of Saltash squeezed into two small rooms, 'shrimpers, sailors, fishermen and watermen, all "looming large" through a fog of tobacco'. The local women were there too, brushing Wilkie's and Henry's feet as they left, claiming it was an old Saltash tradition to guarantee their safe return, and all for just a few more coins. It sounds like they were royally ripped off – and happy with it.

When they got to St Germans, with everything closed and dark, Dawle denounced it as 'a damned *strap* of a place'. The landlady of the only inn had to be called from her bed (Dawle bellowing from the street that his companions were 'right-down gentlemen, and no mistake'), but at last the travellers were able to get to bed and sleep through their first night in Cornwall. The next day, once Henry had sketched St Germans church, they hoisted their knapsacks and set off to walk eight miles to the fishing village of Looe.

By ten o'clock that night Wilkie and Henry were collapsed on a hill outside Looe, with Wilkie going on (and on) about how wonderful it is to walk when you want to really see and understand a place. How blisters don't matter (just sponge your feet with cold vinegar and pop on another pair of socks). How a knapsack becomes your friend, once your muscles have hardened. And who needs trains, or horses, or stagecoaches anyway? When you can be out and talking to the locals. Or chipping rocks and collecting leaves. This was probably so much hot air (Wilkie had to take to his bed when he went on a walking tour with the genuinely hyperactive Dickens seven years later), but I'm still feeling guilty as I roll my car down the narrow road, squeezed between high wooded banks, into Looe and the vast car park on its eastern bank.

Looe is divided into two – west and east – linked by a famous bridge that is no longer here. Well, there's a bridge, of course, but it's not the one that Wilkie made a beeline for as soon as he could. The original was built in 1411, had fourteen arches ('no two on the same scale', says Wilkie) and it even had a small chapel in the centre (gone by Wilkie's day). Celia Fiennes trotted across the bridge in 1698, counting off the fourteen arches and noting that Looe had 'a great many little houses all of stone' (it still does), and Turner painted it in 1811, but in 1853, just three years after Wilkie's visit, the bridge was dismantled to make way for something less inconveniently medieval. I'll bet the town misses it, now that it's no longer a busy port for the fishing and mining industries, and its main trade is tourism. But how were any of us to know that our future wealth would depend on hoarding our past? Any true Victorian would have laughed at the idea.

I'm here on an alarmingly hot day in April. I have been steeping myself in *Rambles Beyond Railways* for so long that it comes as a surprise to find that Looe is full of cars, buses, neon hairdressers and streets surging with people in branded T-shirts and sandals. What on earth was I expecting? Horse-drawn carts and a pilchard industry? When Wilkie was here, the population of Looe was 'some fourteen hundred; and ... as good-humoured and unsophisticated a set of people as you will meet with anywhere'. No doubt he was happy to be out of London, and fired with holiday enthusiasm. He was certainly excited about Looe's shops:

> Let no man rashly say he has seen all that British enter-prise can do for the extension of British commerce, until he has carefully studied the shop-fronts of the tradesmen of Looe [selling] ... such cosmopolitan miscellanies as wrinkled apples, dusty nuts, cracked slate pencils and fly-blown mock jewellery ...

Oh ... I see.

But honestly, I wouldn't want you to think that Wilkie was just another sarcastic Londoner, chuckling at the rustic lives of the hay-headed locals. There's so much more to him than that, even if he did find it hard to resist an easy joke. He's still young – and the currents of the time flowed with brutish certainty. Later, Wilkie would do what he could to divert them.

These days the shops of Looe would give Wilkie genuine pal-pitations. There's no sign of any 'dusty nuts', but there's plenty of other seaside innuendo on offer, not to mention Cornish crafts, cream, pots, pixies and pasties. Since Wilkie trod these narrow streets we have come an inconceivably long way in our under-standing of what it takes to extract money from a casual passer-by and although we all think we're sophisticated enough to spot and resist the obvious temptations, it isn't long before I find myself tucking into 'Cornwall's best Cornish pasty' (it's not), and browsing a shop enticingly decorated with luminous buckets, nets, beach balls and spades, before leaving with a baseball cap and a pair of shorts (well, who knew it would be so hot?). Anyway, when you're visiting a place that is so reliant on tourism, isn't it your duty to buy something? To keep feeding the beast.

Looe on a bright blue Saturday in April is all sunshine and seagulls. There's an easy, aimless drift to the holiday crowds. Small boats sway and duck on the tidal river and people gather at the banks to watch – it's low tide now – sitting at café and pub tables or shuffling up and down the western side, from the fishermen's wharf to the nearby beach, gazing at the boats and imagining another life. The air is salty fresh. Some of the boats are offering deep sea fishing (mackerel! shark!) or a trip to nearby Looe Island, where once, long ago, there was a great and ineradicable infestation of rats. It was only ended, or so Wilkie tells us, when every person then living in Looe – men, women and children – got up early one morning and caught, cooked and ate the whole damn lot, with vindictive relish, ferociously smothered in onions.

Rats or no rats, I'm eating a huge white doorstep of a bacon sarnie, perched on the side of an overturned barrel at the front of a cheery quayside café, listening to my fellow customers get to know each other. Two of them had recognized each other's Kentish accents – and so, I am pleased to say, had I. North Kent, probably, close to the south-east London border, although I'm no Henry Higgins; I just happen to have grown up in Kent. In fact, could Professor Higgins even pull off his party trick now, of placing the status and provenance of any British person he met, based only on the way they spoke? His (or Shaw's) point was to expose English snobbery, although you would think, wouldn't you, that with the amount of exposure it has received over the centuries English snobbery would have shrivelled and died a long time ago. Wilkie, though, lived in a time when the children of Looe could 'congregate together in sober little groups, and hold mysterious conversations, in a dialect which we cannot understand'. No one here today seems to be speaking a Cornish dialect (and the last native speakers of the original Cornish language had all died off by the time Wilkie arrived), but now I come to look about me, there aren't even any *children*. Perhaps they're all at the beach.

The elderly Kentish couple are in Looe on a train trip from home, and their new, younger friend is a Man of Kent who 'moved down here five years ago'. His daughter and her husband 'live in Spain now and are always posting food on Instagram'. 'Oh,' say the elderly couple, 'our two grandkids live in Oz and are on holiday all the time. Thank heavens for Skype.' I have Wilkie on my shoulder, listening to this strangeness, but I actually think what would strike him most (once he'd got used to the idea that his 'all-conquering Railway' had set everything and everyone in motion, and that so much and so many had been smoothed and spread across the globe, and once he'd stopped marvelling over our smartphones and motor cars, our plastic straws, bare legs and miraculous teeth), I think what Wilkie would notice is just how *subdued* the town of Looe has become.

Looe is still, as Wilkie wrote, 'one of the prettiest places in England'. It has a lovely (thank you, Enid) holiday air and a zip and sparkle to its streets. But it's no longer unusual in the way that Wilkie once found it. Of course it's not – but when Wilkie was here he found himself swept up into a boat race and bazaar when 'all the women fluttered out in [the sun's] beams, gay as butterflies. What dazzling gowns, what flaring parasols, what joyous cavalcades on cart-horses, did we see on the road that led to the town! What a mixture of excitement, confusion, anxiety, and importance, possessed everybody!' Until, predictably, it rained with shattering force, and everyone raced for the tea rooms, except for three German musicians who continued to honk gloomily through their brass instruments, and the usual 'inveterate loungers', and 'seafaring men who cared nothing for weather'. The party continued indoors, with everyone bawling and rushing around with 'steaming teakettles and craggy lumps of plumcake'. I'm told this is now a fair description of Looe on New Year's Eve, with added strong lager; but on the day I visit I'm just one of a low-decibel crowd of middle-aged tourists, drifting through the tourist shops, fretting and cooing over the silver charms and the lace.

Wilkie took the rain as a sign to leave Looe. He had stayed much longer than he'd intended, kept in thrall at the inn by 'the smiles of our fair chambermaid and the cookery of our excellent hostess'. Even today there's something more to Looe than its tourism; at the very least, you will find that the fishermen still gather at the wharf to sell dressed crabs and fresh mackerel. Many are heavily bearded in a muscular, salt-lashed way that'd put a Shoreditch *flâneur* to shame. Wilkie, at this stage in his life, was still clean-shaven – he was yet to grow the all-encompassing beard that would come to dominate and define his appearance. That came three years later, on a trip to Italy with his new friend Charles Dickens and an artist called Augustus Egg – all of them beardless at the time – and I think it was Wilkie, if I'm reading the letters right, who first grew a tentative moustache (mocked by Dickens) that over the next few months spread and enveloped his cheeks and chin and then tumbled in profusion to his chest and eventually flared and crackled like a hairy living counterpoint to his great domed forehead. Beards became immensely popular with Victorian men in the 1850s as a way of flaunting their imperial masculinity, and even, it is said, as a tribute to the soldiers of the Crimean War (who had no way of shaving), although I suspect that Wilkie's era-defining whiskers probably had more to do with laziness than anything else. He always dressed with flamboyant disregard for convention, but he was a notorious sloven. Especially once the laudanum took hold.

Wilkie and Henry headed north for Liskeard and I speed after them. We pass under disused railway bridges and race by steep banks of young grasses and ferns and great floods of primroses, dizzying, oceanic outpourings of yellow that drag at my heart. We are leaving the narrow coombes and dense woods of Looe far behind. The sky widens and stretches – the colour seems to leach out of it – and then I know I'm on the right track because 'a single turn in the road brought us suddenly to the limits of trees, meadows, and cottages; and displayed before us, with almost startling abruptness, the magnificent prospect of a Cornish Moor'.

Wilkie dismissed Liskeard as an 'abomination of desolation'. After encountering 'a nonagenarian old woman with a false nose, and an idiot shaking with the palsy', he checked into the worst inn in Britain, where the landlady reluctantly handed him and Henry two sheets each and left them to make their beds in a room with nothing but six immense wooden tables ('like dissecting tables waiting for "subjects"'). We've all been there. I remember staying with Anna in a B&B in Kingsteignton in south Devon in the late 1980s where the smell of rancid chip fat mingling with air freshener was so powerful that I actually wept pine-scented tears of oil. The landlady could not have been kinder. 'Don't worry about Norman,' she chirruped, as she steered us towards the stairs and past a small dark room in which some large, dank animal seemed to shift and stir. 'He's normally the life and soul of the party. But he's been a bit off colour of late.' I spent the night sweating and tangled in the nylon sheets, waiting for Norman's

soft tread on the carpeted floor, his hand on the doorknob and
a rattling, unhinged whisper: 'It's time to PARTY'. But when we
got down the next morning, as early as was decent, there was
Norman at the breakfast table, a dowdy man with sad eyes and a
repertoire of heartbreaking jokes. We each had a fried egg slopping in oil – and were far too polite to turn it away. Wilkie should
count himself lucky for Liskeard's corned beef, about which he
made such a dreadful fuss.

I stop for lunch in an empty pub in St Cleer (where is everyone?),
and accompany Wilkie down the hill to the ruined remnants of St
Cleer's Well, a fifteenth-century shrine dedicated, so Wilkie tells us,
to the honour of St Clare, the twelfth-century founder of an order
of nuns (the 'Poor Clares') who gave up all their worldly goods
to pursue a life of healing, charity and prayer. Wilkie mooched
around the well, while Henry sketched, pondering how things had
changed since the days of St Clare, nuzzling at the crumbling,
ivy-clad walls (the Victorians loved a good ruin), musing on the
power of the ancient church that once so innocently linked 'the
beauty of Nature and the beauty of Religion', the loss of faith
in his own day and the 'melancholy language of desolation and
decay'. And I find myself doing the same, except now the well
(enfolding its holy spring) has lost even more of its old magic. There
are new houses here, crowding right up to the surrounding low
stone wall; several cars are parked a couple of yards from the well
itself; and just across the road children are shouting at the school
gates (it's the end of the school day), although this is a cheering
sound. Wilkie wrote about the 'cottage-girls' who greeted him
shyly by this well, over 150 years ago.

Wilkie was offered a drink from the holy waters by an old
woman (she brought him a glass for the water and a rose from
her garden) and he wrote that the only thing that hadn't changed
in 400 years was the little pool itself, still 'pure and tranquil as in

the bygone days', although I'm sorry to report that all you'll see now is a sludgy puddle with a couple of plastic bottles rammed up underneath an iron grille. What's more, according to John Betjeman's *Shell Guide to Cornwall*, St Clare had nothing to do with St Cleer – the latter was a Celtic saint whose shrine was presumably placed on a much older site of worship. Something pagan. So Wilkie was all over the place, although he surely has a point when he says:

> There has been something of sacrifice as well as of glory, in the effort by which we, in our time, have freed ourselves from what was superstitious and tyrannical in the faith of the times of old – it has cost us the loss of much of the better part of that faith which was not superstition, and of more which was not tyranny.

And here indeed stands Wilkie, at the midpoint of the nineteenth century, with the furnaces lit and the iron wheels churning, straying into the lost corners of ancient Cornwall with the railways howling at his back; and there's Watt and Darwin and Marx just ahead or all around; and everything is aflame and unmoored and on the move; and Wilkie, even though he's right in the middle of it, can see the revolutionary power of what they are doing. And it is! It's dazzling. The planet-stripping energy and wealth that is being unleashed. And it is also heroic, the courage that is needed to create these things and to face down the ingrained tyranny of the old beliefs. Although, as Wilkie sips his water by the holy well, he understands that something else is also being left behind, unnoticed in the noise and excitement. And now, today, I'm not even sure we know what that was. It's not faith or God. But there's something. A continuum or a connection has been broken and here we are, 150 years later, surging forward, full steam ahead, all alone and seemingly out of choices. Or no longer in any position to choose.

I don't know. Perhaps all I can say for certain is that I'm staring into the once holy waters of St Cleer and there are two discarded plastic bottles pressed up against an iron grille. So I pick them up. There's got to be a recycling bin around here somewhere.

Wilkie's father, William, was a moderately successful artist, painting in the traditional manner of the time. In 1822 he was commissioned to accompany King George IV on a trip to Scotland (where he arranged to meet and then married Wilkie's exuberant mother, Harriet). As the years passed, William became a staid sort of man, obsessed with the finer points of religion, carving out a comfortable living, treading a conventional path: the kind of artist people turned to when they wanted a commemorative portrait or landscape, nothing to frighten the horses. Charles Dickens, flush with success from the publication of *Nicholas Nickleby*, became one of his clients in 1839, asking William to paint him 'a seashore with figures' for £100. Dickens met the father long before he knew the son.

As Wilkie drifted around St Cleer's Well, he found himself lost in a reverie about his father. William had died three years earlier and Wilkie missed him, although he perhaps didn't miss having to account for his time or choice of career. The money he'd been left was also useful (Harriet was holding William's characteristically modest but solid estate, to share between Wilkie and his older brother, Charles). In 1836, when Wilkie was just twelve, William had taken his family to Italy and France for almost two years, interrupting Wilkie's sporadic schooling and igniting a lifelong passion for travel, mystery, antique ruins and painting – and where,

walking with his father, he 'first learned to appreciate the beauties of Nature under guidance which, in this world, I can never
resume'. When he returned to Rome seventeen years later, his
travelling companions had to put up with a number of excitable
tales that suggested it wasn't only ancient ruins that Wilkie was
exploring in his early teens. 'Wilkie', wrote Dickens in a letter to his
sister-in-law, Georgina Hogarth, 'in a carriage one day, [gave us]
a full account of his first love adventure. It was at Rome it seemed,
and proceeded, if I may be allowed the expression, to the utmost
extremities – he came out quite a pagan Jupiter in the business.'

The first thing to know about Wilkie, I am learning, is that
he is a storyteller. In later years he would be acclaimed as a man
who could weave a thrilling tale and puncture some of the most
absurd hypocrisies of the age, especially when it came to the
inequitable treatment of women; but it is also true that, even as
he produced his sensational, campaigning novels from his solitary
home in Marylebone, he was secretly installing one, and then
two, mistresses (and their families) in separate houses around the
corner. It's like my mother said, a man with a beard always has
something to hide. Just ask Enid. In 1838, when the Collins family
returned at last from their foreign trip, and the fourteen-year-old
Wilkie found himself enrolled in a grim little boarding school in
Highbury, the only way he could keep the dormitory bully from
beating him every night was by telling him ever more fantastical
stories. Entertain me! Or feel the pain. Wilkie was a proper little
Scheherazade all his life, but I imagine the habit started here.

You'll understand, then, if we don't take everything in *Rambles
Beyond Railways* at face value. With the day getting older, Wilkie
and Henry headed north, deeper into the Cornish moor. They
passed Trethevy Quoit, a Neolithic dolmen that looks rather like
one of the advent houses that my family attempts to make every
year out of slabs of gingerbread and icing, the main difference

being that 'The Place of Graves', as Wilkie called it, has been standing on this spot for many thousands of years and still hasn't disintegrated into a slew of sticky pastry. It's peaceful here in the late April sunshine. Fields and hedgerows have grown up around the stones – and Trethevy Quoit is so much part of the landscape that, despite its size, a dog walker strolls past and doesn't even spare a glance. New housing has been built a few yards away, just beyond a wire fence and a ditch. I look over and there's a woman in white sitting on the nearest balcony, sipping a mug of tea and reading a novel (there is! I mean, it's cream-coloured leisurewear or something, but still: she's a woman; in *white*). And she's close enough to start a whispered conversation. 'Is that the road to London?' I want to ask 'with nervous, uncertain lips', but I'm worried she might start giving me directions (why indeed wouldn't she?), when I don't actually want to go to London.

When Wilkie was here the Quoit stood alone in 'a barren country', but then (and now) its 'aboriginal simplicity … renders it an impressive, almost a startling object to look on'. Startling, yes. In many other countries there'd be a car park and a hullaballoo of kiosks and cafés; here you can jump up and take a restorative nap on the Quoit's sloping roof, a great twenty-tonne hunk of immovable granite. And yet, well over 4,000 years ago, someone somehow lifted these immense stones and placed them here. No one knows why.

Wilkie loved mysteries. His stories are constructed out of intricate layers of conspiracy, confusion and dread. For most of the time, the truth is elusive, or teased at, or obfuscated by a multitude of voices. There is a sensational secret at the heart of his most famous novel, *The Woman in White*, but to get to it his characters have to unpick a tangle of subterfuge and lies, before they can approach the chilling truth. Along the way, Wilkie exposes and rails against some contemporary injustices, although he's no

Dickens. In fact, can you imagine Dickens walking past the now defunct Caradon Mine, as Wilkie did soon after leaving Trethevy Quoit, and having nothing more to say than: 'far beneath the embankment on which we stood, men, women and children were breaking and washing ore in a perfect marsh of copper-coloured mud and copper-coloured water.' Children? Who cares that the water is 'copper-coloured'? There are *children* working in the mine. Dickens would have had a letter to *The Times* out by nightfall and a novel in the shops the following year.

No, what Wilkie cares about is the *story*. No one else but Dickens could write such nail-biting serial cliffhangers (Dickens knew this and used Wilkie as much as he could in his magazines, even hiring him as a staff writer on *Household Words* for a while). Wilkie was aware of criticisms in his lifetime that he sacrificed character for plot, that he was more concerned with a rattling good yarn than he was in exploring the complexities of human affairs, and he even self-consciously tried to do something about it with his later novels. But I don't think the criticisms are remotely fair. Just look at the way he uses different narrators in *The Woman in White* to build an intricate picture of the characters' thoughts and lives. He had passion and empathy. What other (bearded) Victorian writer could have created the heroic Marian, who drives the investigation into her cousin's sinister husband, even if Wilkie almost ruins his proto-feminism by giving her 'a masculine mouth and jaw' and dark down on her upper lip that is 'almost a moustache'? He does the same in his detective story, *The Moonstone*, mixing perspectives, giving women a voice, but this time thickening the fog of mystery with a blow-back of opiates.

By the time he was writing *The Moonstone* in 1867, Wilkie was irrevocably addicted to laudanum. (If you're wondering about the recipe, it's a tincture, and easy to prepare: simply dilute one part opium or morphine with ten parts brandy; flavour with a dash of cayenne pepper, ether, hashish or anything else that comes to hand; shake; dose yourself generously as pain or inclination dictate.) Key passages of this dreamily intricate work were dictated to Harriet, the daughter of his first mistress, Caroline Graves, when he was in great pain and desperately swigging on the drug. It was said that when Wilkie was on a trip to Switzerland, he had to send a friend to go and buy his supplies from numerous separate chemists, because individually they couldn't provide him with the quantities he needed. By 1885 he had been taking so much for so long that his surgeon said he was consuming enough 'to kill a dozen people'.

Wilkie, like any good addict, always said that he wasn't affected, but from very early middle age he suffered from gout (cripplingly), headaches, rheumatic pains, agues and weeping eyes and couldn't survive without regular infusions. He was living in a time when laudanum was freely available over the counter; and had grown up in a household where his mother, Harriet, could say to her anguished friend Samuel Taylor Coleridge (who, to be fair, had a much more tortured relationship with the drug than Wilkie ever did): 'Mr Coleridge, do not cry; if the opium really does you any good, and you *must* have it, why do you not go and get it?'

Amen to that.

I wonder if there was any blister-soothing laudanum in Wilkie's knapsack on this walking tour of Cornwall? He was certainly familiar with the drug two years later, when he wrote to his mother from a seaside holiday with Dickens and his family that 'the sea air acts on me as if it was all distilled from laudanum'. Perhaps the sea air was enough this time. He was a young man and a vigorous one: and he covered the miles. I'm struggling in his wake as we make our way over the moor, with the rock formation known as the Cheesewring as our goal, although for now I take a breather (as did Wilkie) among the three ancient standing stone circles known as 'the Hurlers'. The stones in one of the circles are remarkably well preserved, although it seems a curtailed attempt was made to re-erect some of them in the 1930s, so it's hard to know how many of them were standing when Wilkie passed by.

Wilkie reckoned there were only two possible theories for their existence: they are either the remains of 'a Druid Temple'; or they are the petrified bodies of local men who went out to play ball on the Sabbath Day (the 'hurlers') and were turned into pillars of stone for their wickedness. He preferred the latter explanation; and it's possible, of course; although I also have to break it to him that the stones are almost certainly not the remains of a 'Druid Temple' either – or rather, they are not the creation of what we now think of as Druids. I have a killjoy booklet by Paul White to hand, *Druids in the South-West?*, and he is adamant that the Druids had nothing to do with the 'building of the West Country's megaliths'. 'Druids', with their golden scythes and mistletoe and white robes, that is; and their belief that all living beings' souls are connected and intermingle at our births and deaths. They probably came much later than these stones – and were obliterated by the Roman armies at Anglesey. Although, really, what do we know? Only that we are treading a land where the Druids and their ideas are making yet another tentative comeback.

A stout middle-aged man in faded, high-crotched orange dungarees, with dark curly hair cascading out from underneath a Breton sailor's cap, is striding purposefully around these stone circles, directing an elderly couple where to sit (his parents I guess), and all the while talking loudly about himself and his needs and desires and hopes and gripes. It has to be his parents. No one else would put up with it. His decrepit father totters off to go and sit by himself next to a stone at the opposite edge of the circle and I watch with an uprush of sympathy as he painfully and oh-so-slowly lowers himself to the ground. The babbling man's mother remains with her son and she listens mutely to his endless, energetic complaints, many of them directed at his father: 'What's he doing?' 'Why's he sitting there?' 'Why doesn't he come back?' 'He's too old.' Wilkie also talked a great deal, in an easy, sweet-tempered flow, although he was interested in what other people had to say, and he found an outlet for his teeming brain in the books he created. Perhaps Babbling Man is one of our greatest living authors, or artists. Not that it matters, of course; we must all find our way out. But not to be able to fall silent in this wondrous place, when the wind drops and the late April sun caresses us with soft paws and strokes the lichen-coated granite and an intoxicating aroma of bog and spent sunshine is rising from the tussocky earth; and in fact when the souls of the Celts themselves might be here, in these stones and grasses, waiting to infuse us with some ancient, transformative magic … I mean, please; this is babbling agony.

To the Cheesewring, then – they'll never follow us there. Wilkie described this tower of rocks, set on a pinnacle on the edge of the moor, as 'the wildest and most wondrous of all the wild and wondrous structures in the rock architecture of the scene'. He went on: 'If a man dreamt of a great pile of stones in a nightmare, he would dream of such a pile as the Cheesewring. All the heaviest and largest of the seven thick slabs of which it is composed are at the top; all the lightest and smallest at the bottom.'

As Wilkie and Henry approached the Cheesewring, they were waylaid by a roar of welcome from a gang of awesomely drunk Cornish sightseers. All men, it goes without saying. Henry (the nervous artist) bolted for cover, saying he had to go and sketch, so Wilkie was left alone to share the lads' beer, and one of them 'violently uncorked a bottle and directed half of its contents in a magnificent jet of light brown froth all over everybody'. A true Cornish welcome, they bellowed, although the beery bonhomie soon turned sour because Wilkie was so eager to get past them and up to the top. I only mention it because I'm not sure this sort of thing happens very often any more – at least not to me.

I scramble up the final hill as the sun sinks closer to the horizon and settle myself on some rocks, at the very top of the plateau, just back from the Cheesewring (or Wringcheese as it was called by the eighteenth-century antiquarian the Revd William Borlase). I think I'm alone and get quite a shock when a crow gives a half-strangled yelp and then grunts like a disaffected hog. What strange ghosts must lurk here? Almost immediately a Scottish couple emerges from behind a pile of granite. 'Excuse me, but is this the Cheesewring?' they ask, pointing to the rocks I'm sitting on. 'Well, no,' I say, gesturing down the hill at the seven large granite slabs, each one larger than the next, all precariously balanced on top of one another. 'I think that is.' We agree it is an extraordinary sight. And they wonder if I know how it got there, so I say: 'I'm afraid everything I know is at least 150 years out of date, but according to Wilkie Collins (you know?), the Cheesewring was probably not built by Druids, as people once thought, but is a natural geological formation, although it's possible the Druids may have cleared away a few stones and some detritus to give it its shape. Also, the Druids almost certainly used the top of the Cheesewring to make speeches to their tribes – and made secret sacrifices up there.' They take this strange and archaic explanation in their stride. They nod wisely. And then they disappear rapidly down the hill, leaving me to wonder if Wilkie would be pleased to think his erratically researched holiday book was still being quoted all these years later, and its dubious opinions absorbed and spread and repeated as gospel. Or perhaps the Scottish couple just thought I was unhinged.

I've been enjoying pottering around the eastern fringes of Cornwall, but it still comes as a relief when Wilkie all of a sudden plunges deeper into the county, rattling through the sixty-odd miles from Liskeard to Helston at the head of the Lizard Peninsula, without saying a word about any of it. Despite his earlier maunderings about the joys of hiking, I have a strong suspicion he and Henry may have taken a coach. Wilkie quotes Laurence Sterne in *Tristram Shandy* approvingly: 'I think it very much amiss that a man cannot go quietly through a town and let it alone, when it does not meddle with him.'

Bad weather kept them trapped in Helston – 'the dullest of towns' – thinking dark thoughts about its inhabitants – 'a riotous and drunken set' – and its 'superlatively ugly' church. With the rain slenching down on Wilkie, it's worth mentioning the popular theory, resisted by many, that weather shapes character. Nirad Chaudhuri believed it. Here he is in his book *A Passage to England*: 'the weather has very largely entered into the formation of the Englishman's mind, and the training of his sensibilities. It has made him responsive to changes in the environment, capable of meeting surprises of all kinds, both pleasant and unpleasant'. Or, to put it another way: 'After experiencing the English weather I had no difficulty in understanding why Englishmen became so offensive in India, losing their usual kindliness … Their sense of proportion broke down.'

The only thing going for Helston, said Wilkie, was its festival, 'the Furry', held every year on 8 May, when the whole town dances all day and capers through the streets, hand in hand, garlanded with flowers and leaves. Or so he'd heard, although he never saw the thing (and was relying on Richard Polwhele's 1803–8 *History of Cornwall* for a full account of 'these extraordinary absurdities'). Wilkie could be supercilious about folk traditions, but the Furry was still going 100 years later when the surrealist artist, and local writer, Ithell Colquhoun visited in 1954 and 1955, and she relates how the town gathered to dance (especially the school children, but in the end everyone, including the local 'worthies'), and she describes the dance winding up and down the streets and in and out of the flower-clad houses, while 'the figure is executed as a foursome by the first two couples and so on down the chain'. Ithell was alert to mystic undercurrents, and she says that some locals thought the dance had originated in honour of the sun god, and was brought to Cornwall many thousands of years earlier by settlers from Egypt. True or not, in the 1950s the streets were also alive with jugglers, boxers, palmists, magicians and acrobats and Ithell found herself buying a remedy made from 'holy thistle' from 'a Gypsy Lee'. When she opened the package later it contained some sage-green tablets, a pixie charm and an address in Lincolnshire 'where one could write for advice'. The pills, she said, 'smelled like the unguent of the witch-coven'. The sad fact is, Wilkie didn't get to experience any of this – and nor did I. The key, it seems, is to visit Helston on 8 May; or otherwise avoid the town.

Wilkie was equally scathing about the next place he visited, mainly because it called itself 'Lizard *Town*' and he thought this absurd when it was no more than a few muddy little streets and rickety cottages, seething with 'ducks, geese, cocks, hens, pigs, cows, horses, dunghills, puddles, sheds, peat-stacks, timber, nets'. Maybe someone was listening, because it's just plain 'Lizard' on the Ordnance Survey map now, even though the number of houses has multiplied and the livestock and everything else has been tidied away, replaced by tubs and window boxes heavy with flowers and (on this hot, still, dusty day) a lingering aroma of chip fat. I wonder, as I wander up and down the few spruce streets, if David Icke has ever visited Lizard Town. You would think he should, because he believes (in case you haven't been keeping up) that humanity is being ruled by a master race of lizards, who have disguised themselves as our leaders – and surely Lizard Town would be a good place to explore his theory. Although it does then occur to me that this may be exactly what they're expecting.

When Wilkie was here the local mothers were holding a 'smallpox' party. Anyone with a baby was waiting at the inn for the local doctor, who had brought 'a lot of fine fresh matter' down from London and was going to vaccinate every baby he could lay his hands on. If you tried to do the same thing today the town would be in an internet-fuelled uproar, but in those days all you needed was a doctor's certificate, some impressive whiskers and your word would be God's. I can't make up my mind which of Lizard's two pubs was the smallpox inn, so I have a drink at both – and although the Top House seems most likely (it has an open, early Victorian feel), the woman behind the bar insists it wasn't built until 1860, and I'm not going to argue. I then crack my head on one of the offensively low (fifteenth-century) beams in the Witchball and, like Wilkie (although what drove him out was the thought of the 'fine fresh matter'), I hurry back into the sunshine.

If you live in a city (as most of us do), you will know what it is like to inhabit an atmosphere laced with diesel fumes, human detritus and grit. Strangely, we don't generally notice the air that we breathe, unless we're standing at a junction and a bus is coughing grey toxic particulate smog straight into our lungs. But the truth is that the city air is killing us. We all know it, even if we try to put that inconvenient fact to one side, along with so much else. Perhaps we're waiting for a time when we're less busy? Or, as if by magic – just like that! – a day when our governments are not working to placate the fossil fuel lobbyists. I mention it because the air on the walk to Lizard Point is so dizzyingly fresh, so sparklingly *clean*, so ozone-rich as it blasts in over the point from the south-west seas, that I can feel my brain being pummelled and scoured and positively derailed by the unaccustomed giddying glory of it all. This is the air – better than laudanum! – that would have transported Wilkie and Henry as they strolled along the narrow path, fringed with tamarisk and myrtle, that took them to 'the southernmost land in England'. Breathe it – and weep.

Wilkie was excited to find that many footpaths in Cornwall run along the *tops* of the thick stone walls that divide the fields – and I am excited to find that this is sometimes still true. It is early afternoon and there are no clouds in the clear April sky. The fields are green with fresh new grasses and blackthorn blossom is frosting the hedgerows. Down by the Point there are neat clumps of thrift edging the paths, their first pink buds getting ready for the summer months; and I am happy to find (and identify) delicate violets and forget-me-nots. I'm told there is sea asparagus here, and Cornish heath, but the main plants you'll see, clinging to the cliffs and open ground, are the bright yellow flowers of the Hottentot fig and the rapidly spreading, fleshy, succulent jellybean plant. Neither of these would have been here in 1850. They arrived, somehow, by ship or garden, from South Africa and Mexico respectively. And now they dominate England's southernmost tip, to the great delight of many thrill-seeking tourists (they look spectacular, especially in the late summer when the jellybean plants turn a lurid red), and to the despair of most conservationists, who agonize over the effect this is having on the fragile native clovers and fringed rupturewort.

It is a dilemma, how much to intervene – and whether, indeed, there's any point, given the vigorous glee with which these inter-lopers have spread – although the National Trust volunteer I meet at the cliff edge seems sanguine: why not let them thrive here, he wonders, and make a stand for the more delicate native plants further along the coast? The language of invasion and resistance creeps into our conversation, almost every conversation, about non-native species. None of us can help it – it shouldn't really

mean anything – but it is good to remember that these are *plants*
we are talking about. The National Trust man knows that, of
course. And there are indeed very good reasons for resisting the
spread of many non-native species: it's not just so we can save
the poetry and magic and diversity of what we have, but there
are diseases to combat and ecosystems at risk. As climate change
accelerates, things are going to become even more complicated:
are our native species best placed to adapt to the coming storm
(and droughts)? Or should we welcome African and Mexican
plants to our shores? Is nature in fact going to find its own way –
and should we therefore abandon the Cornish heath (a rare white
heather now found only on the Lizard) to its doom? Be assured
that the debate around what happens to Britain's flora and fauna
in a time of unprecedented globalized trade and massive climate
upheaval is ongoing and lively – and possibly even fruitful – but
it has nothing to do with the *human* cost of the same. Even so.
The Mexican jellybean plant is coming! Retreat! And regroup at
Kynance Cove.

The walk along the cliffs from Lizard Point westwards to
Kynance Cove is empty and wild, even on a blazing hot Sunday
afternoon in April, but the Cove itself (which Wilkie described as
'the place at which the coast scenery of the Lizard district arrives
at its climax of grandeur') is thronged with happy people. There's
a car park here only a short scramble from the beach, and some
three to four hundred cars, which may explain the crowds. Also,
as Wilkie knew, low tide is the time to be here, when the beach
expands and some thrilling caves emerge from the waves – and
that's 3.30p.m. today, so we are bang on schedule.

Wilkie headed down the steep path to the beach, leaving
Henry to sketch from the clifftops. It was August and he felt quite
alone, although perhaps the 'deep mist' kept people away. More
likely, this gadding about on beaches would have been something

strange to the Cornish people of the day, unless they were looking for food or wrecks. A guide materialized to show Wilkie the
rocks and for the next few hours he was steered and pushed and
cajoled up 'Asparagus' Island and past the 'Devil's Throat' and
the 'Devil's Bellows', slipping on the wet rocks, almost plunging
to his death more than once (he claimed), sometimes standing
on the shoulders or even the face of his guide, who taught him
one of life's more valuable lessons: 'never scramble your toes
about, where toes have no business to be.' They gathered wild
asparagus from the summit of Asparagus Island and the guide
told him tales of smugglers and wrecks and fishermen slipping
under the waves in the winter storms. I look at the steep sides of
Asparagus Island (down which a skinny young man is currently
bounding with improbable grace, like a carefree Barbary ape)
and decide that Wilkie was either lying or he really did find a
guide who could, as he says, have taken a drunken man 'up and
down Asparagus Island without the slightest risk either to himself
or his charge'.

I am happier following Wilkie into the caves, walking tall in the
'great, irregular, Gothic halls' before we 'wriggle onward a few feet,
serpent-like, flat on our bellies'. Enid would *love* it here, among the
smugglers and the dark hidden caverns. Children run in and out,
yelling. I follow a father as he leads his very solemn six-year-old
son round one of the shorter routes. Outside, people are charging
into the sea, hoofing up the waves, swimming and flapping their
polystyrene bodyboards, kicking plastic footballs, and shouting
with joy in the sunshine. The beach is alive with holiday delight.
Picnics and windbreaks cluster between the rocks. A young woman
has sculpted a mermaid from the wet sand and is now lying with
her head on its lap. Just past her, closer to the foaming sea, I am
amazed to find a single living starfish in a rock pool – amazed,
that is, to find it has survived so much human freight.

The poet Tennyson was here, in Kynance Cove, two years before Wilkie, jotting in his notebook: 'Glorious grass-green monsters of waves. Into the caves of Asparagus Island. Sat watching wave-rainbows.' Wilkie is also enraptured by the sea, 'as it rolls and rushes and dances in the wind' and almost stays too late ('the surf dashes nearer and nearer to our feet') – but then he didn't have the shrieks of children to warn him or the stampede of oiled bodies rushing to the lonely (but *lovely*) café that overlooks the bay. I find a spare corner of a trestle table and watch the wave-rainbows from on high. I'm sitting with a couple of lean Americans who have ordered at least two dozen cream teas – towering plates of fluffy scones, huge troughs of claggy yellow cream, buckets of jam – but this apparent surfeit suddenly makes sense when a straggling, exhausted party of their friends appears, sweating and heaving from the walk from Lizard Point, some of them close to tears, many too old, I would have thought, for this sweltering adventure – and I watch as they collapse with cries of astonished delight into the arms of this incomparable Cornish feast.

I hear they are on a cruise ship, making its way round the coast. What would Cornwall be without its tourists? Now that the mines and the pilchards ('a Cornishman's national pride', says Wilkie) have almost gone, tourism is the apparent key to prosperity. In 1850, when in other parts of Britain there weren't enough jobs to go around, Wilkie could write: 'The number of inhabitants in the county is stated by the last census at 341,269 and … the supply of men for all purposes does not appear to be greater than the demand.' Wilkie found the people happy and busy and fruitfully employed. There were 'ten thousand persons – men, women, and children' working in the fisheries. He thought the 'inexhaustible mineral treasures in the earth, and the equally inexhaustible shoals of pilchards which annually visit the coast' meant that the people of Cornwall would always prosper. Nowadays the population of

Cornwall is about 550,000, although that number is almost irrel-
evant when you consider that there are over five million annual
visitors and rising.

In the 1964 edition of the *Shell Guide to Cornwall* John Betjeman
lamented his lost world: 'Cornwall has changed so much in
appearance since the first edition of this guide was published in
1933 that now, thirty years later, the text has had entirely to be
rewritten.' On he went: 'Roads have been widened, blocks of
houses have been taken down in picturesque ports to make way
for car parks; petrol stations proliferate ... In the holiday season
lorries and cars trailing caravans and boats block lanes never
intended for such heavy traffic.' According to Betjeman, before
the great upheavals of the mid-twentieth century the only people
who visited Cornwall were 'fishermen, golfers and artists'. He
manages to make it sound like they were all wearing tweed. The
changes, every one of them unutterably awful (he would swear to
that), had happened in the years since he was a boy and 'everyone
in the village had oil lamps and candles' and 'a journey to the
nearest town and back was a day's expedition'.

Ithell Colquhoun, renting a shack further down the coast, wrote
in 1957: 'I have never spent a whole year at Vow Cave and am
sorry now that I did not do so before Lamorna became, during
the summer months, uninhabitable.' And I remember my own
first Cornish holiday, aged eight, in 1971, when the sun blazed
and the surf rolled and we had miles of golden sandy beaches all
to ourselves. Didn't we? I certainly remember my first trip to the
Mediterranean a couple of years later. We were spending ten days
in the hills of Provence, not far from Mont Ventoux, and we had
been promised a day at the seaside, even though my father (my
kind, gentle, but – he'd be the first to admit – somewhat gloomy
father) explained that there was almost no point in going, what
with the insufferable crowds and the rank pollution (discarded

picnics and plastics and French effluent) and the fact that the
once pristine Mediterranean Sea (the wine-dark sea of Homer
and Dumas and Matisse) had been poisoned and blighted with
oil spills and emptied – dragged clean – of all its teeming fish
and every last scrap of sea life. And I remember heading south
in our white Triumph 2000 Estate, with the cicadas shrieking at
the open windows from the hot, scented hills; and how we surged
over the last rise and there, laid out in front of us, was a vision of
such potent beauty – the light leaping from the radiant sea, the
almost empty beach glittering with ochre and gold – that we were
all briefly struck dumb. And then we were seized with laughter,
hysterical from the car journey, my mother too, overcome with
wonder and joy to see this heart-stopping, undeniable beauty; and
the look on my father's face – amusement? disappointment? – as
he started to explain (and then quickly stopped) that what we
think we can see is not the same as what there is.

I'm not saying my father was wrong. In fact, and alas, today
the Mediterranean is sicker and emptier than ever before (and still
undeniably blue and lovely). And Britain's own seas and shoreline, that once seethed with whales, walruses, dolphins, pilchards
and puffins, are silent and sodden with invisible plastics. We all
understand this in theory. But we are also having to contend with
something known to conservationists as shifting baseline syndrome,
the bewildering and endless realignment of what constitutes
'normal' – from Wilkie to Betjeman, from Ithell to us – so that
we can no longer remember, or have no first-hand knowledge of
what it was like to see butterflies thick in the meadows and starfish in every rock pool. We are rightly suspicious of our golden
childhood memories, but none of us ever lives long enough to
notice that the tap of life is being screwed shut.

When Wilkie was here in Kynance Cove he was alone, in
August, apart from his friend Henry (sketching on the cliffs)

and his indefatigable guide; and now here we are in April, and there are 400 vehicles in the car park and cruise ships disgorging tourists into the bay. I'm not saying that's wrong: who are we to say who should or should not be enjoying this extraordinary cove with its rainbow waves and shimmering rocks? Not John Betjeman, let's hope, nor me. Back in Wilkie's time most people had to work hard just to scrape by. But there's no avoiding the fact that there are an awful lot of us these days, on the move and keeping busy, scurrying up and down the land, nosing along the coast, looking for a lost lane or a lonely beach, and all the while buying and using and accumulating and shedding an unfeasible amount of stuff.

Imagine what this beautiful cove was like 150 years ago. And be honest. Wouldn't you rather have it all to yourself – maybe you and a few others – as Wilkie once did?

Then again, who wouldn't? I mean, I know I would.

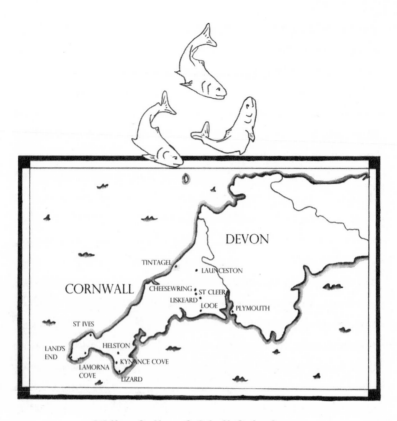

Wilkie Collins & Ithell Colquhoun,
Lamorna Cove to Launceston, 1850 and 1950

THREE

Pilchards to Postcards

'Influences, essences, presences, whatever is here
– in my name of a stream in a valley I salute you; I
share this place with you.'

ITHELL COLQUHOUN, *THE LIVING STONES*

Incidentally, I'm starting to wonder (even worry) about Wilkie's travelling companion, Henry Brandling. Wilkie hardly mentions him, except when he tells us that he has wandered off to make another sketch. We know that Wilkie wrote to a friend, Charles Ward, from Penzance, not far from here, unsuccessfully pleading with him to join them: '*Here*, sir', coaxed Wilkie, the lifelong sensualist, 'we live on Ducks, Geese, Chickens, tongue, pickled pilchards, curried Lobster – Clotted cream – jam tarts, fruit tarts – custards – cakes – *red mullet*, conger eels – salmon trout'. Charles, another artist, had been on a painting tour to Normandy with Wilkie three years earlier (Wilkie had created some pleasant sketches); and it was probably Charles, ten years older than Wilkie, who had led the young boy-man out into the Roman night for his adolescent adventures, where 'he proceeded, if I may be allowed the expression, to the utmost extremities'. I get the sense that Charles Ward was a lot more fun to be with than Henry, who was perhaps a rather nervy man, a friend from the Royal Academy of Wilkie's undeniably neurotic older brother, Charles ('Charley') Collins.

Henry's family, the Brandlings, were coal and now railway potentates in Northumbria. His father, like Wilkie's, had died recently – and he too was seizing the chance to pursue his artistic ambitions (there's a certain irony to this trip 'beyond railways'), albeit with rather deeper pockets than Wilkie's. But he's a hard man to trace. He was slightly older than Wilkie; and his public art trails off soon after this Cornish adventure; and if I'm looking at the right Charles Henry Brandling in the census for 1881, he ended up living in Cheltenham aged fifty-eight with his wife Mary (thirty-four), four children, a servant called Emily Griffin, and with his profession listed as 'Artist Architectural Drawing'. By the time of the 1891 census the household had swelled to eight children, one exhausted wife (forty-four) and three servants. He died in 1897. I think that's him – although what I can tell you is that if he's the poor deluded, borderline insane, 'Henry Brandling' who is the subject of Peter Carey's gripping 2012 novel *The Chemistry of Tears*, in which he travels to Germany from Northumbria to have a giant clockwork duck made for his ailing son, then it's no wonder Wilkie wanted to keep his distance. My suspicion, founded on absolutely nothing, is that Wilkie wanted Charles Ward along because they were both enthusiastic visitors to local prostitutes (in Rome, Paris and beyond), as were Wilkie and Dickens. But Henry (as seen in *The Chemistry of Tears*) would have been, in Wilkie's eyes, a bit of a prig.

Wilkie and Henry were marching hard, despite all that hot lobster and clotted cream, to get to Land's End. ('The Land's End!' raved Wilkie. 'There is something in the very words that stirs us all.') He pretends that he has visited St Michael's Mount ('so well known to readers of all classes … that they will surely be relieved rather than disappointed if these pages exhibit the distinguished negative merit of passing the Mount without notice'); and skips along the coast from Lizard Point to Land's End almost without comment. He does, though, give a passing nod to 'the beautiful coast scenery at Lamorna Cove', and I make a brief detour there with Anna – who has joined me for this stretch – so we can explore the place where the surrealist artist, writer and mystic Ithell Colquhoun lived and worked.

Ithell Colquhoun was born in 1906 in British India. She had come to know this part of Cornwall during the Second World War and then, when the war ended, she fled a disastrous marriage to a Belgian surrealist husband (and there's a combination of words guaranteed to bring disorientation and dismay), and found and settled in remote Lamorna, renting a small corrugated iron shed in the woods, next to the river that flows from the head of the valley to the rocky cove and the sea.

She was looking for seclusion and, as she writes in *The Living Stones*, her extraordinary memoir of her time here, it was 'in Lamorna that I first saw the falling of dew, and it was at Penberth that the shifting of the landscape-veil first presented itself to my clear sight, disclosing – what?' She cherished her solitude, here in the 'valley of streams and moon leaves, wet scents and all that cries with the owl's voice', even though 'any sign of introversion is, in a woman, particularly suspect'. 'An introverted male', she went on, may be acclaimed 'a genius ... but an introverted female? Society is slow to grant her a place at all.'

Lamorna valley may be horrible in the summer months, as Ithell once lamented, but on this weekend in April all is quiet. A tiny tarmac road leads down and through the wet, wooded valley, and at an even tinier fork in the road either continues along the coast to nothingness or drifts into a cul-de-sac and – Ithell would hate this – a large tarmac car park overlooking Lamorna Cove.

Ithell Colquhoun was one of the first prose writers to try and describe the deeper magic of a place. Not just to show what we think we see (the glory of the woods and the trees, and the songbirds she cherished, and the river that danced at the edge of her field), but through solitude and *kaif* – a direct experiencing of the moment – she opened herself to the shifting of the 'landscape-veil' and described, with as much accuracy as is possible, that sense we all get, the feeling we all know, that there is something else around and within us that is neither obvious nor apparent but is none-theless present and vital, except it's just out of reach or slipping past the corner of our eye, and even perhaps other-dimensional. It's there, though, even if we keep on missing it. We just need to find – or remember – another way of seeing.

None of this would have occurred to young Wilkie, despite his love of sensation and drama, and with all his feeling for super-natural undercurrents. The rocks are the rocks. The Druids are strange – but gone. And the last of the 'superstitions' – folkloric festivals and holy wells – are 'the best evidence of the low state of education among the people from whom they are produced'. That was not Ithell's belief. She knew that 'certain places need people as much as certain people need places' and Lamorna became her life: 'I am identified with every leaf and pebble.' She was told that Lamorna Cove was where 'the Atlanteans, fleeing from cataclysm, first landed' and she described the spirits and emanations of her valley and the force ('the Michael-force') that flowed through everything. But most of the time she is transfixed by what she can see right in front of her: the birds, she says, have a brighter plumage here, the sky has its own tone of silver, and 'the hedgetops in summer are bright with the tiny pink stars of stonecrop'. She writes with poetry and grace and humour – some-times anger – and I promise you will find yourself sharing and transformed by her visions.

We couldn't find any kind of memorial to Ithell, even though the valley is littered with plaques commemorating the artists and writers who have shared her love of this magical valley, but we do find the site of her corrugated iron shack, now rebuilt as a trim little hut with Velux windows and well-scrubbed stone walls. It is the primrose time of year and the patchy ground around the house (what she called her 'Irish garden', but is really just a thinning of the woods) has clumps of primula, narcissi and anemone growing among the sycamore and birch. Beyond is 'her' field, green in a clinging mist, and the stream where she would sometimes sunbathe naked, hidden from the road, and watch the dragonflies making love, 'emerald and black, or turquoise and black'. The valley is damp, from the mist and the streams that run to the nearby cove and from last year's leaf mould in the woods, now being forced aside by a rising tide of bluebells. It's not raining – away from this valley we have left behind a sunny day – but everything here is slick and slippery to touch, including the soft spring leaves of the lime trees that crowd close to the narrow road and the top of the new wooden gate that blocks the way to Ithell's old home.

Ithell was certainly not the first or last to make her way to Cornwall looking for a deeper connection to an ancient land. She was followed by countless others (artists, of course, but also academics and antiquarians, magicians and witches, neo-pagans, bards, mystics, Druids, occultists, weekend hippies …), all on the trail of standing stones, stone circles, pulse spots, ley lines, Gaia, Arthur and Merlin, Celtic crosses, the White Goddess, petroglyphs, runes, crop circles, UFOs, labyrinths, Wicca, Elysium, Camelot, Atlantis, and so on. It's a long list. And as Ithell said, 'Cornwall has an attraction for the seeker, bearing as it does traces of those sunken countries Lyonesse and Atlantis … people, irresistibly drawn, will jettison their prospects and come down here to find not only a living but a life worth living.' There has also been a resurgence of the old beliefs and customs from within Cornwall, perhaps starting in 1928 with the re-energizing of the 'Cornish Gorsedh', the gathering of the Cornish people and their robed bards. Wilkie, on the other hand, would have told them all to go back to school.

Not far from Ithell's home, on the other side of the valley, there's a hotel described in the *Time Out Guide to Devon and Cornwall*

as 'bringing a sprinkling of glitz to Britain's furthest reaches'. A
sign on the road is advertising cocktails and views over Lamorna
Cove, and so – with the light fading and the magic hour upon
us – we climb some sweaty wooden steps through a neglected
hillside garden and push the door open into a white, minimalist
reception area. Despite *Time Out*'s excitement, the place seems
utterly unsuited to this valley and in fact some kind of process of
uneasy osmosis is already taking place: an atmosphere of decay
from the surrounding woods has been drawn inside and is possibly even now seeping up the walls. There's no one around. My
mind is filled with Ithell and her belief that this valley is especially
haunted by ghosts, poltergeists and spirits – none of them ever
hurt her, she said, but still – and as we poke around the empty
white corridors and peer through some French windows at the
deserted, windblown terrace, a feeling of distress, of something
being unpleasantly wrong, creeps up on us. Neither of us wants
to say anything. We just walk back fast towards the reception –
and we're almost there, with the long corridor behind us, when
a family emerges from the far end. They have a large dog with
them. Now, I'm not brave about these things – aged seventeen
I had to walk out of *The Shining* – but there's something about
deserted hotels that is *horrifying*, and I whip round to seek solace
from Anna only to find she has already fled out of the door and
down the hill back to Ithell. I turn around again and the people
and their dog – a Rottweiler, as it happens – are almost upon
me and they haven't said a word – not a word! – but why would
they? – and I want to say something about cocktails or cream teas
but before I can do that one of the women looks into my eyes with
such fathomless despair that I find myself lurching back against
the reception desk unable to move or speak until they are clear of
the hotel and – I see this now – heading up the hill to their large
black MPV in the car park.

And that is Lamorna Cove: disturbingly empty off-season; but rammed, they all tell us, in the summer. Ithell left for a more isolated part of Cornwall in the late 1950s, exiled by the traffic and the noise, before returning, years later, to die. People were becoming disorientated, she felt, and unable to concentrate on anything because of their addiction to the clamour of modern life, especially the ceaseless background drone of the radio. The *radio*, bless her.

Anna and I go and stand in the cove. There's a café behind us, opened in 1952 (Ithell would have taken her tea here), but now closed and neglected. Apparently, as I write this, the little cove, its buildings, rocky beach, deserted quarries and shoreline, are all up for sale (for a handsome price) – and of course I dread the thought that someone will see an opportunity here for something irrevocably destructive. Even though I could absolutely murder a cup of tea. Ithell would have agreed, but then she ends *The Living Stones* with this thought, that despite 'the forces ravaging the valley today … there is that which resists the encroachments of man'. She mentions the quarries, abandoned for no good reason, and now lying derelict and 'so', she says, 'vanish all who would profane Lamorna's precincts!' I would only add, for any prospective buyer, that there's a very unpleasant smell coming from the seaweed on the (utterly inaccessible) beach. I really wouldn't bother if I were you.

I'm sorry, that was a distracting detour, but we are now back on our way to Land's End. Wilkie was more than a little excited.

> Something like what Jerusalem was to the pilgrim in
> the Holy Land, the Land's End is … to the tourist in

Cornwall. It is the Ultima Thule where his progress stops – the shrine towards which his face has been set, from the first day when he started on his travels – the main vent, through which all the pent-up enthusiasm accumulated along the line of route is to burst its way out, in one long flow of admiration and delight.

Yes, *yes*, YES! The Land's End.

It suggests even to the most prosaically constituted people, ideas of tremendous storms, of flakes of foam flying over the land before the wind, of billows in con-vulsion, of rocks shaken to their centre, of caves where smugglers lurk in ambush, of wrecks and hurricanes, desolation, danger, and death.

The *Land's End*! When Wilkie finally got there, hiking up from the south-east (through some of the most magnificent scenery in Cornwall, he tells us), traipsing past the pub that is the First and Last Inn in England (it still is), he had to ask a guide to lead him to the actual Land's End because there was no way of telling where it was. It was the same when Celia Fiennes visited in 1698 (although 'the people here are very ill guides'). The land, she said, terminates in a 'peak of great rocks which runs a good way into the sea' and, having drunk some 'very good bottled ale' (but only, she stresses, 'for curiosity sake'), 'I clamber'd over them as farre as safety permitted me.'

Today, it is easy to find Land's End without a guide. You can just drive up to the car park entrance and a heavyset, middle-aged man with copious tattoos, death's head finger rings and armloads of silver bracelets will take your £6 and suggest in a voice of East End gravel that, 'not to worry', what you are about to experience 'offers all sorts of retail delights'. The car park is huge but, on this grey April day, it is actually depressing to find it so empty. We get out and there's an argument going on nearby between a very young boy and his parents: 'You won't get to play with the dinosaurs if you behave like this.' 'Sorry, daddy.' 'Get in the car please.' 'I'm *sorry*, mum.' The boy climbs into the back of the car and sits there, gulping down his tears behind the rain-smeared window. A dark tang of tragedy settles on the day.

A low complex of grey-white buildings now provides frame and flavour to the Land's End: the place, Wilkie tells us, that 'fills the minds of imaginative people with visions of barrenness and solitude'. There are places to eat (and who doesn't love a pasty?). Places to drink (Celia would have appreciated the Land's End Bar and its array of bottled beers). A place to sleep (the Land's End Hotel). There's 'Arthur's Quest' – 'experience the legend' – and an 'interactive experience' from the film company Aardman, featuring all our favourite characters (fun, it says on the sign, for all ages). Wallace. Gromit. Shaun the Sheep. There's a West Country Shopping Village and a Trading Company and a Clothing Company and an exhibition space where we can hear all about the 'End to Enders', the people who have hiked or cycled or otherwise propelled themselves from John o' Groats to Land's End. There's a 300-foot-high statue of a Cornish Bard, wearing midnight blue robes woven from the feathers of local seagulls, in one hand holding aloft a precise replica of the Horn of the Nation and in the other an unsheathed Excalibur. Except, no, there isn't. In fact, as I stand outside the portals of Arthur's Quest, I catch myself thinking that all of this could have been a whole lot *worse*, which of course is true, and after all there are at least three young families here and they seem to be having fun – or at least none of the children are actually sitting on the tarmac and screaming. That would be their parents. Although if you are already thinking like this – that someone could have found a way to make the most iconic landscape in England even more jarringly commercial than it already is – then it is probably time to leave. But only once you have battled through a bitter wind and taken a selfie at the signpost that marks the furthest point of your long journey westwards.

The walk back from Land's End took Wilkie and Henry past 'some of the dreariest' views in Cornwall and into 'the large seaport town of St. Ives', where he spent a couple of days drooling over the pilchard industry. The sight of the Cornish fishermen provoked Wilkie into some of his best writing in *Rambles Beyond Railways*, especially the moment when a great pilchard shoal was sighted from the clifftop (by a frantic man waving a bush, known as a 'huer'), and the boats rushed out to encircle the shoal with nets, and the pilchards were trapped and dragged from the churning sea in baskets and whisked to shore, where dozens of men were waiting with shovels:

> standing up to their knees in pilchards, working energetically; the crowd stretching down from the salting-house, all along the beach, and hemming in the boat all round; the uninterrupted succession of men hurrying backwards and forwards with their barrows, through a narrow way kept clear for them in the throng; the glare of the lanterns giving light to the workmen, and throwing red flashes on the fish as they fly incessantly from the shovels over the side of the boat ...

It is a scene of wild industry. It seems like the whole town is there – men, women, children – all working frantically to a plan. Wilkie is awestruck by the sheer quantity of fish being caught: in 1850, the year he was in St Ives, 22,000 hogsheads of fish were exported, mostly to Spain and Italy; at about 3,000 pilchards per hogshead, that's over 66 million fish pulled from the Cornish seas and dispatched to the griddles of the Mediterranean. Despite what Wilkie witnessed, the vigour of the fishing fleets and the apparently limitless abundance of their prey, the pilchard industry withered and almost died in the 1920s: overfishing, a collapse in demand, foreign competition, new offshore fishing methods … take your pick. There's been a very minor revival of late, although the days when the people of St Ives would gather together as one to pull their wealth from the sea are long gone. Nowadays they're more likely to be working alone, harrying the tourist shoals, or servicing the second homes.

Enid Blyton came to St Ives in 1943, on honeymoon with her second husband Dr Kenneth Darrell Waters, who years later destroyed any letters and diaries from this happy time. They were drawn, presumably, by the romance of the place and its wondrous light. Enid, wasting nothing, inserted a salty St Ives seadog into at least one of her Famous Five adventures. The unearthly, aquamarine light is certainly what attracted the artists (Barbara Hepworth, Bernard Leach, Patrick Heron and many others), which in turn led to the opening of Tate St Ives in 1993, which now powers the art-tourism industry. From pilchards to postcards. On the day Anna and I visit there's an exhibition about the response of artists to the words of Virginia Woolf, and I am delighted to find at least one Ithell Colquhoun on display, which is especially pleasing because she was never much welcomed by the art establishment: too esoteric, perhaps, and never quite abstract enough for the St Ives hardliners of her time. I spend a happy few moments standing in front of one of her nakedly suggestive works, called, I thought, *Come into My Cave*, although right now I can find no record of any such title.

We wander through rooms decorated with the art of Vanessa Bell, Dora Carrington, Gwen John and Laura Knight. It's interesting, our enduring reverence for these 1930s artists and writers. It must (perhaps!) be because of their sense of certainty, which probably sounds odd, given how restless and unhappy many of them were. But they shared a culture, however much they railed against it. Virginia Woolf said that the world had fractured in 1914, cutting us loose from everything that had gone before – farewell, Wilkie – but I think it's obvious that the artists in these rooms have inherited, and are reacting to, a common set of Victorian sensibilities. So perhaps it is only now, 100 years down the line, that we can truly say we are adrift from the past.

I leave Anna in St Ives, pondering the replacement bus service back to London, and make haste after Wilkie, who by now is walking much faster 'than the reader may have perceived'. We arrive at Tintagel, one of the places, Wilkie tells us, 'associated with the quaint fancies of the olden time … and romantically, if not historically, reputed as the birthplace of King Arthur'. Not that the citizens of Tintagel care about any foolish historical doubts: their long single street is buttressed with shops selling Arthur cakes and scones and sweets, Merlin pasties, jewellery and wands, plastic Excaliburs and knights' helmets and goblins and the skulls of dragons, and tarot cards and crystals and of course the Holy Grail itself (and why didn't the questing knights think of that, for goodness' sake? You can buy one here for a tenner). The shops are closed now (the light is failing), so I am saved from buying any pewter, or Celtic pipes, and instead find myself staring with mounting distress at a mug decorated with the suddenly very personal message 'You Sir are a Knob'.

It wasn't always this way. In 1806 someone opened a lead and silver mine nearby, down at the headland at the foot of Tintagel Castle. They called it 'King Arthur's Mine' and although it probably wasn't working in 1850 when Wilkie visited, it was up and running again a few years later. There were also quarries along the coast, sending slate out to sea from little Tintagel Cove, or bringing it inland for the local builders. This must be one of the reasons, I am thinking now, that the main tonal note of Tintagel is grey – slate, stone, and a sweeping hinterland of car parks – and, as the first squall of rain arrives from the north, I find myself succumbing to the kind of creeping dread that comes when you're far from home on a cold night in a bleak town on a grim, dark headland. And you've just been insulted by a mug. I scuttle back to my B&B and lie on the lonely bed, feeling fairly sure that Ithell (and indeed Wilkie) would have found better ways to occupy themselves than watching Tom Cruise leap from tall buildings in *Mission: Impossible – Rogue Nation*.

The next day is bright and clear and I find I have misjudged Tintagel. The shops are no longer tawdry but enticing. The quartz rocks and amethyst rings are aglitter in the sunshine. A car races down the high street, stops outside the Cornwall Hospice Care charity shop and Bill Bailey leaps out and rushes inside (or a man who looks just like Bill Bailey, quite bald, but with a residual festoon of long hair flopping over the collar of his heavily fringed suede jacket). What can the hurry be? Two minutes later he's back outside, clutching a vinyl record, and then he's into his car and speeding out of town.

I follow a footpath to the castle and walk through wet fields where the only sound is birdsong: the high notes of blackbirds, the drowsy purring of a wood pigeon and the raucous shouts of the crows. Wilkie doesn't mention the Norman church near the cliffs at Tintagel, which is a shame, because it's one of those places (or perhaps it's just one of those moments) that are pregnant with holy otherness. The church is Norman, but with traces of its Saxon predecessor, and there's an old woman inside, arranging bunches of daffodils, primroses, irises and other spring flowers near the font and up the nave and around the side chapel. If Wilkie were here (and who's to say he's not?) he'd call her a 'peasant woman' and ask her about the church and hand her a small tip before leaving, but I stay silent and we sidle round one another, the woman breathing heavily as she shuffles and distributes her flowers. There's a memorial here to a fourteen-year-old cabin boy from the Italian barque *Iota*, which was 'wrecked by a raging gale' in December 1893 and, despite the heroic efforts of the local men, who saved the rest of the crew, the boy was drowned. You can hear the sea from here, a constant presence of menace and joy. A few half-remembered words of Larkin slip into my head, and I find myself loitering in this quietly serious place longer than I had intended.

Philip Larkin's fellow poet, John Betjeman, wrote with evocative force about the ruins of Tintagel Castle, which sits on an island just yards from the rocky coast, in his *Shell Guide to Cornwall*. 'Let us all', he exhorted, 'save those with weak hearts and heads, dare the steep path which crosses from the mainland to the island.' Ithell was also here, contemplating the 'vertiginous view' and crossing to view the remains. When Wilkie made the journey it was 'by a steep and somewhat perilous path; so narrow in certain places, where it winds along the verge of the precipice, that a single false step would be certain destruction'. A couple of years earlier Tennyson must have made it over while researching *Idylls of the King*, judging by his notebook: 'Rainy and bad, went and sat in Tintagel ruins, cliff black and red and yellow, weird looking thing.' (It's good to know that even the greatest poets falter in their descriptions sometimes.)

The local National Trust man is initially keen to dispel any notion that the castle may have had anything to do with Arthur. The castle, he says, was Cornwall's first holiday home, a medieval indulgence and never much used. But, he adds, digging is still taking place on the island, uncovering all sorts of intriguing evidence of the place being an important trading base, where some kind of local power, perhaps in the sixth century, dealt with Mediterranean merchants and Vikings. He's clearly desperate to say the name, so I say it for him: 'Arthur!' Well, yes, maybe, he mutters, but in truth I'm just standing here killing time because I'm absolutely terrified of heights – it gets worse every year – and I can already see, peering through the ruined gatehouse, that the route to the island is more, much more, than I'll be able to manage.

It is the sight of a tour party of elderly Germans heading down the stone steps that persuades me to stop talking to the National Trust man and follow them to the island. They are soon far ahead, dancing across the narrow wooden bridge that spans the raging seas, and I inch after them, heart racing, one step at a time, hanging on to the fence with sweaty hands. Sometimes people want to pass me coming the other way, but there's something in my eye that makes them all stay on the side of the path closest to the suicidal drop, leaving me to clutch and moan at the cliff face. At one point, after the bridge, I decide that I might as well spend the rest of my life here, halfway up the path to the island, or maybe I'll just wait for a helicopter to winch me out (or drop food parcels), or perhaps that woman in high heels, who is now sauntering up the path with her dogs and two young children, can lift and coddle me to safety.

I am so shaken by the time I reach the island that I can't take in anything. I have books by Ithell Colquhoun, John Betjeman and Wilkie Collins jostling together in my bag, and I try and distract myself by imagining them all meeting for tea. But I'm

also thinking, did Betjeman even come here? There's something ambiguous in his writing ('save those with weak hearts
and heads') – I bet the fat fraud never even went anywhere near
Tintagel Castle. And Wilkie too – he seems to imagine there were
'sheep cropping the fresh pasture, within the walls which once
echoed to the sweetest songs, or rang to the clash of the stoutest
swords of ancient England!' No sheep could possibly live here.
He dreamed that up in the pub.

I totter towards the safe centre of the island, leaning into a
wind that feels strong enough to fling me over the cliffs. And I am
watching the people who have also made it to the island: toddlers,
yes, but also geriatric women with sticks and immensely larded men
and young couples strolling hand in hand, laughing and taking
selfies at the crumbling cliff edge. The best thing, I am thinking,
is to imagine a time *beyond* this moment, when I'm safely back on
the mainland, possibly under a duvet, when all of a sudden – *sweet
Jesus!* – the figure of DEATH appears out of a light mist, standing
gaunt and terrible on a promontory on the far side of the island.
Is there no one else here who can see him? I don't dare ask. I look
again and see that of course it's not Death – it's a tortured metal
statue of Merlin, or maybe Arthur, with his hood and cloak and
staff – and there are people even now walking around him and
up to the very end of the island (step away from the *edge* you
FOOLS!), but I've had enough. I'm heading back. They're not
so bad, those steps, if you do them sitting down.

Wilkie was far braver than I am. For much of his life he was
tormented by ill health, in particular crippling outbreaks of gout,
and his eyes would often flare up agonizingly. Through his writing
years he had to put up with some vicious reviews (and there were
plenty, despite the raging success of *The Woman in White*); mockery
in the press; his repeated failures as a dramatist (*The Moonstone*
flopped and his 1882 tragedy, *Rank and Riches*, had the first-night

crowd howling with unwanted laughter); and a tour of the US that was received with indifference and even walkouts (this was especially galling after Dickens's predictably triumphant progress a few years earlier, but Wilkie's readings were, by all accounts, limp). Of course Wilkie had his many successes. In 1863 one critic acclaimed him the 'King of Inventors'. But above everything he was *resilient* and he burned with an unquenchable energy. Nothing, it seems, could staunch the flow of his words.

Wilkie wrote *Rambles Beyond Railways* in a few weeks in the autumn of 1850. He could churn it out, just like Enid, although the inventiveness of his language never fails. From Tintagel, with their thoughts already on home, Wilkie and Henry headed for one last sight, the lonely waterfall of 'Nighton's Kieve'. (Wilkie's mother had moved house while he was away on this jaunt, into a much grander place than he thought they needed or could afford, and he was anxious to get back; but he relented when he saw his new room and workspace.)

The coastal path could not be lovelier on this gentle spring day, with a smell of fresh bracken and salt in the air. There are very few people about, but with my nerves shredded, I keep them cliff-side as we cross paths. Wilkie remarked on the extraordinary good humour of the Cornish people, even though, he said, they had a tendency to stare at strangers, and it's true there's an aura of goodwill, a cheery hello and piercing eye contact from everyone who passes. A small fishing boat chugs into an empty bay and anchors just offshore, where it bucks and turns in a mild but friskily insistent swell. I sit on a slab of granite to watch it for a while. In the early days of Tintagel Castle someone watching from this place, probably using this handy granite seat, would not have had a clue what might be about to appear next over the horizon: traders, raiders, slavers, invaders … and Wilkie would have imagined that this one boat was an outlier from the great

Cornish fishing fleet, scouting for pilchards; and now, the boat just sits there, riding the waves for a few minutes, and then turns and disappears up the coast.

A path by a busy stream leads inland towards Wilkie's waterfall. There is no one on it. The water slips and fizzes over the rocks and at one point flows sideways into a low dark pool, fringed with reeds, trembling underneath an old hawthorn tree, still immersed in its winter slumber. With Wilkie on my mind (and, I suppose, his friend Millais), I half expect to see Ophelia here, floating on her back, with flowers spilling from her hands. I walk up to a place where two small streams meet, their waters skipping lightly over two large flat stones, the banks tumbling with primroses and a scattering of dandelions, and with an unexpected bounty of beetles crawling among these beautiful yellow and golden flowers. A seagull gives me an old-fashioned look from a nearby rock. My head, of late, has been so filled with what has gone wrong with our natural world – and our inability to halt the onrush of destruction – or even agree our part in it, let alone what needs to be done – that I am unprepared for this surge of life, the hum of ancient magic in this enchanted valley. It feels like a place before humans. There's peace here, and a lively insistence that the world will carry on. Of course, we humans are here. We are everywhere. There's a vapour trail in the sky and a scrappy wire fence at the top of a steep bank; and I'm still following the well-trodden path that twists uphill by the side of the restless stream, although what could be more enticing and romantic than that?

Another fragment drifts into the day.

Up the airy mountain,
Down the rushy glen,
We daren't go a-hunting
For fear of little men;

I have a feeling Wilkie would have scoffed at this piece of Victorian doggerel, although as he and Henry blundered uphill and downhill in search of their waterfall, they were blocked every inch of the way by a 'miniature forest of vegetation' – 'weeds, ferns, brambles, bushes, and young trees' – quite possibly 'commissioned', he grew to believe, 'by some evil genius of Fairy Mythology to prevent mortal footsteps from intruding into the valley'. You would have thought all Wilkie and Henry needed to do was follow the river upstream, but instead they ended the day entangled in 'a labyrinth of overgrown bushes which might have bewildered an Australian settler'. So he left frustrated and without ever seeing the waterfall. Perhaps he would have had better luck if he'd tried calling the place by the name everyone else knows it by: St Nectan's Kieve, named after the last lonely home of a sainted Celtic hermit. Inevitably, and in a rather too pat exemplar of their different characters – meandering Wilkie, supercharged Charles – when Dickens had visited here eight years earlier he marched straight to the source and splashed around in its waters.

To get to the sacred falls today, all you need to do is follow an easy path past St Piran's Church, described on a nearby sign, for some reason, as 'sadly now restored'. Our resentment of change runs deep. When Nirad Chaudhuri was travelling the land for a few weeks in the late 1950s, he was taken by an English friend to see 'a pretty village, and pointing to a section of the street, [the friend] said, "That bit is quite unspoilt." Nothing more, not a word to explain what *unspoilt* meant in that context, though the notion of an unspoilt place was so very English.'

Leaving the restored church, you must head through a wet and once wild wood of pine, sycamore, rhododendron, laurel, bamboo and ferns, passing little stone cairns by the side of the stream and ribbons and wind chimes in the trees. Or maybe you can take advantage of the new car park that is being carved into the hillside and walk straight up to the kiosk and pay your admission fee and borrow some wellington boots and head down to the falls, where there are yet more ribbons and joss sticks and a mysterious mélange of Hindu, Celtic and Buddhist artefacts, and here, standing in the holy waters, you can grope around for the pulse of St Nectan or any last trace of the Knights of the Holy Grail. But I have decided I'm sticking with Wilkie.

The valley is famous not just for its original hermit, but for two women who, inspired by St Nectan, came to live here in medieval times. This gives Wilkie the chance to roll out one of his trademark stories. The women, he writes, were harmless – they just wanted to be alone – but 'there was something so sinister and startling about the unearthly seclusion and secrecy of their lives, that people began to feel vaguely suspicious, to whisper awful imaginary rumours about them, to gossip over old stories of ghosts and false accusations'. And so the locals started to spy on the women, and they thought they could hear them talking in a 'diabolical language of their own', and who knows where this would have led except one of the women died, and then the other, without ever saying a word to the locals; and Wilkie, standing by a ruined cottage, which he is convinced is the one in which the two women once lived, manages to get quite spooked, and notices that the air in this place is unusually still and heavy, and that 'the evening is at hand, and the vapours are rising in the wood'. So he hurries away to the bright wide spaces of the coastal path.

One hundred years later, Ithell was also here, on the trail of the two women who were persecuted for wanting to be alone. And here I am, as another day ends, standing inside one of the derelict buildings that must, I am sure, be the same one that Ithell and Wilkie described, except now the walls and trees are hung with ribbons and dried flowers and the thick sticky mud underfoot has been trampled and churned by many other visitors. There's a low square hole in one wall, where the footsteps lead, and on an impulse I stoop to crawl through – I am wriggling, I cannot help but feel, through some primordial channel – and there, on a granite wall, are carved two small early Bronze Age labyrinths. Or maybe that's what they are – there's a chipped and faded sign that seems dubious about their age – but I am surprised to find them here at all, because Wilkie never mentioned them, nor did John Betjeman. But Ithell, whom I should have read with more care, knew them as the 'Troy Stones', and although she thought they didn't look ancient (or perhaps, she said, they had been recut in recent times), she also believed that they might 'even now be used to instil the secrets of circle and cross'. Is that what is going on here? Is that why there are so many footprints and so many tokens of remembrance and worship?

Do certain places hold human memories? Is there a way for us to open up to those memories and connect to the essence of a rock, or a holy spring, or a landscape? A landscape that is shaped not just by the physical impact of humanity, but also by our acts of worship and spirit? Ithell would have said so. We just need to remember how. She believed the spirits of the successors of St Nectan were here, near these immemorial mazes, inhabiting and infusing the walls and the trees. She could feel their presence and hear their call.

The labyrinths on the Troy Stones look like a cross-section of a human brain, or even the Tree of Life. They are simple and satisfying. Perhaps, as Ithell says, they allude to the dance called the 'Walls of Troy' that could lead us to the afterworld and back. It is no coincidence, she says, that the leaves on the trees by the stones are dying of a blight that you won't find in any other part of the valley. The spirit of St Nectan – and the message of the stones – is not necessarily benign. But what do we know? Do we think there is something otherworldly, just out of reach of our daily

reckonings, stirring among these woods and ruins? Or is that just
projection? I mean, is the act of standing here, opening myself
to the spirit of a place, as Ithell suggested, of standing alone with
my senses quietened and receptive – isn't that just going to make
the appearance of the numinous more likely?

All I can say for certain is that there is beauty and wonder
and a thread of familiar belonging in the rocks and the soil of
this lonely place. And I had known nothing about the stones and
their associations before I squeezed through that slippery window.
I had to read Ithell more carefully, later, to pick the meaning
from her words. But standing here in front of them now I feel a
rising sense of awe. And then, something black – a crow, I am
sure – shifts behind me in a tree and all of a sudden I can't wait
to follow Wilkie, away from these walls and the insidious woods,
and back down to the fading clarity of the coast.

There's one last visit. And time for one last story from Wilkie
about the behaviour of a profane sea captain who was bringing
bells from London for Forrabury Church, but instead brought
down the wrath of God on his head and was drowned with all
his crew, which is why, to this day, there are no bells in the tower
of the church. But Wilkie's heart is not in it. He is keen to get to
Launceston, and Plymouth, and back to his mother and friends in
London, although he is also dawdling in the churchyard because
'at this point we leave the coast, not to return to it again … and
with this evening, our pleasant days of strolling travel are ended'.

It is hard to leave. Our path will cross with Wilkie's again, that
is for sure – there is unfinished business – but even so, like him,
I am finding it difficult to leave the churchyard and return to the
restless upheavals of London. I stroll past weathered graves rising

from thick grass, and by chance (chance?) find myself in front of a battered grey tombstone.

In
Memory of
WILLIAM FREDERICK DAVY
Who met with an Accident
and was Killed at Trekeel
ON THE NORTH CORNWALL RAILWAY
14TH JULY 1893
Aged 14 Years

IN THE MIDST OF LIFE WE ARE IN DEATH

+++

THIS STONE HAS BEEN ERECTED BY HIS
FELLOW WORKMEN AS A TRIBUTE OF RESPECT

The railway begins and ends my Cornish journey, marked by the death of another fourteen-year-old boy. Wilkie was lucky enough to get to Cornwall just before the railways arrived, but there were many in his day (William Frederick Davy, child labourer, presumably being one) who had mixed feelings about the changes that had been unleashed. No one, though – then, or now – questioned its inevitability; and it was only much later that people started to wonder about the cost. Ithell, in an unhappy moment, and reflecting on the turmoil and possibilities, and the great smoothing brought by the railways and the roads, fell back on Yeats. 'The ancient spirit of Cornwall, if not of all the Celtic countries', she lamented,

Must ramble, and thin out
Like milk spilt on a stone.

Well, we will see.

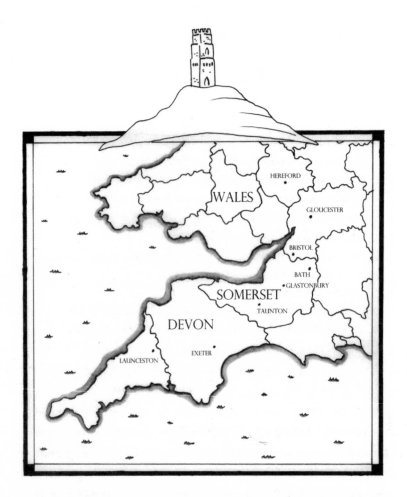

Celia Fiennes, Launceston to Hereford, 1698

FOUR

Backtracking

'… if all persons, both Ladies, much more
Gentlemen, would spend some of their tyme in
Journeys to visit their native Land, and be curious
to inform themselves and make observations of the
pleasant prospects, good buildings, different produces
and manufactures of each place, with the variety of
sports and recreations they are adapt to, [it] would be
a souveraign remedy to cure or preserve from these
epidemick diseases of vapours, should I add Laziness?
It would also form such an Idea of England, add much
to its Glory and Esteem in our minds and cure the evil
itch of over-valueing foreign parts …'

CELIA FIENNES, *THE JOURNEYS OF CELIA FIENNES*

I seem to be taking a long time to go a very short way, or, as
Martin Sheen came close to saying in *Apocalypse Now*: 'Cornwall,
shit, I'm still only in Cornwall.' The plan, I hope you remember,
is to travel around Britain in the footsteps of (mostly) famous
writers, without leaving any gaps, and without straying from
their recorded path, passing from one to the next in one smooth
movement, so thank God for Celia Fiennes, who in the 1680s and
1690s managed to ride on horseback across the whole of England,
clip-clopping through every county, most of them many times,
while keeping a detailed journal for the benefit of her astonished
family. It wasn't the kind of thing an unaccompanied woman did
in those days, but it has turned out to be very useful 330 years
later. She was nothing if not thorough.

Celia was in Launceston in 1698, on her way back from Land's End (and the inn where the beer was so fine). Wilkie was heading through on his way to Plymouth and the London train. So we can hook up with Celia and make haste for the Welsh border, even though, as she complains, the miles are very 'long' in these parts. And they were – longer here in her day than around London, although perhaps shorter than they were in the North. The statute mile was only defined in 1593 and first included on a map in 1675. Very few people in 1698 knew how far they were travelling, or when they could expect to arrive. It sounds quite appealing.

Why was Celia spending so much time riding obsessively around England, with a spare horse and a couple of servants to hack down the undergrowth and frighten away the highwaymen? The roads were in a miserable state, much worse than they had been in the Middle Ages, and a long way from Roman splendour. There was a real danger of armed robbery. Accidents were common. There were storms, floods and mudslides. The accommodation (if any) was shockingly bad – flea-infested, dirty, often rude – and Celia brought her own sheets and stayed with her widespread and generally well-off family whenever she could. She liked to pick over other people's homes, turning up uninvited (but always, apparently, welcome) and giving detailed descriptions of their houses, gardens, wealth and activities. She said she travelled for the many healing spas, claiming her health needed tending, but she could hardly be more robust. Really, she just wanted to get away from home and see the world. Social historians have been thankful ever since.

Celia rattled through Launceston, pausing to look back from a hill outside town. She'd found it 'pretty large', but the streets were tiresomely steep. The best houses, she decided (and there were only two or three of them), were built in the London style by 'some Lawyers'. The rest were 'old houses of timber work', which shows better than anything what it was like to live in a time when people did not fight to hang on to the buildings of the past, for the simple reason that they knew they could make something better. Something less poky and medieval. Celia loved high ceilings and sash windows and she was thrilled to be living through the first stirrings of what would evolve into the Georgian housing boom. Nowadays, of course, people are more likely to try and preserve what they can, against the wreckers and the developers, but that's not because they cannot move on (or not only that), it is because they have learned that whatever comes next is almost certain to be mortifyingly ugly.

Celia had hope for the future. I don't think this was unusual for someone living in her times. She was excited by signs of industry and loved to see such immense quantities of coal being mined and transported on her travels. At the side of a river between Taunton and Bridgwater, having crossed a large common 'of deep black land which is bad for the rider but good for the abider, as the proverb is', she paused among willow trees at a place where barges were unloading coal into sacks, and watched as pack horses took it further, to 'places all about'. This 'is the Sea coale brought from Bristole' she tells us (with her atrocious spelling), 'the horses carry 2 bushell at a tyme which at the place cost 18d. and when its brought to Taunton cost 2 shillings; the roads were full of these carryers going and returning.' She liked industry, as well as a tidy profit. It was her Puritan heritage.

She also liked Exeter, mostly because it reminded her of London. Celia divided her time between Newton Toney near Salisbury, where she was born and her stepmother still lived, and Hackney, a village on the eastern edge of London, where her sister Mary was living with her husband, a merchant called Sir Edmund Harrison, and their five children. London was the place she loved best, despite all the travel. She was thrilled by the new buildings and marvelled at the extraordinary daily spectacle of the new St Paul's Cathedral rising from the ashes. She also enjoyed fashions – and was there for the coronation of William and Mary to pass judgement on the new queen's gold tissue robes and crimson and ermine mantle stitched with gold and silver lace and the huge mound of her hair which was set with diamonds and 'at the least motion brill'd and flamed'.

In Taunton ('a very neate place'), Celia was struck by the fact that all the country women were dressed the same, 'wrapp'd up in the manteles called West Country rockets, a large mantle doubled together of a sort of serge, some are linsywolsey, and a deep fringe or fag at the lower end'. What is all this? I am not sure I need to know – it already sounds lovely enough. The women's mantles were deepest red in the winter and egret white in the summer. Although, come to think of it, there's more than a hint of *The Handmaid's Tale* in the image of the West Country women roaming through Taunton market and Exeter, Plymouth and beyond, baskets in hand, red (or summer-white) mantles flowing behind them.

Celia was born just two years after the return and coronation of Charles II, and thirteen years after Charles I had been executed. The country had been torn apart by a brutal civil war, famously dividing friends and families. Her own grandfather, William Fiennes, the Eighth Baron and First Viscount Saye and Sele, was a fervent Puritan and one of the leading figures in the plot to constrain and ultimately overthrow Charles I. It is likely that the whole thing was planned at his home in Broughton Castle. He was a clever, scheming man, known as 'Old Subtlety', although his enemies suggested it was just pique and wounded pride that led him down the road to revolution, and there was nothing especially bright about him except that he stood out in comparison to his idiot peers. Celia's father, Nathaniel, was a colonel in the same cause, somehow contriving to lose the heavily fortified city of Bristol to Prince Rupert without firing a shot. There was a song about it at the time:

> But as soon as he heard our great guns play,
> With a flea in his ear he ran quite away ...

It has a rousing chorus, culminating in the words – no doubt roared around the Royalist campfires with a great sloshing of beer – 'Which nobody can DENY ... Huzzah!'

Celia had been steeped in Puritanism, which makes her open-minded enthusiasm for almost everything she saw in her battered (but recovering) country all the more impressive. Mind you, she was very careful what she wore when going for a healing dip in one of the many spas she visited. In Bath she donned a huge yellow canvas dress, 'stiff and made large with great sleeves like a parsons gown; the water fills it up so that its borne off that your shape is not seen; it does not cling close as other linning which looks sadly in the poorer sort that go in their own linning'. So she floated amorphously in the waters, enfolded in a vast tent, while curling her lip at the 'poorer sort' who were splashing about in skimpy swimwear.

At Glastonbury (or 'Glassenbury' as Celia calls it) she visited what was left of the abbey and the tower of St Michael's Chapel on the top of the Tor. She threw stones into the cellar of the abbey and heard 'a great echo', which came from the Devil who was guarding his treasure, or so said the local country folk. She inspected the famous Glastonbury Holy Thorn, which had sprung from the ground in the place where Joseph of Arimathea had struck his staff. Cromwell's soldiers had chopped it down not so long ago, during the wars, but an offshoot had been found in a local pub garden and now it was flourishing again, blossoming every year on 7 January – Christmas Day in the old calendar. And so it would be today, or its descendants would, if it didn't attract quite so much vitriol. The latest assault was in December 2010 when it was mown down by a man with a chainsaw. Whether people resent its beauty, or mystery, or religious associations – or whether they just hate trees – is unclear. Perhaps all of the above.

Glastonbury, of course, is now famous worldwide. And almost every year a Festival blossoms here. But it can also be a glum place, in almost any season, drained of its magic, strenuously touting its crystals and astral charts, trampled flat by pilgrims, undone by the avid attentions of its wide-eyed inhabitants. I don't believe 'magick' should be spelled with a 'k', unless, like Celia, you can't spell. Or maybe I have never stayed long enough, nor waited till dawn to witness the Somerset mists swirling around the Tor, and seen the black tower rising like hope from a ghostly white sea. Many people swear to the power that resides here. Ithell would have pointed out the significance of the name of the church, St Michael's (and Michael, as she told us, 'is germane to all other dragon-slayers from Perseus to Hercules and St George, since Michael is the Uranian aspect and St George the human manifestation of the same being'). Celia would have recoiled from this kind of talk, but please do not imagine that I am doing anything other than trying to understand. Wherever the currents take us, it is surely enough to know that others have always taken these readings seriously.

In the late twelfth century Henry II tried to kill the Arthur myth stone dead. He was worried that the Welsh in particular still clung to the belief that Arthur would rise again in their time of need, and having announced that Arthur was definitely buried at Glastonbury, along with his wife Guinevere, he ordered that their bodies should be dug up. He seemed to know (he said it was a prophecy) that Arthur was lying sixteen feet below the surface – and sure enough, when the monks got digging, that's exactly what they found. The skeleton of a huge man and, said Gerald of Wales, writing soon afterwards, 'a tress of woman's hair, blond and lovely to look at, plaited and coiled with consummate skill, and belonging no doubt to Arthur's wife'. One of the monks leaped into the grave to seize this gorgeous braid of hair and it turned to dust in his hands. 'In their stupidity the British people maintain that Arthur is still alive', Gerald sneered, eager to impress Henry II, but it is time to accept that 'the fairy-tales have been snuffed out'. He would be surprised to see Glastonbury today.

I should say at this point that I am following Celia's route in reverse – tracking back into the past – but it is the only way I can get to Hereford. Celia is having a great time hopping around the spas and baths of Somerset. At a place near St Vincent's Rocks she found a 'hott spring of water which looks exceeding clear and is as warm as new milk and much of that sweetness'. In Bath itself she notices the very fine new Hall that had been built since she was last there, ready for the 'balls and dancing'. It is not long, now, till the arrival of Mr Darcy, and Celia slips into yet another pool of hot steamy water. Celia, by the way, did not ride naked around Britain, as some people think. That was Lady Godiva. But she may, even so, be the subject of the nursery rhyme, 'Ride a cock horse to Banbury Cross/To see a fine lady upon a white horse'. Or that's what the people of Banbury would like you to believe, having spent money on a big, tourist-friendly statue. 'Fine lady'/'Fiennes lady', you see? There's the proof.

You may also be wondering about the coincidence in our surnames. It's all very simple. Celia Fiennes' grandfather, William Fiennes, is my great $^{(x\ 10)}$ grandfather and her father, Nathaniel Fiennes, is my great $^{(x\ 10)}$ uncle, which means that Celia is my first cousin ten times removed. She never married and didn't have any children, so I am not her direct descendant (it is her uncle James who is my great $^{(x\,9)}$ grandfather), although I can already sense that this may be more information than anyone outside my immediate family should be expected to endure.

But it's a familiar question, isn't it? Usually innocent, but not always benign. Alive with preconceptions. 'Where are you from?' Or, to put it another way, 'Who are you?' 'Where did you come from?' We like to know. Of course we do. Even if the question can imply something about belonging, and something about the person asking it, that has started to make us feel uneasy. The implication 'Do you belong here?' can follow softly in its wake – unspoken (at least most of the time) and also (most of the time) never intended at all. To say it again, it is human to want to know. But I am also aware how uncomfortable this question can be, how downright hostile, and indeed how easy it is for me, a middle-aged white man, to travel this land, on the trail of Celia, my first cousin ten times removed, and not have to worry (or not that often) about my welcome or my right to be here. Apart from anything else, I am in the happy position of being able to stare at Celia's 330-year-old signature ('Fiennes' with a flourish and a swirl) and think: I once practised my signature in exactly this same way. That feels like it's worth something.

Well, leaving aside for now other more troubling considerations, it turns out it's not worth very much. In his book *A Brief History of Everyone Who Ever Lived*, Adam Rutherford shows that everybody living in Britain today who has at least some European ancestry is descended from the Emperor Charlemagne. He says it is simple mathematics. And if we had only managed to keep detailed records, we would discover that all modern Europeans (with a trace of European ancestry) are in some way related to absolutely *everyone* who was alive in Europe just six hundred years ago – assuming they left a line of descendants. It is surprising. If you want to know more, you'd be far better off buying his book, but what this means is that it is likely – not certain (more generations need to elapse), but it is likely – that you too are descended from someone in Celia's immediate family. Not from her – she never had any children – but someone. And in fact, Rutherford goes on to say, 'the most recent common ancestor of everyone alive today on Earth lived only 3,400 years ago'. Cousin.

We will see Celia again (we'd be lost without her), but I am going to race past Bristol. It is an inspiring place, I know that, and 'a very great tradeing citty ... and is esteemed the largest next London'. Celia loved the market and the magnificent stone cross, and when she was here the harbour was full of ships carrying 'coales and all sorts of commodityes to other parts'. Three hundred years ago those 'commodityes' included slaves, although I have no idea if that's what Celia meant. In 1698, when she rode through, the gruesome transatlantic trade was about to ramp up into another, even more intense phase. The monopoly of the Royal African Company had been broken that year (up till then it had exercised exclusive rights to trade with the African continent) and the first Bristol-owned ship was about to leave the city for the Caribbean, picking up a shameful cargo of enslaved African men and women. Celia didn't have anything to say about that. Although, as we know, her silence is not unusual.

In August 1846 (150 years after Celia rode through the city), the escaped American slave Frederick Douglass arrived in Bristol from London. His explosive autobiography, *Narrative of the Life of Frederick Douglass, an American Slave*, had just been published and he'd been forced to flee and seek sanctuary in Britain. He was put up in Bristol by the abolitionists John Bishop Estlin and his daughter Mary. He was still only twenty-eight years old and he toured Britain for eighteen months, speaking over 300 times to enthusiastic audiences, drawing crowds of thousands, crammed into churches, theatres and halls. When he returned to America in 1847, after a group of British businessmen had helped buy his freedom, Mary wrote that 'many hearts had followed him'.

Slavery had been 'unsupported on English soil' since 1772 and finally abolished across the British Empire in 1833, but Douglass was the force who reignited the anti-slavery movement and spread it across the globe, borne aloft by surging waves of British outrage and self-satisfaction. After he spoke in Edinburgh, over 10,000 women sent a petition to Washington demanding an end to slavery. And in Bristol, the day after he arrived in the city, he thrilled a crowd in the Victoria Rooms with the soaring passion of his speech (but not before the mayor had surprised the local paper by pouring Douglass a glass of water).

'You may', Douglass began, have 'heard of America, 3,000 miles off, as the land of the free', but the truth is that the real sound coming from the South 'is the clank of the fetters and the rattling of the chains, which bound their miserable slaves together, to be driven by the lash of their driver on board the ships for New Orleans, there to be sold in the market like brutes'.

A few days later Douglass was in Exeter, making 'A Call for the British Nation to Testify Against Slavery'. He realized that he needed Britain's help in the fight against American slavery, or at least the support of its people, even though anti-British sentiment in America might make this support counter-productive. But as he said that night in Exeter:

> [Slavery] is such a monstrous system, such a giant crime, that it begets a character favourable to its own exist-ence, vanquishing the moral perception, and blinding the moral vision of all who come in contact with it; and a nation has not the moral energy necessary to its removal.

Douglass knew exactly how to tickle his patriotic, West Country audience, and to a final crescendo of wild cheering he shouted:

> I will go to the land of my birth, I will proclaim it in the ears of the American people, whether I'm in a state of slavery or freedom, while I have a voice to speak it shall be raised in exposing the guilt of the slave-owners, and in contrasting the munificent freedom of monarchical England, with the slave-holding, man-stealing, woman-whipping, degradation of democratic republican America.

Anyway, I'm going to slide past Bristol and Bath, lovely as they are. Time is short and they're quite busy enough reassessing their own histories without any help from me.

We can also miss Gloucester. It's 'a low, moist place' says Celia, and she had 'the worst Entertainment' and 'strangers are allwayes imposed on', and there were very few books in the library and that should be warning enough. Celia stayed outside Hereford with her cousin, Pharamus Fiennes (I mention this so I can write his long-vanished name), and when she rode into the city thought it was 'a pretty little town of timber buildings, the streets are well pitched and handsome' and there were plenty of fish in the 'thick and yellow' river. Celia never did venture into Wales. She had heard that 'the inhabitants go barefoot and bare leg'd' and were 'a nasty sort of people'. But waiting here in Hereford, in the year 1188, about to embark on a long tour of the country, is Gerald of Wales – and he can explain quite how wrong she was.

Gerald of Wales,
South and Central Wales, March and April 1188

FIVE

'I'll Be Your Mirror'

'Wealth and violence seem to sustain us in this life,
but after death they avail us nothing.'

GERALD OF WALES

I cross the border that separates England from Wales on a minor road near Presteigne, just north of the A44. It is an early morning in June and a dense mist is rolling down the green hills and seeping through the hedgerows. With visibility squeezed to a few awkward yards, I am driving slowly with the windows down, the car's engine clattering off the high banks of the narrow lanes and the wipers flapping and squawking at the murk. On either side, the verges are radiating wet new life: hawthorn blossom, red campion, cow parsley, flowering nettles, a twist of woodbine and the last of the native, 'English' bluebells. 'Araf', says the first sign in Welsh: easy does it.

I stop at New Radnor and the mist seems to lift a little, or turn wetter. A mizzle, let's say. The English language is awash – drenched – with ways of describing the stuff that falls from the sky. I'm afraid I can't tell you about Welsh, but it surely won't be any different. In Kazuo Ishiguro's novel *The Buried Giant*, set in a post-Arthurian time of invading Saxons and traumatized Britons, much of the land is veiled and muffled by an impenetrable fog. Something unspeakable is being hidden – the truth, perhaps, about what really happened when two peoples met. An ageing Sir Gawain even appears out of the gloom. It is an unsettling book, and it asks impossible questions, in a halting language, about what we choose to remember – and what it may be better we learn to forget – about the worst of crimes. But when did you ever hear of a border being agreed with a smile and a friendly handshake? Someone has always lost something.

I am following in the footsteps of a man called Gerald de Barry, otherwise known as *Giraldus Cambrensis* – or, in plain English (a language he despised), Gerald of Wales. And this is how he starts his book *The Journey Through Wales*:

> In the year AD 1188, Baldwin, Archbishop of Canterbury, crossed the borders of Herefordshire and entered Wales.

The border would have been in a different place in 1188, deeper into what is now England and closer to Hereford, I imagine, and the transition from one country to the other was more significant than it is today, albeit less abrupt (there's no avoiding the signs bidding us all 'Croeso i Gymru'). Archbishop Baldwin was leading an urgent mission into Wales to sign up recruits for a third crusade to the Holy Land. The previous year Jerusalem had fallen to Salah ad-Din (or 'Saladin, the leader of the Egyptians and of the men of Damascus', says Gerald), and Baldwin had been ordered by Henry II, 'the king of the English', to persuade the ferocious Welsh fighting men, especially their famous archers, to 'take the Cross' and travel to the Middle East to help reverse this cataclysmic outrage. Gerald, the Archdeacon of Brecon, whose Norman grandfather had married a Welsh princess, had been brought along for his diplomatic skills and his blood ties to almost every important Welsh family in south Wales. It was not known, until the mission arrived, quite how welcoming some of the Welsh would be.

There was another, and not just incidental, reason for Baldwin's trip: it would give him a chance to preach in all four Welsh cathedrals and thereby affirm Canterbury's (and England's) precedence over the Welsh Church. This second part of the mission was causing Gerald a great deal of angst: it was his fervent wish that one day the Welsh Church, with its spiritual base in St David's, would become independent of Canterbury and England and report directly to the Pope in Rome. It was the way things had always been, he believed, until the invading Normans had demoted St David's to a mere bishopric, answering to the Archbishop of Canterbury. There was very little evidence for this (although in his books Gerald manages to manufacture plenty), but it was a cause to which the quarter-Welsh Gerald would devote much of his life. The truth is, Gerald longed to become the next Bishop of St David's himself (one of his Norman uncles had held the post for many years) – and Gerald, who was ambitious, not to mention acutely aware of his own talents, allowed himself to dream of a moment when the Bishop of St David's might one day morph into the Archbishop of All Wales.

None of this was ever going to happen, not so long as there was a Norman king on the English throne. If they allowed the Welsh Church to secede, then they might as well allow the whole country to go its own way. Most of Wales was independent at the time of the trip, but the Normans were palpably hungry for more of what they didn't yet have. Twelve years earlier, in 1176, on the death of his uncle, Gerald had fought a bitter campaign to succeed him as Bishop of St David's – and had only lost because he was, in the eyes of Henry II, suspiciously and dangerously Welsh. It was Henry, of course, who in 1170 had (perhaps accidentally) ordered the murder of the Archbishop of Canterbury, Thomas Becket, for showing too much independence. All of this was recent history to Gerald, but his ambitions were taking him to a dangerous place.

The man who had beaten Gerald to the Bishopric of St David's, a Norman called Peter de Leia, was also riding with Baldwin, presumably keeping his distance from the acerbic and voluble Gerald. It was here in New Radnor, at the end of a long day's ride from Hereford, that the archbishop gave his first sermon on the taking of the Cross and as soon as it was over, with the final 'Amen' floating away into the surrounding hills, Gerald leaped to his feet and hurled himself at Baldwin's feet, vowing that he would follow his king and Church on a death-or-glory crusade to the Holy Land, so help him God. He was the first person in Wales to take the Cross, or so he tells us, just as he makes a point of mentioning that the next person was the current Bishop of St David's, Peter de Leia (too slow, Peter, too slow …).

What we know about Gerald comes almost entirely from his own writings. At the time of the trip he was about forty-two years old, a tall, vigorous man, breathtakingly handsome (as I say, Gerald is his own source), with strikingly shaggy eyebrows and a piercing eye. He had grown up in Manorbier in south Wales in the castle of his Norman father, probably learning Welsh from his mother. He spoke Norman French by default and wrote, he tells us, in 'the most beautiful Latin'. (Alas, I'm no judge. After spending ten years not learning the language, all I can say for sure is that being able to misquote Latin epigrams does not make you Disraeli.) He compared the speech of the English to the hissing of geese, and saw no need to understand the witterings of a humiliated peasant race. He was brilliant and shrewd and always destined for the Church, and was sent away aged eight to study with the monks at Gloucester Cathedral, before heading to Paris as a teenager to learn philosophy with the best. He was hugely ambitious (the diocese of St David's might as well have been carved on his heart), witty, questioning, energetic, scheming, combative, loved a good story (the wilder the better), but he became bitter in later years when his dreams of St David's were thwarted. Baldwin, whom Gerald dismissed as an amiable but ineffectual holy man totally unsuited to the post of archbishop, would have been delighted to have him along for the ride, even though it wasn't long before he found himself having to read out loud from Gerald's books every night of the trip.

It is peaceful here, and still early, high above New Radnor on the Norman earthworks, in the place where Gerald pledged his allegiance to the Holy Cross. There's no other trace of the castle: its stones were removed long ago to feed the walls of the church and the villagers' homes. All that remains is a series of stepped, damp, grass-covered mounds and ditches, and a vast ancient ash tree, only just coming into leaf on this first day in June, a solitary hawthorn surrounded by the stumps of other fallen trees, dense clusters of nettles and, on the southern slope, above some advancing elder trees, a mazy rush of golden young buttercups, muted in the drifting fog. An army of moles has been busy enjoying itself in the absence of any human interference; and far below in the village I can just make out a child's bright yellow trampoline in one of the back gardens. A sheep on a distant hill gives a petulant bleat from out of the mist.

A lot has happened in the 830 years since Gerald, Baldwin, Bishop Peter and their accompanying retinue of clerks, clerics, servants and soldiers gathered around this hill. And yet, really, not so much.

In 1188, Wales was ruled by a chaotic jumble of Welsh princes and Norman knights, the latter taking care to acknowledge the primacy of their king, Henry II. In the south, the most important Welsh leader was the Lord Rhys. He had come to New Radnor to greet Archbishop Baldwin, who had not only brought Gerald with him to keep things civil (Rhys was one of Gerald's many Welsh cousins), but also Henry II's most powerful adviser, Ranulph de Glanville, who was here, not so subtly, to make sure that the Lord Rhys wasn't going to give any trouble. Once that was clear, he headed back to England. It was a time when 'wealth and violence', as Gerald put it, were the ultimate answer to anything, with violence usually the more certain route. In 1063, just before the Norman Conquest, Harold, the last Saxon king, 'had marched up and down and round and about the whole of Wales with such energy that he "left not one that pisseth against a wall"'. According to Gerald it was only because of the destruction wrought by Harold and his English soldiers that the Norman kings had managed to subdue Wales. Now the south of the country, and the border with England, were studded with the castles of Norman lords who had grabbed what they could and held it against Welsh retaliations and sometimes each other. Gerald's Norman grandfather was one of these lords who'd chosen to blend bloodshed with diplomacy and marry a local Welsh princess.

Baldwin and Gerald were travelling through a violent land, although I doubt they'd have been under any threat. They had their soldiers, after all – and anyway their arrival in a town or village would have been a major thrill to almost everyone. Here was the Archbishop of Canterbury, the first ever to visit Wales, and he had the God-given power to forgive sins, heal the sick, cast out the devil and excommunicate the wicked. People would have rushed to come and hear him speak; in Cardigan, Baldwin was almost crushed to death by a frantic surge of would-be crusaders. So although Gerald and Baldwin sometimes grumbled about the state of the roads (there were none to speak of, apart from the remnants of a Roman road along the south coast) and the godawful weather (this is Wales), and Baldwin fretted about the crusade – despite all that, I get the feeling they were both thoroughly enjoying themselves.

From New Radnor the recruiting party made its way west to Castle Crug Eryr, where they signed up the Welsh Prince of

Maelienydd, 'despite the fears and lamentations of his family'. There they turned south, probably past the little church of Glascwm (rebuilt since Gerald's day, although it's possible the same yew trees were there to welcome us both). Inside the church there's a sign marking the 'safe return' of five local men from the 1939–45 war; and just next to this, propped against a wall, is a white wooden cross commemorating Oberleutnant G. Brixius of the German Air Force, who died when his plane crashed nearby in 1942. Gerald would have approved, I reckon. Despite his many criticisms of the English, Welsh, Flemish and others, he had a thoroughly medieval understanding of what it means to be human. A race may be punished or rewarded for its behaviour (the Welsh, for example, had been driven to the western edges of Britain because of their well-known and unfortunate predilection for incest and homosexuality), but we are all one family under God.

The route south took Gerald through Hay-on-Wye, once deep into Wales, now a town on the border. The travellers were met by a great crowd of would-be crusaders, running towards the castle, 'leaving their cloaks in the hands of the wives and friends who had tried to hold them back'. The annual literary festival is in full swing and I sit for a while under the walls of this castle, with the bunting flapping above and a smell of venison burgers and cumin hanging in the air. Despite the use of the Welsh language on almost every poster, street sign and handout, Hay during its festival is thronged with English-speakers, most of them, it seems to me (as my eye drifts down a bewildering list of quinoa and kelp smoothies), from the suburbs and surrounds of England's wealthier cities. Well, that's fine, let's hope (for here I am), and it is undeniably better that these mostly sensitive and eager-to-accommodate (but at times utterly oblivious) foot soldiers of English globalization should be wearing their Hunter boots rather than the chain-mail shirts and iron gauntlets of Baldwin's day. But let's not kid ourselves how we got here. As Ithell Colquhoun once wrote about her beloved Cornwall, a part of Britain less secure in its otherness: 'The Cornish language did not die a natural death; it was executed like a criminal by the oppressing Saxon power.'

The dominant local Norman baron of the day was a man called William de Braose and he ruled over Hay, although his main base was at Brecon Castle, just a short walk from Gerald's official home in Llanddew. He was an undeniably violent man, fond of stealing Church property and slaughtering the locals, but Gerald is strangely silent on all of this, instead claiming that de Braose was so pious that it became quite boring the number of times he invoked the Lord's name in everyday conversation and correspondence. Maybe Gerald was trying to get his backing for his St David's schemes. He also slobbers all over de Braose's wife, Mildred ('a prudent and chaste woman'), even though she is better remembered for her terrifying brutality – she ate babies, you know – and was starved to death, with her son, in King John's dungeons once her husband was safely out of the way. Gerald also has surprisingly little to say about his local town of Brecon, so it's interesting to go and stare at the bald statements of power – castle and cathedral – and wonder where that power has gone today. Not the cathedral, that's for sure. It feels sleepily Trollopian, although its elegant east side was only made possible with an infusion of de Braose's blood-drenched plunder.

Baldwin had turned south at Brecon, still keeping close to the border, heading for Abergavenny, Cardiff and the south coast. Gerald keeps us amused, as he must have done Baldwin, with a succession of miraculous tales. There's one about a woman in the north of England who sat down without thinking on the wooden tomb of Saint Osana and found herself stuck there, unable to move, until the people came and stripped her naked and whipped her for the crime. It was only once she had prayed and wept for forgiveness that her 'backside' was unglued. And, as they trotted along, Gerald told Baldwin about Brecknock Mere (we know it as Llangorse Lake), to the east of Brecon, which sometimes turns bright green, or flows with red blood, and at other times is covered with gardens, ornamental buildings and orchards, and harbours the most delicious eels and pike. There was a legend that the rightful ruler of the land could conjure the birds of the lake to sing to him; and once, when the Welsh lord, and Gerald's great uncle, Gruffydd ap Rhys ap Tewdwr was riding at its side with two Norman knights, in the time of Henry I, all the birds did just that, thronging Gruffydd with song and acclamation, while ignoring his Norman friends, and Gerald must have taken pleasure in telling Baldwin just what Henry I had said when he heard this story:

> By the death of Christ, I am not the slightest bit sur-
> prised. It is we who hold the power, and so we are free
> to commit acts of violence and injustice against these
> people, and yet we know full well that it is they who are
> the rightful heirs to the land.

Gerald, who was only one-quarter Welsh at birth (whatever that might mean), nonetheless *felt* Welsh, or he did when writing his book, or riding through the country's green valleys. Later, when he wrote his *The Description of Wales*, a companion piece to his *Journey*, he devoted the second half of the book to describing how to conquer the miserable place, and denouncing its hopelessly divided princes and its greedy, incestuous, drunken inhabitants. And that was after spending the first half praising its people (no longer homosexual, he is happy to report, as they had been 'in their more prosperous days', but sober, brave, nimble, hospitable and kinder and more quick-witted than any other Westerners). Like any of us, Gerald was able to incorporate or balance more than one identity at a time. Or perhaps he was just acutely conscious of not offending his powerful, Latin-reading audience.

I am tracking Gerald and his captive listeners down the Coed Grwyne Pass, now home to the Grwyne Fawr reservoir. A couple of miles to the east is Llanthony monastery, which Gerald loved (he takes most of one chapter to tell us how it had grown into the very emblem of noble monastic life, until it was corrupted by the 'boundless extravagance of the English'), but he seems not to have visited the place on this trip. Time was pressing and as fussy little Archbishop Baldwin no doubt said: 'Hurry along, now, Saladin's army isn't going to defeat itself.'

It was in this wild and wooded pass, so Gerald tells us, that fifty years earlier the Welsh had ambushed and murdered the Norman Lord Richard de Clare, ruler of Cardiganshire. Apparently he had ignored the advice of the local lord, dismissed his heavily armed soldiers, and come prancing down the path accompanied only by a few servants and preceded by a minstrel singing his praises. It sounds very Monty Python ('I would fayn walk this way alone,' trilled Lord Richard, before being hacked to death along with all his followers). Gerald is quick to point out how 'rash and inconsiderate it is to take no heed at all of the advice given by those who are trying to help us'. Perhaps he was smarting from some recent slight. He was a man who bore a grudge for decades, and rewrote passages in his books several times over the years to amend his verdicts on those he felt had betrayed him. The Plantagenet kings, for example, he described in the end as an 'accursed race' and said he'd wasted his time dedicating his books to Henry II ('no interest in literature', God rot him) and 'his son and successor in vice, Richard'.

The woods in the pass are still dark and gloomy, especially with the familiar mist drifting through the trees. From where I'm standing, all alone, halfway up the eastern slope, I can hear the Grwyne Fawr river splashing along the valley – and there's laughter, too, coming from the direction of the reservoir. A cuckoo calls and calls again. Perhaps this was the route Gerald followed, down to the River Usk and on to Abergavenny and the sea. There were no maps, of course – only local guides. There are beech trees here on the edge of the pine woods, and hawthorn, rowan, hazel and ash. Plenty of sycamore, too, although there wouldn't have been any here in Gerald's day: the species only arrived from mainland Europe in Tudor times.

It is hard to stand even in this remote place and try to piece together how close any of it might be to what Gerald and Baldwin once knew. For starters, most of the trees are close-packed conifers, arranged into straight rows for harvesting. Britain only has one native pine tree (the Scots pine, or *Pinus sylvestris*), and I can't see any of them here. More to the point, in Gerald's day there were no plantations, just the remnants of the wildwood. On the other side of the valley a huge, surgically neat square of woodland has been carved out, the timber driven away, leaving behind a churn of wheel ruts and splintered bark. Well, they'll be back again another day to plant more trees (we hope), and this time they may even include a fringe of native species (sustainability and diversity have found their way into the modern foresters' handbook); but when he came this way Gerald would have ridden through a wild tangle of oak, hazel, thorn and ash, or stopped to rest under an ancient and solitary pine among an outpouring of wildflowers, and the sound of the birds and the insects would have been all-enveloping at this time of year, and so much more than just the bickering of crows in the mutilated woods, and a sudden shriek of alarm from a single blackbird, and the low rumble of distant machinery.

Can a landscape be old and tired and used up? Put it another way: if we wanted to recreate Gerald's world, right here, in this

isolated valley, what would we have to remove? The pylons, poles
and wires, of course. Wheel tracks. Tarmac. The RAF Tornado
that has just now come screaming overhead. Fencing. That tum-
bledown, red-brick building. The reservoir. The four parked cars.
The cling of diesel. Any last trace of chemical pollutants and
pesticides. Crisp packets and plastic bottles. Footprints with tread.
Vapour trails in the sky (if we could see them through the fog).
All recent arrivals from the animal and plant kingdoms. (Every
bit of this is something the makers of historical dramas must be
horribly familiar with – as well as the inevitable scrawling letter
pointing out that the larch tree was only introduced to the south
Wales valleys in 1837.) Perhaps we should just squint, block our
ears and noses, and stare at an oak leaf.

But we can't stop there. We have to think about what we'd put
back in. Wolves, for example – they were still here in 1188, deep in
the broadleaf forests, although there was a bounty on every pelt.
And beavers. They'd been hunted to extinction all over England,
but they were hanging on not far from the Grwyne Fawr valley,
as well as in a last few refuges in Scotland. The pine marten.
Red squirrels. And don't forget the songbirds, in lost abundance,
with their spellbinding songs of rapture. Eagles overhead. Beetles
underfoot. The fish that leaped and splashed in the river. Honey
bees and storms of butterflies feeding on a glittering mosaic of
flowers. The spreading bellflower and the bastard balm. And
people. This valley would have had its people, who moved south,
not so long ago, into the new mining towns and villages and
booming cities.

Would you go back? If you could? I am alone here, on a
narrow path, with the pine forest pressing dark and close, and
surely it is reassuring to know (the odds at least are against it) that
I am not about to be dragged into the woods and murdered by
a local cutthroat. And when Gerald rode this way he had much

to say about the miraculous gold and silver staff, kept in a local church, that was 'particularly efficacious in smoothing away and pressing the pus from glandular swellings and gross tumours which grow so often on the human body'. Well, yes indeed. And thank God for antibiotics. 'Shifting baseline syndrome' works both ways: and most of the time we are oblivious to the advances that sustain us. If I had been lucky enough to be born Gerald's twin in 1146, and not some powerless peasant, I would have been dead of an exploding appendix long before I was able to make this trip. But I do wonder if there is anything we've left behind, do you think, in our centuries-old quest for the perfect picnic spot – the one that is always just around the next corner? Surely we could have called a halt many times and said, 'This is great, with its gorgeous view. Let's stop here.' Couldn't we? And when was that, do you think? And where? And who exactly would it have all been for?

And here comes Enid again, spreading out her tartan rug for tired limbs in the flower-filled meadow. There is ginger pop, and strawberries. Skylarks are calling and hovering in the cloudless sky. There's honeysuckle and dog roses in the hedgerows. Harvesters at rest in a field of mown hay. A ruined castle on a green hill. Hot dusty lanes. A distant sparkle on the blue sea. The village shop and the beaming bobby. 'You young scamps run along.' Sunlight …

No. We have to press on. But I have allowed myself to drift deep into the pine forest and I am now lost on a faint track, with the mist clinging to the cheerless trees. A dark silence is paring the courage from me. I walk on slowly. The battered remnants of an ancient lime avenue are either side of the path. The trees must be hundreds of years old. There are roots everywhere, huge, exposed, sinuous, weathered, slippery and humped with earth and moss. The path is tenuous and the walking is hard. One of the lime trees has fallen, taking two or three pines with it, but it is still alive, its branches reaching for the light, even as the canopy closes over its fallen body. This is a miserable place. Bereft of humanity and life and yet at the same time suffocated by our ceaseless needs. Or so says Gerald – and he quotes Isaiah: 'Woe unto them that join house to house, that lay field to field, till there be no place, that they may be placed alone in the midst of the earth.'

We have drained the wild from this world, even in the empty places.

I am alone in a dark wood. And I cannot begin to describe the rush of joy when I stumble and slip to the edge of the forest and there are the fields with their cows and the hawthorn in blossom, and the mist has lifted (I would never have known), and the sky is a heart-hugging blue, and down below is the glitter of the river I thought I was following but had lost.

It is an easy walk from here to St Issui's Church, where local legend holds that Baldwin preached on his journey, although Gerald makes no mention of this. It is a tiny church, rebuilt since Gerald's time, but still very old, perhaps fifteenth century, and no one is quite sure why Baldwin bothered to make the journey, if indeed he did. But the little place still feels important, carved into the steep hillside, with a tumbling drop to the hazel-fringed river, a long way from the nearest town or village. I stand in the small green churchyard, among the mouldering tombstones, and a woman stifles a cough from inside the church. There are violets, forget-me-nots and countless daisies springing from the grass and a smell of ripe daffodils. There is happiness (and more) in the air. If Gerald were here he would not have wasted the opportunity to set us straight:

> Those mountain-heights abound in horses and wild
> game, those woods are richly stocked with pigs, the

shady groves with goats, the pasture-lands with sheep, the meadows with cattle, the farms with ploughs. All the things and creatures which I have mentioned are there in great abundance, and yet we are so insatiable in our wicked desires that each in its turn seems insufficient for our needs.

Nothing has changed.

I speed past Abergavenny, where Baldwin preached and Gerald expends a few more evasive, mealy-mouthed words about the murderous William de Braose, who – he doesn't tell us – once slaughtered several unarmed Welsh guests in its castle. At Caerleon Gerald stopped among the ruins of the old Roman city and marvelled at what was left (much more than now) of the 'immense palaces' and the extraordinary sophistication of the pipework. Gerald believed King Arthur had once held court here; and he has a few salacious tales to tell about a soothsayer called Meilyr, an incubus, some beautiful women and their demons. There is no sign that any of this stuff is any less real to Gerald than his descriptions of the sheep in the fields, because as he says when quoting St Augustine: 'I will neither put a limit on divine power by denying it, nor strain the bounds of credibility by accepting it.'

Cardiff was not a big town in Gerald's day – it was a castle and not much else – and indeed even by the year 1800 the population was still no higher than about 2,000. Today, the population is almost 350,000, their forebears brought here by the power of coal and the immense wealth it generated. Gerald saw it coming, as he gazed out on the nearby hills:

Many of nature's riches still lie hidden from us, undis-
covered as yet because we have given no attention to
them, but the diligence and careful enquiry of later
generations will no doubt reveal them.

Although in truth Gerald was predicting an outpouring of soothing
oils and 'sweet honey' from the local rock, not black coal.

    After their adventures in the woods, Baldwin stopped at Cardiff
Castle, 'where it stands so nobly on the River Taff', for yet another
of his recruiting sermons (and just think how often the English
have turned up in the centuries since, with the same grim purpose
in mind). The original castle keep is still here, on its green hill,
raised by William, the first Norman king, surrounded by the later
medieval walls and towers and Victorian halls, and I go and sit
at the very centre, with my back propped against a rough stone
wall, and I look up to where the floors would have been, through
to a roofless blue sky. The place is busy, with queues forming on
the narrow stone steps to reach the very top of the tower. People
have arrived here from across the globe – China, Malaysia, India,
the US – and I am sitting in the sunshine wondering if any of us
actually know anything at all about what we are looking at (I'm not
sure I do), when I hear a young black man from Brazil or Portugal
absolutely boiling over with enthusiasm for the intricacies of the
motte-and-bailey and the crumbling keep. And that makes me
happy, because I hate to think that this knowledge might one day
evaporate (and 'ramble, and thin out/like milk spilt on a stone'),
and it feels safe in his hands. And then his older friend, or perhaps
it's his father, starts to tell him about the time the Welshman Ifor
Bach kidnapped William, the Earl of Gloucester, from inside
Cardiff Castle – and this, I realize, because I'm sitting here reading the very same thing, even as he talks, is a story that Gerald
tells in *The Journey Through Wales*. Gerald longed for posthumous

fame, especially once he realized that his worldly ambitions were out of reach, and if he's not now squirming with delight in his grave, or jumping up and down in the celestial heights, then there is no afterlife.

Down below a bass guitar rumbles with bone-squeezing power. There's a concert just getting started on the great green sweep of the castle grounds and the people of Cardiff have arrived in large numbers, as well as the travellers from distant lands, to listen to Sister Sledge, the Fratellis and the Hackney Colliery Band. Gerald was well travelled for his day, across England, Wales and Ireland, and also France, northern Italy and Rome, but most people never went anywhere, unless they found themselves swept up into a war or – as was the case here – a crusade. When Gerald and Baldwin (the Normans) preached to the Welsh and English, they would speak in French or Latin, and their audience wouldn't understand a word, although it didn't stop them from volunteering with hysterical enthusiasm. Later, in Llandaff, as Baldwin spoke, the English stood on one side and the Welsh on the other, 'and from each nation many took up the Cross', united by religion and war.

In 1188 the differences between the Welsh, Normans and English were pronounced: ethnic, linguistic, cultural. The English were beaten, their leaders killed or exiled and replaced by Normans. In their turn they were helping the Normans colonize the Welsh. Gerald considers the English 'bumpkins', but you only have to read his chapters on how to conquer the Welsh in *The Description of Wales* to know that Gerald the Norman knew all about divide and rule and every other little trick that the English and Welsh, now operating as the British, would eventually bring to their own colonial expansion.

Also living in south Wales, near Haverfordwest, were a very large number of Flemings, who, Gerald tells us, were 'hostile to the Welsh'. They had been brought in by Henry I to help keep the locals compliant, behaving 'vindictively' and 'submitting the Welsh to shameful ill-treatment'. Apparently these Flemings, as well as being quick to fight and good with the wool trade, were able to see into the future by reading the right shoulder blade of a ram, once it had been boiled and stripped of its meat. It is a shame this useful knowledge has been lost, but there is now not a trace of any Flemings left in south Wales, although it's entirely likely that their descendants live on in the town of Haverfordwest and its surrounds.

The simple question that Kazuo Ishiguro is asking in *The Buried Giant*, it seems to me, is whether it is better for people to forget the past, or face up to it. There could well be different perspectives to this question, but the answer may still be the same. Also, to be more specific, should different peoples (tribes, ethnicities, nations), who have at one time slaughtered and enslaved each other (and the traffic may have been one way or both ways), and who have been participants, willing or unwilling, in atrocities, even genocide – is it better or even possible that they live in a cloud of forgetfulness, or should events be disinterred and scrutinized? This question will not go away, but the answer, or at least the first step, is surely obvious: we need to clear away the fog, and listen, hard, to the survivors.

I wonder what the psychic Flemings would have said about all this. I remember sitting with Anna in the bar of a hotel in Beijing, on New Year's Eve 1988, with the protests of Tiananmen Square already brewing, having travelled by train and boat from London across Sweden, the Soviet Union and Mongolia, and we were talking to a Québécois and a Welshman who were only just back from visiting Tibet (what a world, Gerald, *what a world!*). We were the only four people in the bar and we wanted to hear about Tibet, still so strange in those days, but the man from Quebec had nothing good to say: it was 'boring'; Tibetan culture was doomed, the Chinese would see to that; there's no point in complaining or resisting … every nuance and difference in the world will one day be ironed out, and that is a good thing; an end to conflict and wars. The boredom will save us. 'Yes', agreed the man from Wales, himself, I would have thought, like the man from Quebec, just another member of yet another minority trying to keep its shape in a homogenizing world – 'yes, it will all go one day, soon, and I won't miss any of it.' I could have noticed that there was desperation in his eyes, not acquiescence; but it wasn't until many years later that I came across R. S. Thomas's brutal, anguished dismissal of the Welsh and their culture:

> An impotent people,
> Sick with inbreeding,
> Worrying the carcase of an old song.

Anyway, I got drunk. And I can safely say it was the worst New Year's Eve I have ever spent, and I speak as someone who has mingled with the crowds in Trafalgar Square, and heard the chimes at midnight, and seen the vomit floating in oily clumps in the churning fountains. Some of it mine.

Speaking of which, Cardiff city centre on a sunny Saturday lunchtime in June is a lovely place to be. The streets are wide and bright. The shops and the covered markets are busy with a merry crowd. The drinkers are out of the pubs and on the pavements, easing into the long day. I pass a hugely energized gang of young men in black-and-white polo shirts with the words 'Ben Jackson's Stag Night' on their breasts and lager slopping from their glasses. Round the next corner I find myself pushing past a man looking like Sherlock Holmes, and several women dressed as babies and bears. Close to the St David's/Dewi Sant Shopping Centre there's a large bronze statue of John Batchelor who, I can tell you now, was a local Liberal Victorian politician, businessman, anti-slavery campaigner and 'friend of freedom'. If Gerald found himself standing here today, in front of this imposing statue, he would probably assume that Batchelor was a pivotal hero to the people of Cardiff and Wales. Although he'd more likely be distracted by the man in a romper suit drinking beer from a baby's bottle.

What else would Gerald think? His was not a literate culture, so he'd surely be impressed and overwhelmed by all the writing everywhere, on the shopfronts, in the newspapers, bookshops and on the magazines carried so casually. There's lighting overhead – the electricity! – and a neon blaze from the shops. And the music. It's everywhere, thumping from speakers and howling from the mouths of buskers. And although Gerald knew the Welsh as a musical people and very fond of the harp, he would not have been prepared for this incessant rhythm. Shops, shops, shops, all of them laden with goods and bounty from every corner of the globe, not that Gerald would know, but he would marvel at the mounded fish from the seven seas spread on the icy counters (the ice!), the sweets in every store, the sugar and the spices. So radiant and shiny. The colours! Our palette has stretched and it now glitters and throbs with gold and silver and hot pinks. And of course there's glass in the windows, so much of it, and in our hands. And even on our noses. There are the paving stones underfoot, with no dirt or rivers of shit to negotiate, and the cars, trucks, motorbikes and even a unicyclist with a top hat. There's a smell of sun cream in the air (coconut – what's that?) and car fumes and cigarettes and vanilla-flavoured vape oils. Gerald said that no one ever had to beg in Wales, the people are so hospitable, but there's a man here asking for spare change and a smoke, although Gerald would probably sign him on the spot to join his crusade. The people are no taller than in Gerald's day, but their skin and hair and teeth must seem impossibly glossy and (I'm only guessing here) they are – to Gerald's eyes – protein-packed and buoyant with muscle and fat. The clothing is startling: so colourful, and so many layers. The huge spongey shoes, with their laces. The zippers and buttons. The gold chains and hoops and precious jewels on display. The wealth. When Gerald was here in 1188 the people wore the same thin cloak and a tunic, all day and in bed at night; they had no deodorants. If he closes his eyes, all Gerald will hear is the animated 'hissing of geese' – the excitable and incomprehensible yak of the English – although that would also surprise him, because he knew the English as a silent race, 'their outward fairness of complexion and their inward coldness of disposition', whereas the Welsh were warm, voluble and dark. But, with his eyes closed, the Welsh also seem to have disappeared and so, he now realizes, have the Normans.

From Cardiff to Margam Abbey, now an exciting adventure park-land on a hill overlooking the industrial south and the sea, then onwards to Neath and Swansea. Gerald keeps up a flow of stories about fairyland, and the slaughter of the English by the Welsh and vice versa. In Carmarthen, having crossed the River Tywi by boat, Baldwin recruits more crusaders, while Gerald informs us that Carmarthen's name means 'Town of Merlin', because Merlin was discovered here 'as the offspring of an incubus' (that is, his human mother had become pregnant after sex with a male demon, which was unsurprisingly common in those days, but as Gerald always says, who are we to doubt these miracles?). In fact, rather dully, Carmarthen means a sea town with some walls, but that hasn't stopped the locals from erecting a startlingly ugly wooden statue of the Welsh wizard on their high street, complete with pet dragon, staff, peaked hat, cascading beard, snake, wand, horn, owl and what may well be a flask of mead.

I get a pleasant jolt when a man saunters past talking Welsh to his two young sons. There is no reason for my surprise, other than inexcusable London-centricity. As Wyn Griffith says in *The Welsh*:

> to the ordinary Englishman, the greatest of all strange-
> nesses is a strange language in a familiar country. After
> crossing the Channel to France, he expects to hear
> French spoken, for he is in another country. But it is
> always a shock to him, in his own island as he would call
> it, to find his railway carriage – that familiar carriage
> in which he left London a few hours ago – invaded by
> people who speak a strange language among themselves,
> apparently from choice ...

There are probably more Welsh speakers alive today than there were in Gerald's time, thanks to population growth and some vigorous recent campaigning, even if the proportion of Welsh speakers in Wales is much lower. When Wyn Griffith tries to define who the Welsh are, and God knows he's not the only one, he falls back on the language. Without it, there'd be no real difference between them and their neighbours, he says, especially because he cannot, unlike Gerald, find a way to define the Welsh 'race'. And yet this is how Gerald finishes his *Description of Wales*:

> Whatever else may come to pass, I do not think that on
> the Day of Direst Judgement any race other than the
> Welsh, or any other language, will give answer to the
> Supreme Judge of all for this small corner of the earth.

I follow the man and his sons because I want to bathe, briefly, in the sound of their conversation. It is both familiar and incom-prehensible. I feel a thrilling connection to an older land (even though this is happening, now) and back to Gerald, who we are fairly sure spoke Welsh but did not, unusually for him, like to boast about it. I hope I am not lurking in a sinister fashion, but anyway the man and his boys turn in to a barber shop and I carry on to take in the rest of the town. I am looking for a café, but there are surprisingly few. This is nothing like London, where every other place can sell you a jolt of caffeine and every other person is suckling a tub of sweet milky coffee, like a parade of hungry babies, unable to let go of their teats.

It transpires that almost every shop in Carmarthen is a barber. And almost every man and boy, and mother with a boy on her lap, is inside getting a haircut. Gerald is very clear about this:

> Both the men and the women cut their hair short and shape it round their ears and eyes … The men shave their beards, leaving only their moustaches… You can find it in the book which Julius Caesar wrote … 'the Britons shave their whole body except their upper lip.' Sometimes they shave their heads, too, so that they can move more freely.

Gerald also says that the Welsh care for their teeth better than he has seen in any other country, brushing with green hazel shoots and then burnishing them with woollen cloths 'until they shine like ivory'. They also 'daub their faces with shiny warpaint'.

Wales, you see, has always been the home of the tattoo, short haircut, fresh shave, clean teeth and all-over body wax (but always sparing the moustache). I decide it would be wrong not to join them and in no time (there's so much choice) find my scalp being kneaded and delicately teased by an early middle-aged, handsomely coiffed blond man from Neath who is fascinated by the fact that I've come from London and yet even so have entrusted him to look after my hair. I ask for the electric trimmers (No. four; my needs are simple) but he insists on hand-cutting each individual hair with a tiny pair of silver scissors ('I'll bet they don't do this for you in London'), and wants to know how much a similar service would normally cost. When I tell him £13 he subsides like a ruptured bouncy castle. He'd been harbouring a dream to move to London and make his fortune, and although I backpedal, and try to explain that I get my hair cut in Tooting, but in the centre of town he could make much, much more, he's just not listening and a restless unhappiness settles on us both, while he snips and trims through the long afternoon with his sad little scissors. 'Do tell them where you got your haircut', he finishes at last, brightening just a bit, 'when you get back to London.' Ah yes, London. I'll make sure I let them know.

It really is a very fine haircut. And I feel proud to take it to Manorbier Castle, which is where Gerald was born and spent a happy childhood. Gerald doesn't in fact go to Manorbier on his trip with Baldwin, so I shouldn't really be here, but he writes so evocatively about his family home, and it's really not so far off the trail (how he must have pleaded), that I make a quick detour. And what a place to grow up! The great grey castle is still standing on its hill, somewhat decayed and altered since Gerald's day, but I think he would recognize at least one of the towers, and the river still rolls past the walls and down to the beach, where Gerald used to build sand-cathedrals (*not* castles, he tells us) so that his family knew, even when he was very young, that he would be a good man for the Church.

He most certainly stood on this empty grey beach and watched the seagulls and skimmed these flat, red and black stones over the shallow waves. It is raining of course, a slight, drifting, soft rain, but that is what has saved this beach – this country – from ruinous tourism and other, earlier invaders. A man walks by slowly with his large dog, both of them sheltering underneath an even larger red umbrella. The only others here (and this is an afternoon in June) are one happy family, the three young children building dams in the river. It reminds me of my own family's only Welsh holiday, when my brother and I spent a week, perhaps two, merrily pushing mud around in the rain while my parents sheltered in the lee of the camper van and wondered whether to go home early. Mostly (Henry I being an example Gerald would know) the English have packed up and headed for their dry beds rather than linger in this land of clouds. How much more vital and satisfying to invade Bordeaux, they must have felt, with its golden dunes and incomparable wines.

The travellers reached St David's at last, with Gerald chaffing at the presence of the current Bishop, Peter de Leia. He manages, somehow, to call him 'a most friendly and hospitable man'. Or maybe he really did like him, although in the course of a long exposition on why St David's always was and still should be at the head of an independent Welsh Church, Gerald does give Peter a backhanded slap when he says that every bishop sent from England to Wales just wanted to get back to the easy life of an English bishopric. What the place needs, says Gerald, is a *Welsh* bishop.

He then vents some of his spleen by telling us the true story of a man 'in our own days' who 'lying ill in bed' was visited by every toad for miles around. His friends fought the toads with stick and sword, killing them in vast numbers, but in the end they had to put the man in a bag and hoist him to the top of a tall tree, with all the branches removed. Even that didn't help. The toads crawled up the trunk and devoured every last scrap of their victim, until only his skeleton remained.

The Bishop's Palace in St David's has risen and fallen to ruins since Gerald's time, and the cathedral would be unrecognizable. There's a choir practising for a concert tonight, so I sit at the back with a crowd of other sightseers and listen as the small choir, and an eight-person wind section, fills the nave with heavenly sound. I'm thinking of Gerald, of course, who yearned to be bishop here. He had the support of the local clerics and parishioners, but the English establishment was against him, from the king and the Archbishop of Canterbury down.

In 1198, ten years after this trip with Baldwin, Bishop Peter de Leia died and Gerald saw one last chance to get his hands on the prize. He was even elected bishop by the local chapter – and they sent him to Rome to try and persuade Pope Innocent III to confirm the appointment, bypassing the English Church. But the Archbishop of Canterbury, now Hubert Walter, fought Gerald implacably, and King John could not be persuaded to make a decision (well, he told Gerald when he saw him that he was 'right behind him', and told the archbishop the same thing not long after); and after four long years of fight (he was even thrown into prison in France by the archbishop's men, who had been told to look out for a tall man with voluminous eyebrows), he finally gave up. He lived for another twenty years, settling scores in his many books, and died in Lincoln or maybe Hereford aged over eighty.

I leave St David's for Cardigan, on the trail of the still vigorous Gerald, via tiny Nevern Church. The mist lifts a little and I sit on an ancient stone tomb in the shadow of a weeping yew and allow myself to be drugged by waves of wild garlic, until I remember the fate of the northern woman who defiled Saint Osana and I jump down in a hurry. In Cardigan, Baldwin preached in a green field just by the bridge and you can stand in the same spot, only slightly diminished by the passing cars, and contemplate the many miracles that were performed here after his visit, although as Gerald says, 'I have no time to tell you about them.'

The sun is out and I find myself wondering what, today, would persuade the men of Cardigan to gather in excited reverence and then sign up to fight a ferocious enemy in a faraway land. Well, there's the plunder, of course. The forgiveness of all sins. Eternal life. The chance of a bit of sunshine, for Christ's sake. But they must have known that one likely outcome was death or disfigurement. Gerald's book is full of tales of women who try to prevent their men from joining the crusade – and here in Cardigan he tells us about a woman who seized her husband by the cloak and belt and 'brazenly prevented him from taking the Cross'. Three nights later God punishes her by causing her to roll over and suffocate her young boy in her sleep, and she herself 'sewed the sign of the Cross on her husband's shoulder with her own hands'.

The road out of Cardigan is marked as something called the 'Saints and Stones Tour', but I am not to be thrown off the scent of Gerald, who is now making his way along the beautiful banks of the River Teifi. I stop in Cenarth, because it was here, or hereabouts, that Gerald claimed to have seen some of the last beavers still living in Wales. The rest had been hunted to oblivion long before, as had all the beavers of England south of the River Humber, although Gerald had heard that there was also one stream in Scotland where the beavers still lolloped and gnawed and splashed and dammed and got on with their lives far from the hunters and their dogs.

The last beavers of Britain were exterminated by humanity not long after Gerald's tour, as indeed, at one time, were the wolf, the bear, the boar, the ox, the lynx, the walrus, the grey whale, the crane, the osprey, the pelican, the elk and the woolly

mammoth, and so on and on and on ... but now they, and
some of the other lucky species, if they still exist elsewhere, are
making a tentative return. Not here on the River Teifi, as yet,
but in Devon on the River Otter and in two sites in Scotland.
It all seems very grudging. The Scottish government has had to
rush through a law confirming them as a 'native' species in order
to protect them from gun-toting landowners. And the Angling
Trust seems to imagine that the fish are going to be disturbed by
the presence of these large herbivores, with whom, we shouldn't
really have to point out, they once co-evolved. Britain's landscape
was shaped by beavers. They were here long before us, and
they bring abundance in their wake, an explosion of life in the
ponds and dams and purified, meandering streams. They even
help mitigate flooding. It is a catastrophic failure of imagination
to think that we cannot once again share our land with these
wondrous beings.

The beavers of Gerald's day had a sure-fire way of evading
human hunters. They would castrate themselves. It is how they
got their Latin name, *Castor*, Gerald assures us, even though it
actually comes from the Greek word for 'musk'. But it is well
known that humans lust after a beaver's testicles. Not in a sexual
way, I think, although Gerald is not quite clear about this. When
the hounds are hot on its heels the beaver will whip off its own
balls and shake them from a safe distance at the pursuing hunters – and they will immediately call off the hunt. And sometimes
when an already self-castrated beaver is being pursued, all he has
to do is 'rush to the top of a hillock, cock up one of his hind legs
and show the hunter that the organs which he is really after have
already been cut off'.

Sadly, there are no longer any beavers getting busy on the
banks of the bountiful River Teifi on which to test this theory, but
one day, perhaps, they will return. And how much more beautiful

everything would be if the beavers were here, with their shaggy dams spread across the river, close to where it now sparkles in the falls. The salmon would still flail and leap in their season. Dragonflies and frogspawn would dart and roll in the reeds. But even now, the path along the bank, although narrow and awkwardly speared with alder roots, is a magical place, impossible not to follow, slipping in the mud, entranced by the shimmer of midges in the faint, falling light on this long summer's evening. The woods on either side are growing muted, darker, but still gentle with a greening of young ash and sycamore. A wood pigeon gives a throaty purr. And there, just around the next bend in the path, there is a huge greyhound waiting, watching my stumbling approach. There are no humans to be seen. The dog looks as if it has stepped out of the pages of Gerald's book, wilder, more alert ... undeniably medieval. I walk on – perhaps I shouldn't – and the hound, long-haired, I now see, grey, close-packed, rangy, as tall as a wolf, bows from the front and dips its head and wags its tail and then, without warning, leaps up and thrusts its long hard nose into my groin. I just have time to notice that it has no collar – Oh dear God, it's feral! – before I stumble back, shouting and sprawling into a juniper bush, flinging up my arms to protect my throat. And my groin. Sweet Jesus! Do we really want the beavers back? And the wolves? Why ever did I think it was a good idea? I have been transported into a Roald Dahl story. The man who wanted to see a rewilding of the world – our dreary, desiccated world – and who mocked Gerald's faulty Latin and silly ideas about self-mutilating beavers, is now alone in the woods, far from help, about to be castrated by a wild dog. And torn apart by toads.

The dog gives a happy bark and skips away, looking to see if I want to play some more. I really don't. I get out of the bush and turn for home and the dog trots with me, sometimes at my heel, sometimes far behind, or pushing past and loping ahead with eager intent. He has a white-tipped tail and he smiles as he runs, his mouth open, his teeth large and hard and sharp. He's a beautiful dog – and at one point he disappears and although I continue to fret about ambushes, it turns out he has vanished for good. I miss him.

Gerald spent several nights not far from here in the Abbey of Strata Florida. He must have been impressed, because ten years later, when he was fighting to become Bishop of St David's and travelling to and from Rome, he entrusted his precious collection of books to the monks and not long after that they sold them and kept the money. Gerald's life was full of frustrations and thwarted ambition.

There's not much left of the abbey now, but it remains remote and far from the concerns of our hectic world. The carved stone western doorway still stands and low ruined walls trace an outline of the grass-covered great hall. There's an old farm next to the outer wall (although it looks deserted), and a couple of empty houses, with spiders' webs in the windows and swifts calling in the eaves. It is nearly dark now. There's mist in the woods on the surrounding hills and bats in the air. A car crawls past on the tiny dirt road and the driver peers out through the murk. I listen to the sound of his engine as it fades to nothing down the valley. Just to one side of the ruined abbey, next to a dying ash tree, there's a small country church; and next to that, vanishing into the gloom, is a vast graveyard, still very much in use, many of the tombstones freshly carved, but others of immense age, scoured and featureless lumps of stone drowsing in lichen and moss. Gerald stood here once, although that was long before even one of these ancient stones was planted. He would have been talking to Baldwin, or the abbot, or walking alone, and making his plans, or composing his book, and scheming and plotting and turning over the options

on St David's, or maybe just taking the air and listening to these
swifts and thinking about dinner and inhaling the extraordinary
freshness of the wild Welsh night and

                                                              Jesus

    he was a handsome man
                      and what i want to know is
    how do you like your blue-eyed boy
    Mister Death

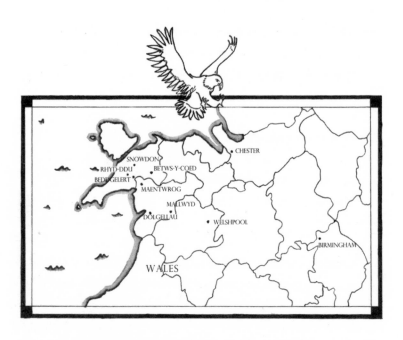

Edith Somerville & Violet 'Martin' Ross,
Welshpool to Chester, June 1893

SIX

'Lorf? – Why, I Thought I Should 'a *Died*'

'You were a nice woman to write with.'

LETTER FROM MARTIN ROSS
TO EDITH SOMERVILLE

After leaving the Abbey of Strata Florida, Gerald and Baldwin turned their horses north towards the rest of Wales, most of it at that time still under the control of Welsh princes, following the coast and keeping the mountains of Snowdonia to their right. There is a lake, Gerald tells us, hidden among these crags, where only one-eyed fish live; and another on which a floating island drifts and blows; but Gerald himself skirted around the edge of the mountains and was not able to witness any of these wonders, although he did share the story of the giant eagle that lands on the highest peak every Thursday, far above the world of man, and waits with bloodthirsty intent for the epoch-shaping battle that Merlin had prophesied would take place on that particular day of the week, even if, maddeningly, he neglected to give us the month or the year. You could have set your week's calendar by it.

I don't know if the prophecy had been fulfilled by 1893, but over 700 years after Gerald had ridden this way the Irish writers Edith Œ. Somerville and Violet Martin (aka Martin Ross) were struggling up the slopes of Snowdon, silently cursing their guide and keeping an eye out for eagles. They were gathering material for a series of travel articles and a short book, which would be published two years later as *Beggars on Horseback: A Riding Tour in North Wales*.

They had started their journey a few days earlier in the town of Welshpool, staying at the Royal Oak Inn, 'with its thick walls and polished floors, and its associations of the old coaching days', while they negotiated with shopkeepers for suitable horses. The Royal Oak still stands stolidly at the foot of the high street, but I'm sorry to say that the gas lamp on a stone pedestal that once stood just outside in the road has been removed to make room for buses and cars. There's a fading photo of the thing in the corridor of the Royal Oak and, true to Somerville and Ross's description, it looks like it was the one and only focus of Welshpool life, attracting the town's loafers who 'turned to look after us like sunflowers to the sun'. Perhaps visitors were a rarity in those days. Or maybe it was the unfamiliar sight of two young women travelling together, encumbered by safety skirts, riding habits and wide-brimmed hats, their hired horses reeling under over-stuffed holdalls, shying and zig-zagging down the high street, before galloping off to 'the unknown and the unpronounceable'.

Despite the skittishness of their new horses, Somerville and Ross were both entirely at home in the saddle. They rode side-saddle (that is, with both legs arranged down the same side of the horse), a feat of great strength and control that also required the rider to sit for hours with her shoulders up and straight and the bottom half of her body twisted awkwardly to one side. Not surprisingly, in later years Somerville was plagued by sciatica in her right leg, although the pain was never enough to keep her off a horse for long. Ross didn't survive to suffer the effects of side-saddle riding, although the tumour that killed her, everyone believed, was caused by a terrible fall she had taken seventeen years before her death. Ross was short-sighted, which made every outing a peril (on the day she fell she seems to have ridden into a fence without seeing it), but – like Somerville – she was fearless.

Anyway, I'm going to call them Edith and Martin, the latter because when Violet Martin first met Edith Somerville in Drishane, Castletownshend, Edith's family home in south-west Ireland, there were at least two other Violets lurking among the numerous cousins and aunts, so she was dubbed 'Martin' to avoid confusion. And then, when they published their first book together, 'Martin' evolved into 'Martin Ross', in honour of her family home in Galway. The fact that she published her books under a masculine name (and Edith used the androgynous E. Œ. Somerville) must have helped when their bestselling *Some Experiences of an Irish R.M.* appeared. Many people read these tales of hunting and happy anarchy, narrated by a genial, put-upon, cigar-loving, irredeemably innocent English major working as a resident magistrate in rural Ireland, and assumed that the authors were men. Edith and Martin never hid their identities – they were well known in their lifetimes – but the publishers were probably pleased. In those days it was believed that men were less likely to read books written by women. In certain categories, I mean. Hunting, for example. And humour. It wouldn't happen now.

Edith was thirty-five years old in June 1893 and Martin was thirty-one. They were cousins, like almost every other member of the Anglo-Irish gentility, but they hadn't met until the year 1886, when Edith was twenty-six and Martin twenty-three. Edith wasn't even that interested in Martin at their first meeting. She was older, popular, busy, with a wild beauty, and she may have felt her life was already replete with five younger brothers and a sister, an eccentric mother, cousins and friends. Anyway, she was about to head off to Paris to study art. It took some effort from the more introverted Martin to get her attention, but Martin knew what she wanted. Edith ignored the first letter, sent to her in Paris in March 1886, as you can tell from the somewhat querulous tone in the second, posted on 19 May:

My dear Edith, You know and you should blush to know
that there is no reason in the world why I should write
to you – but there are people to whom it interests one
to write irrespective of their bad qualities and behaviour … you are a 'popular girl' – a sort that I have always
abhorred – so bear in mind that theoretically you are in
the highest degree offensive to me.

Edith came back from Paris later that year, she and Martin met
again, and before long they were visiting each other as often as
they could, even though Martin had her own eccentric mother
to attend and her own family's crumbling big house to patch and
worry over. But they exchanged dozens of long letters, written
deep into the night, and one time they met, in 1887, it was Edith
who suggested that they should try writing a book together. They
mockingly called it 'The Shocker', presumably in an attempt to
deflect the hilarity of Edith's hyperactive family, who couldn't see
why anyone would want to write a book, rather than play croquet,
or row in the bay, or come hunting, or photograph each other
in outlandish fancy dress. Much is made of the poverty of the
Anglo-Irish gentry at this time, as Ireland changed around them,
living in their big old decaying houses, unable to collect any rent
once the tenants stopped paying, and it's true that several families
lost their homes, or left them to rot – but, still, it doesn't sound *so*
bad. If you want to know what it was like, you only have to read
Somerville and Ross.

Edith and Martin were writing to make money (and who but
a fool would do anything else?), because money, for them and
every other unmarried Victorian woman, meant a modicum of
independence. And when 'The Shocker' – real title *An Irish Cousin* –
came out in 1889 they were rewarded with an instant commercial
and a critical hit ('It is very much like a dream – that I should sit

down and write about a flourishing critique of the Shocker in the *Athenaeum* – but there it is, in black and white,' purred Martin in a letter to Edith in September). Edith's mother was still wringing her hands (it was all so agonizingly *outré*), but the rest of her family was pleased, even if they persisted in treating the whole thing as a joke. None of them seem to have recognized the deep seriousness of Edith and Martin's ambition. Or understood how high they could fly. Perhaps we've all been misled by their modesty and talent for self-ridicule. Or even their sense of proportion.

There are other reasons. For one thing, they lived the life of a class that was under siege for its unwarranted privilege, even if, by 1890, much of that privilege and wealth was draining away, and they would insist on writing about dogs and horses and hunting and the curious marriage rituals of their tribe, albeit with the most acute and all-knowing eye. And they quoted, or transcribed, the speech of their servants and the local country folk, along with the rising middle classes and their own kin, which many (especially in the early days of the Irish Republic) found insufferably patronizing, however accurately it was done, or suspected that they were being laughed at, even though they never were – it was always *with*. And later, when Martin died, there was the awkward fact that Edith carried on writing for both of them, communicating with Martin through a spirit medium and refusing to remove Martin's name from the title page of any of their books ... not even the ones that were written long after Martin's death.

Martin's mother was impressed by *An Irish Cousin*. So was her son, Robert, who had shirked his responsibilities as the lord of Ross House to become a successful composer of light verse in London, playing up his Irishness for the stage. He was the author of the very popular *Ballyhooly*.

All together now:

Whililoo, hi ho, let us all enlist you know,
For their ructions and their elements they charm me;
We don't care what we ate, if we drink our whisky nate,
In the Ballyhooly Blue Ribbon Army.

In 1893 this nonsense was rocking them in the aisles in London, while Edith and Martin were working when they could on their one truly great novel, *The Real Charlotte* (the three, even greater, Irish R.M. books are collections of interconnected short stories). They had also discovered a demand for travel journalism, and had been making trips to Denmark and Connemara (on a cart). Their Welsh jaunt fitted into this series: there was money to be made and they could escape the financial anxieties of home for a while.

Edith and Martin left Welshpool abruptly ('there are no suburbs'), breezing along 'the white road stretching westward into the unknown'. The sun blazed from a cloudless sky, the hedgerows were soft and drowsy with dog roses and elder bushes of every shade of pink and cream, the honeysuckle flowered in thickets and intoxicating perfumes filled the air:

> The thought of them takes the pen from the paper in indolent remembrance of that first ride between the Montgomery hedgerows, while yet the horse-flies had not discovered us, and while the hold-alls lay trim and deceptive in the straps that bound them to the saddles.

And that, if you don't know them, is a typical Somerville and Ross moment. Beauty and laughter, and any pride of achievement, are punctured with a gleeful smile. The straps on their holdalls burst, strewing ridiculous and superfluous objects across the road, the horseflies descended in droves to devour them and their horses, 'and the reign of suffering that ceased not till our journey's end was fairly inaugurated'.

I think Martin wrote most of *Beggars on Horseback*, while Edith sketched and painted and added her comments later. But it is hard to know, and as Edith said, the one doing the writing was usually the one who just happened to be holding the pen. Their separate thoughts, styles and impulses blended together, she wrote, like blue and yellow paints creating a perfect green. If they were apart, they would exchange episodes and ideas by post; if together, they would talk and write wherever they could. The incorrigibly modest Edith always claimed Martin was the greater writer, but there is only a slight falling off in the works she produced after Martin's death (and Edith would simply have seen this as further proof that Martin was still involved).

Edith was perhaps less filtered – she churned with creative energy – Martin more controlled; but both of them shared an extravagant delight in the absurdity of their fellow humans, and they raised each other to heights it is hard to imagine they would have reached on their own. Writing gave them another reason to be together, chuckling over the latest gothic sayings of the Somerville cook, wrestling with the intricacies of plot and character … but, to say it again, their laughter and self-deprecation masked serious intent. If Edith's later books lacked some of the soaring joy of their earlier, collaborative work (but none of the dark humour), well who's to wonder at that? 'My share of the world', she wrote to her brother Jack in an anguish of grief after Martin's death, 'has gone with Martin, and nothing can ever make that better. No one but ourselves can ever know what we were to each other.'

Martin put it very simply in a letter to Edith in 1889: 'Writing together is – to me at least – one of the greatest pleasures I have. To write with you doubles the triumph and enjoyment having first halved the trouble and anxiety.'

On their first night out of Welshpool, Edith and Martin stayed at the old Cann Office Inn, where they lingered late in the gardens among 'the peace of a hundred sleeping roses' and Martin 'caught one of my very finest colds in my head'. Riding on the next day under a hot and cloudless sky they decided that the landscape was very like Connemara: no trees, many sheep, and the hills 'big and mild, with the magnanimous curves of the brows of an elephant'. You can see it all today (with a garnish of tarmac and telegraph poles); we are closer to Martin and Edith than they ever were to Gerald and his medieval wanderings, despite the horses. Most striking of all is the ease with which they ride through Wales, where women travellers rarely ventured alone, encountering (like Gerald) 'a politeness incredible, almost unnerving'. They have no fear of outlaws or wolves. The inns are trim and well-tended. And perhaps (it's just a thought) they expected less than we do today: they drifted through Mallwyd, where they would have stayed at the inn except a 'weird, pig-styish smell pervaded the village', and immediately found and checked into a popular tourist haunt, the Griffith Arms Hotel; whereas I am pulled into a lay-by, 125 hectic years later, drumming my fingers and gnashing my teeth, while my smartphone gropes to locate an elusive network signal, so I can check if the Griffith Arms still exists and then scroll through its star ratings and user comments on TripAdvisor.

In the event, Edith and Martin galloped away from the Griffith Arms, vowing never to return (there was a sharp disagreement over the bill), and they struggled on in sweltering heat towards 'Dolgelly', these days firmly re-established as the town of Dolgellau. Edith had fashioned herself a hat out of bracken and a painting rag, to keep the horseflies at bay, and Martin was delighting in calling it a *puggaree*. The English language was always too small for them. The first book they ever worked on together, not for publication, was a dictionary of 'Buddh', a glossary of the invented language used by Edith's family when there was no adequate word in English available. Words like 'Gub (n.) – A vague pursuing horror, the embodiment of the terror of darkness.' Or 'White-eye (n.) – A significant and chilling glance calculated to awake the fatuous to a sense of their folly.'

The language of their books, including the ones produced by Edith alone, heaves and seethes with its own energy. They had both learned and spoke Gaelic, which may have been a factor. Irish writers (perhaps all non-English writers – and Edith for one *never* described herself as English) often loosen the bounds of the imposed language. You can hear it in Wales, too, a dissatisfaction with what's on offer, along with a lip-smacking relish of what's possible. The rolling momentum of the sentences. '… sloeblack, slow, black …' I grew up in a family that used a large number of made-up words. Perhaps that's normal, but I wonder if it was the influence of my Scots-Irish grandmother from Donegal, seeping down through my mother and aunts. Even when they weren't making up words, Edith and Martin would put commonplace ones in surprising places. They are such evocative nature writers – present, watchful, joyous – but wary of overflowing into vapid effusiveness. Edith was no fan of sub-Romantic gushings and had no time at all for the then (and now) fashionable nature-mystic Richard Jefferies: all that 'rot about Nature' she snaps in a letter to Martin in 1891.

Edith and Martin (and I) stop in Dolgellau to refuel and pick up supplies. I wander into an outdoor sports shop (I am bound for Snowdon), and get talking to a lean and bearded 'mountainy man', as he would have found himself called in *The Irish R.M.*, about following Edith and Martin's route to the summit. He consults his weather chart and stares at my leaky trainers, threadbare anorak and wasted, clerkish limbs with unfeigned concern. 'I'd head up tomorrow. The cloud is low, but a fresh south-westerly breeze

should carry you to the top. If you're setting off from Rhyd-ddu.'
I thank him and buy my mountain essentials: two beautiful maps
and a sugary slab of brown (not white) Kendal Mint Cake. 'The
healthy option,' I josh, limbering up for the most important part
of any hill-walking expedition: excruciatingly bad banter. The
mountainy man gives a short, dutiful, dying bark, like a seal choking on a badly thrown fish, and tells me it gets dark at 8.30p.m.

In Edith and Martin's day every house in the town of Dolgellau
was surrounded on all four sides by a street. The buildings were
big and grey and the shopkeepers stood in the middle of their
homes, ready to reach out to any passing customer from which-
ever direction they chose to approach. There must have been
a deal of in-filling since those days, because now Dolgellau is
arranged into neat streets, with many fewer shops. The major
tone is still grey – sky and houses – but that doesn't do justice to
the place's trim, uplifting appeal. There's a beautiful cricket pitch
on the edge of town, with standing stones on one boundary and
a racing river on the other (it was a sluggish, drought-hit trickle
in 1893). There is no sign of the Angel Inn where Martin and
Edith 'staggered into shelter', drawn by the fact that the landlord's
wife looked like one of Edith's aunts, and while Edith painted an
ancient Welsh woman in a Welsh hat, Martin 'no less enjoyably
to myself, sat on a wheelbarrow in the stable and laid down the
law' to the landlord, ostler and saddler about ill-fitting saddles
and 'warbles'. I, meanwhile, am munching my way through 'the
best bacon sandwich in North Wales', or so it says, and pondering
Edith and Martin's advice that there are three things to avoid in
Wales, although you never can: butter, coffee and bacon. All of
them are 'odious'.

The Grapes Hotel in Maentwrog still stands, where Edith and
Martin stayed on the night before they climbed Snowdon, and the
village is as it was, 'hemmed in between a wooded hill and a river,

lying silent in the velvet gloom'. They were met at the entrance by
a fellow guest from Manchester, his face scarlet with sunburn, who
had just been up Snowdon and 'had felt "that sick and giddy" at
one place that on the downward path two guides had enveloped
his head in a sack and carried him'. His 'rather shy' friend was
playing 'The Man Who Broke the Bank at Monte Carlo' on the
piano in the next room and ever since that night, wrote Martin,
the tune has 'held a horror for us that is not entirely its own'.

> Oo're ye goin' to meet, Bill?
> '*Ave* ye bought the street, Bill?
> Lorf? – why, I thought I should 'a *died*

These days it is Sky Sports on every wall and a cheery hubbub at
the bar. I haven't been here long before I realize that every person
in the packed front room – grandfathers, mothers, toddlers – is
speaking Welsh. Everyone, that is, apart from me ('a pint of Purple
Moose please') and Gary Neville on the commentary ('they need to
get tight on their man, Jamie, *tight*'). And of course, again, I remind
myself that this should not be strange to us tourists. When Edith
and Martin were here they often had trouble making themselves
understood, whereas now the Welsh-speaking population is com-
fortably bilingual. But many English people continue to find this
aggravating. When I was working at *Time Out* in the 1990s (yes,
even there, at the great liberal London magazine), I remember one
of our editors returning from a Welsh holiday and complaining
that people refused to understand him in the shops and he was
'sure that they had been speaking English before I came in'. The
pressure to conform – the insistence on conformity – is relentless;
so I'm very happy to sit here, drinking my beer, listening to people
talk regular pub bollocks through the night. Or at least I guess
that's what they're doing, because obviously I don't have a clue

what everyone is shouting about; and I suppose whatever 'Pam na wnei di ffwcio i ffwrdd, y cont Sais ddiawl?' happens to mean, it's all part of the merry chit-chat of a big night out.

Anyway, the staff and patrons of the Grapes Hotel could not be friendlier. And the morning's butter and coffee could not be any finer. Edith and Martin left early on the longest day of the year, riding through pine forests and oak woods and absolute loneliness, wrapped in their new Dolgellau *puggarees* and remarking on the rarity of the June tourist. The weather was on the turn and the air was growing chilly. They rode through the famously beautiful Aberglaslyn Pass almost without comment ('Mother of God! It's like a circus' is all they'll give us). On the road between the grave of Gelert, which was once a place of pilgrimage for newlyweds, and the nearby village of Beddgelert, they are delighted to observe that 'the distance that separated each bride from her groom was noticeable, and seemed to indicate a desire to economise conversation'. Edith even supplies a drawing of four mournful figures, two brides and two grooms, shambling in single file along the road, heads down, each of them alone with their thoughts.

By this stage of their lives, neither Edith (thirty-four) nor Martin (thirty-one) seemed keen on marriage. Later in the trip, in the Saracen's Head at Cerrig-y-Drudion, they came under the scrutiny of a middle-aged tradesman and his wife sitting in the pub's parlour, 'too entirely respectable to be aware that they were bored almost to madness'. Edith was pursued for much of her life by her cousin, Herbert Greene, a genial, pompous and reactionary Oxford academic, who would propose marriage to her every few months. It is possible she even accepted him once, in 1898, but was saved by the death of her father; and the engagement seems to have been allowed to drift away in the turmoil of her becoming mistress of the family home. According to her biographer, Gifford Lewis, she had also wanted to marry a young man called Hewitt

Poole when she was nineteen, and was devastated when her father decided he wasn't rich enough. I don't know about Martin and marriage – but what mattered most to her and Edith was their independence.

Were Edith and Martin lovers? Many people seem to think so. A quick Google search finds them cropping up on numerous 'Famous Lesbians' websites; and their first major biographer, Maurice Collis, was convinced Edith was attracted only to women. But his book (published 1968) needs to be read through the filter of his times, not to mention the prism of his own prurience:

> Any sexual union with a man had something revolting about it for Edith. Deep in her was a profound distaste for the opposite sex. Ethel [Edith's first great friend] did not suffer from this disability [*sic*] … Edith's deepest feelings, however, were entirely concentrated on her own sex. The emotion, however, was sublimated. It did not include what she would have termed its grosser manifestations [*sic* and, in fact, good grief!].

God knows where he got this stuff, but there he leaves us, more or less, with some misquoted notes from her diaries, until later in the book he re-emerges with Edith's 'disgust' at her sister Hildegarde's wedding, which 'could only be fully explained by a psychiatrist, though perhaps enough has been said earlier in the book to hint at what his [*sic*] explanation would be'.

They loved one another, that much is certain. They spent all the time together they could. They often shared each other's beds. But after Martin's death Edith was horrified when someone suggested people might think they had been lovers and she immediately set about scribbling over what she felt were incriminating phrases and passages in Martin's letters. Gifford Lewis has managed to decipher a few of these censored words and apparently there is no hint of any physical love; instead they are weirdly innocent. In 1919, three years after Martin's death, Edith became close friends with the composer Ethel Smyth and she appears to have reacted with stunned surprise when Ethel suggested a physical relationship. Ethel (who angrily described Edith as 'virginal' and herself as having 'more experience of life stored in my little finger than you have in your whole body') was even more bemused when she managed to persuade Edith to come to Sicily on holiday with her, hoping for some love among the lemon groves, only to find that Edith had asked along her sister Hildegarde and her husband. In the event none of them went.

Well, what do we know? Really? It seems unlikely they were lovers. Not because of the times they lived in – or not especially – but because neither of them seems to have had the inclination. Perhaps they sought diversion in writing and hunting. I guess in the end we have to say that we just don't know. And more than that, I now find myself wondering – and obviously I don't want to come across like a gaslighting Victorian patriarch, or indeed the worst biographer in history, a kind of anti-biographer, the *black hole* of biographers – but I do have to ask: what the hell business is it of ours anyway? Here's Gifford Lewis: 'That Edith was a lesbian has gained general acceptance through an unlovely combination of affected liberalism, ignorant salaciousness and the sad assumption that huge vitality and strength in a woman implies masculinity.'

So – to Snowdon we must go. 'The ascent', wrote Somerville and Ross, 'began as seductively, as gently, as the first step towards a great crime.' The daughter of the landlady at the inn in Beddgelert, with 'compassion in her eye', had suggested they start from the tiny hamlet of Rhyd-ddu instead of from Beddgelert itself, cutting a long preliminary walk out of the journey. They had hired a guide for the trip, a stocky, almost silent man called Griffith Roberts, who had already been up and down Snowdon once that day. We don't have guides any more in this country, or at least not ones who are hanging about at the foot of Snowdon or on the coastal path of Cornwall, waiting for business, like the men who sprang out of the mist to take Wilkie in hand. It wouldn't make any financial sense. But after a few minutes of following Griffith Roberts's unforgivingly broad back, Edith and Martin started to wonder if they wouldn't have been better off with a slightly less vigorous guide: an asthmatic, perhaps, or someone with a club foot.

These days the route to the top from Rhyd-ddu is clearly marked: you just have to park next to the one-track railway station (where the steam train puffs and wheezes) and head up the hill. It couldn't be easier. I am alone, but carrying my lovely new map and what's left of the brown Kendal Mint Cake. Unlike Edith and Martin, I am not encumbered by a full-length skirt, bodice, cinch-waisted jacket, hat and thin-soled leather shoes. There is no one else on the path (how strange that is for a weekend), but then, as the mountainy man had warned, the grey cloud is settling on the heights and there's a chill edge to the stiffening wind. I feel very close to Edith and Martin. Indeed, I seem to be tracking them precisely: an early over-confidence in the easy, grassy gradient is turning quickly into a breathless, heart-pounding, ignominious craving that Griffith Roberts might call a halt. We have been walking for about half an hour, so we are probably not nearly there yet.

When they finally pause, Edith tries to find out if there are still any eagles on Snowdon, as Gerald once wrote, but Griffith Roberts's English is not up to the question. She leaps to her feet and flaps across the mountainside, squawking and shouting about 'big birds who steal lambs' and at last Griffith Roberts assures her that there are indeed plenty of '*fahxes*, oh yess, many fahxes' on Snowdon. Edith sat down, exhausted, and Martin 'laughed a great deal', something she did often: she was famous for her wild laughter, impossible to suppress, which could come at the worst moments, and always at any sign of over-inflated dignity. The eagles were in fact long gone by 1893, although there is now a slender chance they might be making the most tenuous of returns, if only the conservationists and farmers can agree what to do about all these sheep and their helpless, succulent lambs.

The way grows steeper and rockier. Griffith Roberts is taking 'a short cut', and I am certain that I am on his trail, following the occasional signs and my perky little map. We are tracking the path of a stream, shallow in the summer months, slipping over boulders and a deluge of splintered rocks. I find I am standing at the foot of a sharp passage, peering over the beginnings of a cliff, watching distant pillars of mist glide from left to right, while silver filaments of cloud flow above them. It is more or less the last time I see anything, because now the Snowdon mist is upon us. I press on, finding hope in the cairns that lurk in the gloom. They must have been a rarity in 1893. A soft rain has joined itself to the thickening mist, although I could waste a lot of time wondering where one ends and the other begins. Let's just say it's grey and wet, up here on the cold mountain. Despite the fact that the land down below is writhing under the worst drought for many years, there is water all around: in the reeds and squelching underfoot, spraying from the falls, pouring from my hood and blearing my glasses – how on earth could Martin have seen any of this? A blanket of chill damp fog is laid across my shoulders. It is quiet. Heavy breaths and scrabbling footfall. Stones slipping back. No other sound. Water. Sheep. Crows.

A brief tear in the mist allowed Edith and Martin to see that 'the cliff on which we were kneeling ran with a tremendous horse-shoe curve right up to the highest peak of Snowdon'. And that's about where I am, I reckon, when Edith 'made the contemptible suggestion that we should return to Rhyddu and get particulars of the sunrise and the view from the landlady's daughter'. Edith and Martin, you see, were staying (or meant to be staying) overnight at the hotel at the top of Snowdon, and I am starting to think, as I read these words, alone in this fog, that Edith may have a point (and there isn't even a hotel on Snowdon these days), but Martin 'repelled the suggestion with appropriate spirit'.

I have paused (again), this time on the pretence of looking at the twelve tender saplings planted in plastic sheaths just to the side of the path. Once, long before Somerville and Ross came this way – and probably not even in Gerald's day – the slopes of the hills and mountains of Wales were covered in trees. The early settlers and English conquerors made a good job of cutting them down (why give your enemy somewhere to hide?) and the relentless sheep ensured they never returned. Perhaps a pair of eagles, or a pack of wolves, would solve this problem. It is surprising how high the treeline might climb if these saplings manage to take hold, but we are conditioned not to think of our peaks as naturally wooded. We think first of moorland and peat and grouse, and the occasional square of forestry, but this barren landscape is not natural: it requires constant work to keep the uplands free from trees. It is also madness, of course (we need trees for flood mitigation, soil retention, species diversity, oxygen …), but with the climate in meltdown, and the sheep corralled, there might soon come a day when we see juniper, alder and birch near the very top of Snowdon.

There is an ancient wind blowing me up the mountain, ruffling the mist among the rocks. It is cold. I hadn't thought I would be so alone here, just me and the long-dead Edith, Martin and Griffith Roberts. And I had not thought to give Snowdon the absolute respect it is due. But even Edith and Martin, before they started, were saddened by the way their planned route 'degraded the ascent of the highest mountain in England and Wales into a mere episode of the late afternoon'. And I was following them – at least that's my excuse – two Victorian ladies in all their finery, giggling their way to the top, although it's only when they are finally there, shivering in a little wooden hut (because that's all the 'hotel' turns out to be) that Edith admits that on the last narrow stretch, with cliffs on either side wreathed in tormented vapours, she had 'an almost uncontrollable desire to traverse it after the manner of a serpent'.

How does anyone manage to lose his new, beautiful map on the slopes of Snowdon? It can be done, apparently. Round about the point where the mist is thickest and the path least certain. Perhaps I should not have come here alone, but I wanted to enjoy Edith and Martin's company. Their friendship was the bond that defined their lives. In one of the later Irish R.M. stories, 'Harrington's', they introduce us to 'the chicken farmers', two women who have retreated to a small farm on a remote stretch of the Irish coast, one of them a doctor, the other 'very pretty', and recovering from a broken engagement to a gunner ('drink, I fancy, or mad', says Philippa, the R.M.'s wife). I've always thought the portrait of the women chicken farmers must have been Edith and Martin's wistful fantasy of escape, written not long before Martin's death. It showed what might have been possible, if only family and duty had not pressed so hard. A little pink box of a house, on the shore of a small, round lake, far from the suffocating intrusions of others. Tending chickens. But it's really not something they would have thought about for long. Or even much enjoyed.

In the story, Major Yeates, his wife Philippa and their cousin Andrew end up following the chicken farmers to an auction in the ruins of an old mine on the edge of nowhere. They have Anthony, their eldest son, with them, as a treat for not crying when his cake was spoiled on his ninth birthday. Mr Harrington, the last owner of the mine, had committed suicide (although the jury was too sympathetic to call it that), and everything he owned was going under the hammer. Unlike every other R.M. story, there is a twitchy unease running through it like adrenaline in a rat. There is a ghost, and second sight, and a groping, nauseating dash through the pitch-black mine, looking for Anthony, who is lying limp and stricken by a falling rock, and the major (who narrates all the stories) 'felt that sickening drop of the heart that comes when the thing that seems too bad to think of becomes in an instant the thing that is'. I know that feeling too well. I guess we all do.

But anyway I have a horror of black mines, ever since my older brother, also only nine years old, plunged head first down the shaft of a German bunker in Brittany, in the dead darkness of an underground passageway, at the very moment when my mother was saying, 'Hang on, wait, just stop, I'm going to strike a match.' And he was fine, after the weeks in hospital when he drank puréed vegetable soup through a straw, and my parents never slept, and I managed to get myself stung by a wasp so the French nurses would pay me some attention. (I was seven, and sick with worry, and insanely jealous of that damned straw, which was long and could be twisted into all the shapes of a roller coaster. No one in England had ever seen such a thing.) I can replay every second of that time in the bunker, and still hear every word.

Mostly, though, the Irish R.M. stories have no dark shades. They are filled with the bright sunshine of carefree days. Reading them, you would never know (or you would have to read very closely to realize) that Ireland in the early twentieth century was a place of bitter division, on the brink of war. This was deliberate (Edith and Martin knew what sold), but also unavoidable: they really did find life very funny, especially when they were together. They stripped out all politics and put in all the people they met

and knew. Disguised, of course: Edith always claimed that there
were only two characters in the stories drawn from real life, her
sister's dog and a local drunk called Slipper. But this was not true.
I even wonder if the ineffectual but lovable Major Yeates of the
Irish R.M. stories is in any way a nod to the poet W. B. Yeats,
whose work they knew well and whom Martin met for the first
time in 1901, as she described to Edith in a letter:

> Yeats looks just what I expected. A cross between a
> Dominie Sampson [an impoverished scholar in a Walter
> Scott novel] and a starved R.C. curate – in seedy black
> clothes – with a large black bow at the root of his long
> naked throat. He is egregiously the poet – mutters ends
> of verse to himself with a wild eye, bows over your hand
> in dark silence – but poet he *is* – in spite of various
> things – and I got on well with him, so far.

That 'so far' is revealing. Yeats was also born Protestant and
'Anglo-Irish', with its assertive and tormented and distancing
hyphen, but by 1901 he was an Irish nationalist, with no time
for any Home Rule compromises. How to be Irish – who *can* be
Irish? (or British or English) – preoccupied Martin and Edith
just as much as it did Yeats or any of them. Edith, as I say, would
never have considered herself English – her family had lived in
Ireland for hundreds of years – and she could flare into a rage at
the thought of what England had done to her country. Martin
too considered herself Irish, but she was also more conscious of
her family's leading place in the Protestant Ascendancy, and as
opinions polarized, she found it harder to know where she fitted.
On the side of Home Rule, no doubt, in 1901 – devolution that
would have kept links (and much control) at Westminster – but
Martin died in December 1915 and never lived to see the Easter

Rising, the murderous reprisals of the Black and Tans, the burning of the big houses, the birth of the Irish Republic, Civil War and the flight of most of the Anglo-Irish (but not Edith) who represented, whether they liked it or not, centuries of oppression, servitude and famine. There didn't seem to be much room for ambiguous hyphens in the new, independent, Catholic Ireland.

Later on in the day she first met Yeats, Martin was asked to add her initials to a tree that was being decorated by a gathering of 'the literary crowd'. 'WBY did the carving, I smoked, and high literary conversation raged and the cigarette went out and I couldn't make the matches light, and he held the little dingy lappets of his coat out and I lighted the match in his bosom.'

'Lappets'. The thing about Somerville and Ross is that they could never stay serious for long.

I was almost brought to my knees with relief when I met 'Nick from the Wirral' on the slopes of Snowdon, at the moment when the fog was at its deepest. I was skirting edgily along the cusp of the horseshoe leading to the top when Nick came bounding along another path, bearing a high-vis orange jacket and an open tap of merry banter. He was also on his own and had decided on a whim to take a longer route home, over the top of Snowdon, which is perhaps even crazier than it sounds. We made it to the summit together, in thick cloud and a few freckles of snow, and he insisted I arrange myself on top of the triangulation point for a photo, so I could show the world that I was briefly the highest person standing in England and Wales. There was a queue of people waiting to do the same thing, all of whom had arrived by the train that has been slogging up Snowdon since 1896, three years after Edith and Martin made the journey by foot.

The wooden hut where Edith and Martin stayed is long gone, replaced by a vast alpine visitor centre and café, which sounds like a hideous thing to impose on a mountaintop (and it is), but under the circumstances (aftershocks of vertigo amid pangs of mourning for the missing map) also hugely welcome. Edith and Martin shivered through the short night, made even more miserable by thin doses of sleep, hiding under their blankets when they thought someone was going to come and make them admire the sunrise. They awoke in the grey dawn with the certain knowledge that mountains are best viewed *en profile*, from the base – and 'a beautiful view is not a mere matter of miles seen from a great height'. Which certainly makes a pleasant change from the needy posturings of male writers, spaying their way up the mountains of the world, conquering things. The best writers about nature, I decide, as I sip hot tea and peer through the panoramic windows at an impenetrable wall of cloud, are not 'nature writers' at all. Somerville and Ross are the proof.

The descent of Snowdon is a lot easier than the climb. I even find myself giving directions to a bunch of middle-aged men ('just follow the stream bed, you can't go wrong'), reassuring a nervous couple who are worried about the cliffs ('it's a lot easier if you sing!') and, close to the foot of the mountain, joshing with a group of British Asian lads ('Nearly there! One last heave!').

Edith and Martin are grumbling about the litter, 'the soda-water bottle, the sandwich-paper, and the orange-peel', but there is no sign of my map. The smells are more familiar lower down the mountain – there's a dusty whiff of heather in the air – and I am walking slower, wondering why I feel an ache of loss for people I have never met. Edith and Martin (and Griffith Roberts) kept me company every inch of the way, scrambling over the jagged scree and the icy bogs. Their laughter on the slopes was vivid and real. But of course, I do realize, they're not actually here.

All of a sudden the sun is shining, not just here on the lower stretches but also, glancing up, on the peaks of Snowdonia. And there are groups of people heading up in the late afternoon, talking and laughing. Couples. Schoolfriends. Walking parties. Bands of brothers. I was a fool to have wanted to be alone on the mountainside. Thank you, thank you, 'Nick from the Wirral'. None of us should be on our own. Love and friendship are all that matter. I don't know why I feel so shaken (is there such a thing as reverse altitude sickness?), but perhaps it is not healthy to brood too long on the dead, although Edith, and most of her family, would have disagreed. In the 1920s, when armed men were at large in the country, Edith was convinced that the spirits of her dead family, Martin among them, but with Uncle Kendal the most active, had woven a web of protection around her and her home. They laid snares for intruders and whispered messages of horror and dread.

It was Edith's mother Adelaide, and her brothers Kendal and Jocelyn, who had introduced the family to spiritualism. They were enthusiasts from the 1850s. Kendal once levitated his brother, who whipped out a pencil and signed his name on the ceiling, and they all consulted the dead, watched tables float in the air and channelled reams of automatic writing from their ancestors. At first Edith and Martin viewed these antics with detached amusement, but the possibilities of spiritualism seem in the end to have taken a grip on them all, especially once the more aloof Martin had left the scene, or at least had departed this earthly dimension. Edith became a convert, just as the movement grew in popularity with the grieving families and survivors of the First World War.

On 21 December 1915 Edith watched Violet Martin die in the Glen Vera hospital in Cork, having sketched her asleep only three days earlier. She wrote to her brother that her life was in ruins. Six months later, still ravaged by grief ('the deadly details that go to the making of each futureless, featureless day'), she went to dine with a local medium called Jem Barlow and after dinner found herself watching in astonishment as Jem wrote out, in automatic writing, this message from Martin: 'You and I have not finished our work. Dear, we shall. Be comforted. V.M.' From that day onwards Edith was in almost daily contact with Martin (apart from when she went on speaking or horse-dealing tours to the US – apparently Martin had to stay closer to home), and after a while she found that a spirit medium was no longer necessary: she could communicate directly with Martin herself.

There are sixteen books written by 'Somerville and Ross' before Martin's death in 1915; and a further sixteen produced by them afterwards. Of course, Edith was a brilliant writer, much greater than she allowed herself to believe: she always used to defer to what she felt were Martin's superior talents. There were no more R.M. stories, or another *The Real Charlotte*, but the books by post-mortem 'Somerville and Ross' are still powerful, funny, ebullient, sharp – and almost as tightly written. It doesn't really matter if you believe in any of this, or in Edith's version of how it happened, although I do not see why we should be so quick to recoil from the possibility. Of course it can be explained away. And maybe all that really matters is that it was enough for Edith to know – and to be quite open about knowing – that six months after Martin died she was able to talk to her again and resume their writing partnership. And not only that. It was their companionship and friendship, their daily communion, their love – their *laughter* – that had survived the absurd severance of death.

J. B. Priestley & Beryl Bainbridge,
Birmingham to Liverpool, 1933 and 1983

SEVEN

'The Secret Dream'

'And who shall restore to them the years that the
locust hath eaten?'

J. B. PRIESTLEY, *ENGLISH JOURNEY*

I am driving through the outer reaches of Birmingham, on the
trail of J. B. Priestley, who travelled this way in the autumn of
1933, and recorded what 'one man saw and heard and felt and
thought' in a rumbustious book called *English Journey*. But at the
same time I am also hot on the heels of Beryl Bainbridge, who
herself had followed Priestley in the summer of 1983, making a
series of six television programmes about her experiences, while
writing her own (shorter, but just as opinionated) book, also called
English Journey. It feels like I've wandered into a Cold War novel,
following the spies, following the spies. Or, maybe, given Priestley's
preoccupation with Time – and his theory, loosely garnered from
J. W. Dunne's *An Experiment with Time* (and no doubt imperfectly
understood by me) that all time is concurrent and interwoven
and that we can never truly understand someone's life until it
has been lived in its entirety, because our younger selves feed into
our older selves and also (mysteriously) vice versa – perhaps all of
this is happening to all three of us at the very same moment, in
an endless loop of reportage. Am I, right now, jostling for road
space with the ghostly vehicles of Beryl B and Jackie P? And what
about Birmingham itself? The city of eternal, restless reconstruc-
tion. How do we know that this place even *is* Birmingham? Or

rather, is *still* Birmingham? Other than the plethora of 'Welcome
to Birmingham' signs of course. This is a slippery city, shifting,
unfixed, no matter how often you visit (the more often you visit),
and it has never once managed to put an end to an obsessive
fidgeting with its own buildings, public spaces and concrete vistas.

Priestley came in by coach from Coventry. He was thirty-eight
years old and already a world-famous author, launched into literary celebrity by the immense success of his fourth novel, *The
Good Companions* (1929). Even in 1933, he considered himself
middle-aged and in public he affected a bluff, grumbling, pipe-
smoking demeanour, although he'd go on to live to the ripe (and
grumbling) old age of eighty-nine. 'I have always been a grumbler',
he wrote in the Preface to his book *Delight*, 'for I have a sagging
face, a weighty underlip, what I am told is "a saurian eye", and a
rumbling but resonant voice from which it is difficult to escape.' He
said it was his Bradford upbringing. 'To a good West Riding type
there is something shameful about praise, that soft Southern trick.
But fault-finding and blame are constant and hearty.' He liked to
tease, did Jack. At a time of international economic meltdown, he
was now living with his second wife, Jane, and five children, in a
large family home in Highgate, London, as well as a seventeenth-
century manor house in the lush and easy lowlands of the Isle
of Wight. The golden proceeds from *The Good Companions* really
had been good to him, but Jack was restless and anxious to shake
off the too-cosy cobwebs and go and see what was happening to
his beloved land. Especially the Midlands and the North. He was
suspicious of places that didn't make anything proper.

Grumbling away – about the lying manufacturers who'd over-
sold his razor (when he was so looking forward to his morning
shave), and the huge new gaudy pubs on the Coventry road, and
the extreme discomfort of the overcrowded coach – he looked
up and found himself staring at the passing houses and shops

and factories of outer Birmingham. 'Did all this look like the entrance into the second city in England? It did. It looked like a dirty muddle.' Beryl was just as dismissive. But in fact, as I come racing over the flyways looking for an exit, with the lorries howling from either side, and the damp concrete crash barriers framing a whirling flash-past of shiny new towers, vast hoardings and broken-backed warehouses, I find myself thinking: well, this isn't so bad. It may be because I know Birmingham (that is, I know it well enough to get off these roads as fast as possible), but it is also true that there is no longer anything uniquely distressing about what you'll see here. Where once Birmingham was a byword for urban dysfunction, with Spaghetti Junction and the Bullring its crowning glories, the hectic descent into its city centre doesn't even seem especially out of the ordinary. It could be the effects of shifting baseline syndrome (this is the city that J. R. R. Tolkien reimagined as Mordor in *The Lord of the Rings*, grinding up the surrounding orchards and fields and his own childhood hobbity home). Or maybe some of the improvements are finally starting to pay off. The fact is, there is nothing *unusually* ugly about any of this.

Jack was staying in the Midland Hotel and a young, unemployed man carried his bags there from the coach station. As usual, Jack had managed to coax the man's life story out of him (when in the mood, which was often – Jolly Jack! – he was interested in everyone and everything, and he oozed empathy). The young man was twenty-two and had been out of work since he was sixteen, his mother was dead, and his father was also jobless. And at the hotel, Jack tells us, the porter spoke to this victim of an unwelcoming world 'in a fashion that most of us would hesitate to adopt in talking to a mongrel'.

Beryl, after a grim night in an unnamed, squalid hotel, where she ate an evening meal of pie and chips on a tray in the front lobby, had been checked into the Holiday Inn by her TV crew.

And I am staying at the Holiday Inn *Express*, which is infinitely slicker and cleaner and altogether more airless than anything Jack and Beryl could have booked or ever indeed desired. Where would they even have smoked? Jack had his favourite pipes (hundreds of them), and his noxious tobacco, the occasional cigar, the soft packs of filterless tabs. Beryl announced that she should have been sponsored by Silk Cut given the amount of chain-smoking airtime she had given them in the making of the TV series. (And it's true – just watch – it's another world of cigarettes in pubs, cafés, restaurants, town halls, trains, shops, homes and hospitals; and rasping interviews as the smoke billows and blooms.) Neither of them could work or live without tobacco. In fact, it is then, as I ponder their unabashed addictions, and stare out through the soundproofed windows on the fifteenth floor of the Holiday Inn (Express) at a silent grey cityscape of cranes and car parks, canals and wet alleys, that I succumb to an unanswerable urge to hurry out and buy my own first pack of cigarettes for twenty-seven years. To be clear, I blame Jack and Beryl for this bittersweet relapse – not Birmingham.

Down in Birmingham city centre, Jack is of the firm opinion (all his opinions are firm) that 'so long as you keep within a very narrow limit in the centre, Colmore Row, New Street, Corporation Street, Birmingham has quite a metropolitan air … here in Colmore Row you could imagine yourself in the second city of England'. On this particular day I am going to have to narrow down his definition even further, because the view he raves about – from Victoria Square, with Hill Street 'mistily falling away beneath the bridge that the Post Office has thrown high across the road' – is currently blocked by yet more huge hoardings, with an exquisitely rendered architectural drawing of a forthcoming paradise on the other side. I sit (and smoke) on a low wall in the centre of the square, with my back to a lush outpouring of ornamental grasses and yuccas, and admire the sturdy civic confidence of the Town Hall and the city's Museum & Art Gallery. Jack spent a long time in the gallery, hiding from the disappointing streets, admiring the early English way with watercolours. He felt that these painters must have been 'the happiest set of men who ever lived in this country', wandering our lovely land in the years before it was dug up and defiled. What a baggage of lost Arcadias we all carry with us.

Next to me there is a young man trying to secure tickets to see Pakistan at the Cricket World Cup. He alternately shouts into his phone or flails at its screen. 'All gone! All gone!' he wails, 'Bangladesh … Old Trafford … Afghanistan … Edgbaston … Australia, gone, India, gone … Platinum tickets … no … over £200 … no … all gone …' His unhappiness fills the square and bounces off the hoardings with their neurotically optimistic fantasies. The future city of Birmingham, as it is drawn, will apparently be peopled (but sparsely) with elegantly suited thirty-year-olds, most of them white, with purposeful jaws and powerful strides. And here and now, in today's city, it is a Friday, near the end of the working day, and the square is filling up with hurrying people, most of them in small, happy, voluble groups. A young woman with an artificial leg bounds past on crutches, gasping with laughter at her two friends. Unlike the people in the posters, we are all smoking.

When Beryl was here in 1983 it is likely that Birmingham was at its worst. At least, that is the hope. She hated 'the terrible streets' of the centre, but was even more dismayed by her terrifying car ride round the flyways and into the surrounding estates. She was born in 1932, the year before J. B.'s journey, although she claimed, from a surprisingly young age, that she had been born in 1934, and exaggerated how young she was when she hit the major landmarks of youth: leaving school, first job, moving to London. I don't know why she bothered – God knows she was young enough – but by her own admission she always was a compulsive 'auto-fictionaliser', although, as her biographer Brendan King puts it, everything she ever said or wrote about herself was at some level 'existentially true'.

Like Jack, Beryl was already a successful writer by the time she made her English journey. She had written a dozen acclaimed novels and been shortlisted for the Booker Prize twice, but there was still a sense (we can see this now, but even then it was somehow *known*) that her career had yet to take off. After the trip there was a sharp change in Beryl's profile (the TV exposure certainly helped), and there would be many more books, including several increasingly ambitious and high-selling novels, collections of short stories and non-fiction, and a further *three* Booker nominations – but never the prize itself.

Beryl was chosen to follow Jack the Yorkshireman around England, I suspect, because she was 'a bit of a character', with her ciggies and booze and forthright views, but also because she was northern, or at least northern enough for a befuddled southern BBC commissioning editor. She had been born in Liverpool, and grown up just outside, and had her first job at the Playhouse, where she soaked up J. B.'s works, and had lived in the city for a few years with her young family. She had trained herself out of her Liverpudlian accent at some point (Jack rumbled pure Yorkshire all his life), and had lived in London, on and off, from her twenties, and in fact Beryl seems to have regarded her native city with a mix of claustrophobia and regret, but she was still slotted into the box that read 'working-class northerner (female)'.

Initial reaction to Beryl's TV programmes, at least in the letters pages of the *Radio Times*, was hostile. R. E. Lamb from Southwold spluttered: 'Whatever induced the BBC to choose Beryl Bainbridge to make the series *English Journey* (Mondays BBC2)? [She] shows neither the verbal technique of an interviewer nor any descriptive ability ... Even to link her name with that of J. B. Priestley is an insult ...' Meanwhile, (Mrs) Rose Woodford from Exeter wrote that 'having looked forward to watching *English Journey* I am writing to say how very disappointed my family and I were. The narrator lacked both personality and enthusiasm, and indeed, seemed bored with the whole thing. We shall certainly watch no further instalments ...' And Hugh Homan (from Sudbury, Suffolk) was furious that 'smoker' Beryl should have castigated 'a hideously littered shopping precinct' only to stub out her cigarette on the front drive leading to 'the factory that manufactures the cigarettes she so much appreciates'.

Two weeks later, the letters editor of the *Radio Times* fielded a gentle backlash. Beryl was 'a perfect guide, enthusiastic and angry as appropriate' (V. G. W. Welland, Clevedon, Avon); she is 'a lovely human being, cigarette butts and bloody hells notwithstanding' (R. Wardrop, Lytchett Matravers, Dorset); and, according to Frederick Warren from Twickenham, 'the economic depression in the thirties engendered unemployment, poverty and general demoralization in many urban and industrial areas, and the fact that those features have recurred in the eighties is a tragedy, properly highlighted by Beryl Bainbridge'.

In Beryl and Jack's day, controversies played out slowly in the letters pages of fortnightly or monthly magazines, or stretched over several days in the newspapers. I wonder how either of them would have coped in the age of the below-the-line comment. Both of them had to endure vicious reviews. Beryl's plays were rejected. Jack had a 'stinking' review of his biography of Thomas Love Peacock in *The Times*. His friend Horace Walpole wrote to tell him not to worry because the reviewer had always been prejudiced against everything Jack had ever written. But over the years he had his novels praised and savaged, his plays sent back, he stared glumly at empty seats in the theatre, danced on stage to joyous shouts of 'Author! Author!' and lamented early closures. Most of all, he was patronized by a literary class that he had once yearned to join, and then learned to loathe. Virginia Woolf sneered that he and Arnold Bennett were 'tradesmen of letters'. God, the snobbery. They hated his vast success, of course, and immense output. Both he and Beryl were prolific – and that is always suspect to some. And for years Jack struggled to swallow the contempt he felt for these same people (editors, agents, officers, interchangeable Oxbridge dolts) who had led all of his friends (and nearly Jack himself) to bloody slaughter in the First World War. Even though, let it be noted, Jack also loved a good literary cocktail party, and the chance to leave early with someone else's wife. Anyway, to sum up (because we need to get back to the streets of Birmingham and will return later to the wives, husbands, lovers and wars): I am sure Jack and Beryl would have coped just fine in our age of online vitriol and under-exercised inadequates #justsayin.

Beryl is not happy.

> Everywhere we walked buildings were either going up or coming down, or else the roads were being widened to take yet more motor-cars. An endless process of construction and destruction. It seemed there was neither time nor room for pedestrians. We were literally a dying breed.

And Jack has leaped on a tram and headed for the outskirts. Jack be nimble! He was a short man, and broad of beam, but startlingly quick on his feet.

> I only know that during the half-hour or so I sat staring through the top windows of that tram, I saw nothing, not one single tiny thing, that could possibly raise a man's

spirits. Possibly what I was seeing was not Birmingham
but our urban and industrial civilization.

Like I say, perhaps Beryl was seeing Birmingham at its lowest ebb.
And Jack (who fought depression all his life, ever since he emerged
scarred, gassed and deafened from the trenches of the First World
War) had a tendency to despair. Some people have suggested it's
why he wrote so much, and kept so busy, and yet for most of his
writing life he only ever skirted around what happened to him in
the war. He wrote, said his friend John Braine, to forget.

I think that sounds a little too pat. But what we can say (and
I guess will always be able to say) is that Birmingham is still being
knocked around and put back together. It is thirty-five years since
Beryl was here, and if anything the scale of construction is even
more frenetic. At least the cars and trucks have been shuffled a few
roads out from the very centre of the city, but you can still hear
them from Victoria Square, revving and clattering up and down
Queensway. There are car parks, too, at every turn, multi-level
underground vaults and great stacked concrete cubes reaching
to the sky. Temporary parking lots fill the spaces where buildings
recently stood.

Jack was here in a year when car ownership was spreading
fast, despite the miserable economy. There were two-and-a-half
million motor vehicles on the UK roads by 1934 (up from 300,000
in 1920), including Jolly Jack's capacious Daimler, which he had
been using to get around England, along with various coaches
and trains. It was expertly driven by his new chauffeur, who had
been taken on when Jack had shown himself incapable of getting
behind a wheel without provoking a rolling tide of destruction.

Charles Montgomery has written in *Happy City* about how the
motor car was forced into the pedestrian- and horse-friendly cities
of the US. Over 200,000 people were killed in motor accidents in

the 1920s, as people were moved off their streets or mown down. The same thing happened here, although some of our cities proved harder to repurpose. Narrow medieval or Georgian streets cannot be so easily transformed into superhighways. Sometimes plans were delayed long enough for the public mood to turn against the new model of a cascading hierarchy of motorways and roads carving into the heart of the cities. Sadly, that was not true of Birmingham, especially because much of the centre had already been blitzed in the Second World War. In fact, it seems likely that the leaders of Birmingham, and other Midlands cities, and many cities of the North, positively welcomed the arrival of the American vision of the shiny new city of the future, with its free-flowing roads and central business districts and dormitory suburbs. It must have been tempting to set themselves against the smaller, fussier cities of the South. And anyway, as Jack wrote, 'the number of important inventions, from the steam engine to gas lighting and electroplating, that either first saw the light or were first brought to perfection in this city, is very impressive.' Birmingham had always led the way … so bring on the Bullring and the flyovers. But it also occurs to me, as my random wanderings bring me up against yet another queue of idling cars stuck in a reverberating canyon, or inching their way up a clogged slipway, that it could just as easily have been some vindictive Whitehall bureaucrat who was responsible for pressing 'Go' on the whole sorry mess.

The annual Conservative Party Conference is about to start, so as well as hoardings and building sites there are also armed police and new temporary barriers and single-file walkways blocking the views. I follow Beryl along Paradise Way: 'what must it be like in winter when the rain sweeps down and the wind blows the refuse through the concrete tunnels?' People (Jack and Beryl, for starters) have always taken pleasure in kicking Birmingham, but I read what Beryl wrote thirty-five years ago and I think it's likely that the place may actually be getting better – in spite of the interminable improvements. Beryl nearly got into a fight in the graveyard of St Philip's Cathedral with the Clerk of Works and his architect, who were desecrating the tombs with their latest scheme, but she decided she couldn't have an argument on television. So she took it out on them in print. 'We all know', she wrote, 'that architects and planners spend their lives contriving and plotting to eat up the land with their rotten office blocks. And what on earth did they mean by development?' It is hard not to grumble in Birmingham (no wonder Jack was so energized), but if you feel yourself giving in to a weary unhappiness with everything modern, head for the revamped canal, but most especially make haste to the glittering new library, its interlocking outer discs now glowing with soft radiance in the low golden sun on this heavenly Friday evening.

I decide I need a drink. There's a bar in the cellars of the Midland, where Jack stayed, although the hotel has since been rebranded with a pompous new name. Jack would have recognized this as an example of 'Admass', his description of the relentless corporatization of everything, the American-led over-production of pointless goods and the irresistible marketing of glossy, empty lifestyles. Well, he blamed the Americans (as did Enid, you may remember). It is much harder now, almost ninety years later, to remember what differences really exist between them and us. Our different world vision – and people really did feel there was one – was swallowed long ago.

I find a seat in a booth. People are crowding in with happy shouts, spreading out into the low-vaulted rooms. Jack loved a hot fuggy pub. Not being able to find one was something that depressed him about Birmingham. At night in 1933 the city centre was empty, although it blazed with light, and even once he found them, he said, the people were extraordinarily ugly: 'nearly all looked as if life had knocked them into odd shapes, taken the bloom out of their faces, twisted their features and dulled their eyes'.

He was quick to add that nobody had ever called *him* handsome, but many women would have disagreed. He could talk you into bed, said one, with his insistent low rumble. Jack was scornful of his literary contemporaries who got into an angst-ridden tangle about sex. He was, he felt, uncomplicatedly available … and that was something, he also felt, that his first two wives, Pat Tempest and Jane Wyndham-Lewis, had to learn to live with. Or maybe feign ignorance. Jack was mulish on this point. I don't think – in mild mitigation – that he was an especially jealous man, and perhaps he would have been happy for his wives to carry on affairs just as he did. But his first wife, Pat, died of cancer in 1925, just a year after giving birth to their second child – and presumably aware that for the past year Jack had been sleeping with Jane, who was already pregnant with Jack's third child (and Jane's, for that matter, from her own first marriage). Confused? Jack and Jane were married soon afterwards and remained so for twenty-seven years, despite Jack's affairs, having two more children together, until he met the famous archaeologist and writer Jacquetta Hawkes and married her in 1953. And then, possibly, he came to heel.

So, quite apart from all the novels and plays, Jack kept himself busy. Not long before this trip he had fallen hard for the twenty-four-year-old actress Peggy Ashcroft, trailing her moonily from theatre dressing room to restaurant, pleading with her to leave her husband, Rupert Hart-Davis (they'd only been married for a few months), telling his wife Jane to get ready for a divorce. Before things went any further, Ashcroft told him she was leaving her husband, but was in fact going to marry Theodore Komisarjevsky, a visionary theatre director. Jack rolled back to Jane and other, less incendiary affairs. One inspiration for Jack's *English Journey* may have been an attempt to forget all about Peggy Ashcroft.

The city had changed by 1983, and however much Beryl was disgusted by Birmingham's appearance, she was amazed and entranced by its happy crowds of drinkers. 'We had lunch in a noisy pub beneath an Insurance block. Plastic grapes hung from the ceiling and there were hundreds of people, sweating and laughing and knocking back the beer as though they were on holiday in some Mediterranean resort. Everyone merry as crickets, and hungry.'

My bar doesn't have any plastic grapes, but it does have an eye-catching collection of Roman murals, naked satyrs and gilded cupids on the ceiling. The tempo of drinking is picking up (mine included) and a Friday night spirit of fiesta is gusting through the low rooms. In the absence of anything more substantial than a small packet of nuts, I am earnestly chewing over this idea of shifting baseline syndrome and wondering how we can ever know for sure if things are better or worse than they were before. Take Birmingham, for example. Not many people alive today can remember Tolkien's leafy lanes and mill wheels splashing in the river under the old elm trees. We're just happy that the Bullring is slightly less of a shit-heap than it once was. But millions of people also yearn for Tolkien's fantasy life in the bucolic villages of the Shires. The orchards and the water meadows. The carthorses lumbering to market. They must do! That's what the books and films are all about: holding back the destroyers of forests, saving the hobbits' village, defeating the horrors of Mordor/Birmingham. Although I do have to ask: if that's what we really want, then what the hell do we think we are up to in Birmingham? And how come we can be nostalgic for something we've never known, and much of which never even existed?

By the end of the third drink I have convinced myself that Enid Blyton, with her cobblestoned villages and heathery hills, and her profound distrust of strangers, may have had more influence on the thinking of the British than any other twentieth-century politician, writer *or* philosopher.

A hot and hearty crush of people has pressed into the booth and swept me up into their fast-flowing rounds. I am at the bar, talking to a short eager man with a large and immaculately bald brown head. He asks me what I'm doing in Birmingham and I say I'm researching a book. 'Oh', he says, 'I've always thought I should write one. I've had such an interesting life.' This is not the first time I've heard that. But anyway, what? I don't know, because I'm outside, smoking, and a woman yells down the street, 'What's happening in the Shakespeare?' and someone else shouts, 'Later'. I am surprised to see how early it is.

I am back in my booth. Apparently the beer is fine, but we also need something stronger. Spirits! 'The great thing about Birmingham', I am being told, by a slobbery man whose thick earthy thigh has me kettled in the corner, 'the great thing about Birmingham is the people.' 'Do you like the new library?' I find myself asking, God knows why. 'The *what*?!' he roars. 'The library.' He heaves his face towards me, glistening nose just an inch from mine. 'The library? *I fucking love it.*'

More cigarettes in the loud Birmingham night. Beryl would understand. She liked a drink, maybe not so much when she was younger, but later she'd drink before going out and would collapse under the table at dinner, or fall out with her friends, or stop and sleep in the street on the way home. It was because she was so slight, people said, that the alcohol just took her away. You can see her singing in the pub in the Newcastle section of *English Journey*, belting out the old tunes, fag in hand. She looks like she was a lot of fun. People fed her drinks because that's what they thought she wanted, or just to hear her talk. But, really, that kind of determined pull towards oblivion is troubling to watch and – for those who love us – almost impossible to stop.

It wasn't the same for Jolly Jack. He exuded bonhomie, of course, and propped up the bar, pint and pipe at the ready, holding forth, looking ever more Falstaffian as the years passed. There was only one period in his life when he lost himself in drink, just after he'd been wounded in the trenches for the second time, and all his mates were being killed, and he must have thought there wasn't much point in doing anything else; but then he decided, reluctantly, to take the officer training that was being urged on him, and he went back to the trenches, and was gassed, and at last the war ended, and he never went back to live in Bradford but took one of those degrees at Cambridge that were being offered to ex-servicemen, and after that he got married, and worked ferociously to get clear of the poverty, and mostly drank moderately (but I guess with dedication) because as he said, it didn't take much to make him 'a little muzzy' and then slide into 'a spirit of mischievous lust'.

Back in the bar I am startled to hear myself attempting to explain 'sifting basheline shindrome' to a man who seems absolutely thrilled to hear all about it. He then asks me what kind of music I like. The bar (or is it even the same bar?) is thrumming with life and urgent conversation. I am surprised to see how late it is. Double whiskies are the way to keep an evening going, when there are so many beautiful and fascinating people here (how times have changed since 1933, Jack) of so many different ages, shapes and colours, and no one seems remotely interested in going home – and certainly not me, because where would I even *smoke* in the Holiday Inn Express, now that I am re-addicted for ever. It's just perfect here, surfing the tidal roar. Cities are the thing! We're human. We need noise. Movement. Laughter. Screw the Hobbit. I bloody love Brum.

I am standing on the fifteenth floor of the Holiday Inn (Express) staring out at a grey Birmingham morning. I can hear a low male voice rumbling in the corridor and for one ghastly moment I think it is Kingsley Amis, come to administer his patented hangover cure. I might even welcome the distraction. At some point in the night an intruder has blowtorched my tongue and air-dried my eyeballs, before trowelling the inside of my head with wet Brummie cement.

If I can only manage to leave this room, my plan is to head to Bournville, on the outskirts of Birmingham. It is the home of Cadbury World, the vast and glutinous chocolate-themed shop and visitor attraction, as well as the site of the headquarters of the Cadbury (now Mondelez) global chocolate research centre (yum!). The Cadbury factory is also here, which cannot fail to raise a vision of chocolate waterfalls tumbling into Tuscan-brown lakes of caramel and velvet, lapping at the foothills of sugar-dusted, marshmallow mountains under a honeycomb sun. I do know, of course, that reality is going to trample all over this childhood dream, but I have to follow Jack and Beryl.

Bournville is also the village created by the philanthropic Quaker George Cadbury in 1900. He and his brother Richard inherited the chocolate business from their father and in 1879 moved the factory from the centre of industrial Birmingham into what was then farmland, although there was already a railway and a canal. When Richard died in 1895, George dedicated the rest of his life to doing something about his belief that 'the root of most social evils lay in the bad housing conditions in which all too many had to live'. He bought 330 acres of land near the factory and by 1900 had built 300 houses, not just for the local Cadbury workers but for many others on low incomes. Rents were set appropriately. Infant mortality and adult death rates plummeted.

Jack continues the George Cadbury story with a quote from one of the local Bournville publications of the 1930s:

He then handed over the whole property to a body of
Trustees – the Bournville Village Trust – on behalf of
the nation. He thus gave up entirely his financial interest
in it, and secured that all profits ... should never accrue
to any private individual or body, but be devoted to
the development of the Bournville Estate, and to the
promotion of housing reform elsewhere.

He further stipulated that no house could occupy more than a
quarter of its own site, and that one-tenth of the land (quite apart
from private gardens) should be reserved for parks and sports
grounds. Since then, the Bournville Village Trust has boomed
and spread, with many more low-cost houses, and not just here
but in Greater Birmingham and beyond. Their mission remains
the same (at least, so far as I can tell: their published Corporate
Aims gabble about 'customer-focused services' and 'a Digital First
approach', but I reckon we know what they mean; they are also,
for the record, committed to 'Business growth').

Can you imagine any modern-day company owners doing what
George Cadbury once did? You could say there's Bill Gates and
his extraordinary work in global health. But in 1933, as Jack put
it, the Cadburys 'genuinely prefer spending a good part of their
money on their factory and its employees instead of on racing
stables and yachts and Monte Carlo'. He is talking not only about
the Bournville Village Trust, which as I said was never just for the
Cadbury employees, but also the dozens of clubs and schemes
that the Cadburys set up for their workers, including sports halls,
theatres, lectures, conferences, club rooms with billiards tables,
drama, music, games – everything, in short, except a place to get
a drink (and thank God, I find myself thinking, for the teetotal
Quakers). He was told when he visited that there were about
7,000 employees and ex-employees signed up to the various

clubs. Model yachting was especially popular in those distant days, so the Cadburys had provided a small lake. In their turn, the workers clubbed together in 1937 and donated a statue to their employers to commemorate the opening of their lido. God bless them, one and all.

By the time Beryl got here in 1983, things were rather different. She found just five women working on the automated production line (Jack had witnessed many hundreds) and when she went for lunch in the canteen she met a small bunch of grumbling old men looking forward to cashing in their pensions and tending their gardens. The lido and the clubs were closed and the employees were being asked to pay for membership of their own sports halls. But that was far from the end of it. In 2010 Cadbury was bought by Kraft, the US convenience food mega-corporation, in a hostile takeover, accompanied by much hand-wringing in the UK media, who were mostly upset about the trashy inedibility of Hershey bars. The company once known as Cadbury became Mondelez (not on its products, but for the purpose of corporate growth in the lucrative new world markets), and in 2014 its American CEO pocketed $21 million for a job well done. In 2016 the *Independent* ran this headline: 'How one of Britain's best-loved brands went from a force for social good to the worst example of brutal corporate capitalism.' And to round it off, in 2017 Mondelez paid no corporation tax in Britain, despite profits of £185 million. And what do George Cadbury and his one-time workers make of all that, I wonder, as they paddle their yachts in their celestial pools? I bet they're not eating Oreos.

Beryl and Jack were both led around the factory, checking on the workers, but I'm on the 'self-guided' tour of Cadbury World, accompanied by coachloads of sugar-fuelled schoolchildren. We are all handed a couple of bars of chocolate when we buy our tickets. Over in the factory itself I have read that the latest machine is churning out one million bars of Dairy Milk every day, with just four employees to keep an eye on things. There is no sign of even the smallest chocolate waterfall. The tour takes us past lush Latin American dioramas, where a waxwork Mayan, who looks a lot like Cher, is fondling a large wrinkled cocoa pod. Stout Cortés is there too, picking disconsolately at his helmet while a young Aztec woman offers him flowers, or perhaps a mug of hot chocolate. Anyway, that's the theme – the human lust for chocolate – and we find ourselves in Victorian Birmingham, staring at the first Cadbury shop, and then the disembodied head of George appears, talking with a soft but nonetheless grating voice about how superior his chocolate was (and is) to any other version, and a Cadbury employee hands us more bars (a Flake and a Caramel, hurrah), and we sit through a film about the production process where the bench seating shakes us around like so many cocoa nibs and I realize too late, with the chocolate swilling and slopping on an empty stomach, and the schoolchildren erupting all around me like a row of uncorked sherbet fountains, that this is no place to be dawdling with a hangover.

I do find a small chocolate fountain at the end of an echoing corridor. Round the next corner I am given more chocolate (a Boost and a Twirl) and I eat it absent-mindedly. Note for Kingsley: I may have found an alternative cure for hangovers. There are four Cadbury employees here, dressed in white lab coats, decorating eggs and smoothing out trays brimming with brown chocolate, and one of them kindly shows me the quickest way out, which takes me past rooms filled with the Cadbury marketing campaigns of old. Curly Wurlys! Creme Eggs! And here at the end is an animatronic gorilla thumping out the climactic drum solo from Phil Collins's 'In the Air Tonight', with a crowd of forty-somethings filming it on their phones. It was an advert, I am sure you remember, for something or other. I have a suspicion I've found the teachers, and if so they really should get upstairs fast to deal with the sugar-based catastrophe that is unfolding in another part of the building. The rooms are glowing Cadbury purple. Welcome, Jack, to the sticky and addictive heart of admass.

Outside in the autumnal sunshine of Bournville village, just a short stroll from the factory gates, I sit in front of a café, opposite the green, and watch adults gathering their children at the end of the school day. I know that much of the Bournville estate is set aside for people on low incomes, but everyone here seems very well-to-do: sleek, groomed, in no hurry at all. I presume that not much of the housing is occupied by Cadbury workers these days – there probably aren't enough of them to fill half a street. There is a stately, between-the-wars atmosphere, familiar from BBC Sunday night television. Red postbox. Wide pavements. Lines of mature lime trees, their leaves slumped in the gutters. Ducks on the green. Despite the 4x4s humped up on the kerb, I am surprised not to see the children running around in long grey shorts and school caps, stuffing conkers into their satchels. The half-timbered houses look solid and well loved: the irrefutable legacy of George Cadbury.

Jack was uneasy about the Cadbury and Bournville set-up. It was horribly paternalistic. 'No factory workers in Europe have ever been better off than these people', he wrote, but 'it is when one takes a longer view that doubts begin to creep in.' Isn't it disempowering? When Australian workers were offered the same deal – the clubs and subsidized housing and theatre halls – they said thanks, but we'd rather have the money. So Jack chewed it over, dragging in Hilaire Belloc (who thought that this 'servitude' would lead to the decay of genuine democracy), and fretting that the paternalistic employer was 'wrecking the proper scale of values'. The average worker would start to believe that 'he was made for his factory and not his factory for him'. Jack wanted workers to be free of bondage, running their own lives, 'forming associations far removed from the factory', using their leisure 'and demanding its increase, not as favoured employees but as citizens, free men and women'.

Yes!

And somewhere in Poland there are Cadbury workers, with no sports halls or theatres or boating lakes, and certainly no half-timbered village to call home, churning out bars and eggs at knock-down prices for the European market. Except that right now, with automation, it has again become cheaper, and more expedient – at least until the next currency fluctuation or political upheaval – to carry on making the Dairy Milk here in Bournville. But there is one thing we have all lost, since Jack wrote those words – and that is the idea that automation will set us free. Do you remember that? The belief that more leisure is to be welcomed, because it will be paid for. That everyone will benefit from the technologies that replace us. And the reason for our loss of faith, as Jack would be the first to point out, is that the new wealth created by all these labour-saving machines has not spread to the workers and ex-workers and people of Bournville and Birmingham. No. It has flowed up and away and over the hills to 'Monte Carlo'.

J. B. Priestley didn't really want to return to Bradford as part of his *English Journey*, but he did and he dragged Beryl and me in his wake. He was born here in September 1894 and left for good in September 1914, when he joined the army and was sent to France, aged just nineteen. For him there were two Bradfords, the city he was revisiting in 1933 and the other place that was frozen in the pre-war years of his childhood and youth: 'I have

changed, of course; but I think the place itself has changed even
more than I have.' He recaptures that earlier, pre-First World
War Bradford exquisitely in his 1946 novel, *Bright Day* – and not
just the fabric of the city, but also the atmosphere of a place
that is living through the last years of the good times, when the
wool trade on which all its wealth was based was still flourishing
(although the decay was setting in), and the theatres, restaurants
and music and concert halls were buzzing, and the large German-
Jewish community was still welcome. The Independent Labour
Party had been born in Bradford (or Bruddersford as he calls it
in the novel), and his not-so fictional uncle (based it seems to me
on Jack's teacher father),

> still lived in that early optimistic Labour atmosphere,
> before anybody had sold out and before the party
> machinery had grown too elaborate. In those days Merrie
> England, with more good cricket and W.W. Jacobs and
> Exchange Mixture and roast pork and bilberry-pie and
> June mornings in Wensleydale for everybody, still seemed
> just round the corner.

W. W. Jacobs was a writer of escapist short stories, and 'Exchange
Mixture' was Jack's favourite blend of pipe tobacco – and as for
the rest of it, we're not too far from Enid and her picnic blankets.
The whole country seemed to be yearning for those never-never
Edwardian days in 1933. And what is especially worrying is that,
almost ninety years later, it feels like it still is.

Clever Jack left school at sixteen. His father (with dreams of
university) was disappointed, but he found Jack a job as an appren-
tice in the wool trade, where Jack mucked about and bunked off
to walk across the moors (fancying he was Wordsworth) and wrote
all the time, submitting articles to the local paper and even, in

1913, getting one published by a London magazine, the *London Opinion*. Jack's mother had died when he was two and his father had remarried four years later (Jack liked his stepmother) and he grew up at No. 34 Mannheim Road, where now there's a fading blue plaque and a neat front garden and a small child peering from behind a thick curtain. It's a steep, trim little street of low, yellow houses and new dormer windows, with mature rowan trees on both sides (Beryl mentions them) and roses and suburban silence. A young British Asian woman walks past with four young children trailing behind her, the youngest boy dragging a cricket bat.

The family turns onto Bonn Road. There's also a Heidelberg Road round the corner – reminders of Bradford's German-Jewish days. I wonder at what point street names are chosen to reflect a local heritage – or even renamed, although no doubt that would cause difficulties. There has been plenty in the news about the unhappiness of Bradford, especially racial tensions, but also the terrible unemployment rates and degenerative poverty. Bradford is officially Britain's *youngest* city, with one-quarter of its residents under the age of sixteen, and although it now has its own university (unlike in Jack's day, when bright students had to travel to Leeds or beyond), there is inevitably huge pressure for jobs. What also troubles policymakers is the fact that the different communities of Bradford tend to live apart, grouping together in the same areas, many of them never meeting anyone from another background. Or so we hear. Of course, you could see this as a positive thing, with families and communities helping each other in difficult circumstances, but there's also deep anxiety that people of different faiths and cultures never speak to one another – and that, they say, was one of the causes of the 2001 riots.

Jack had predictably robust views on the matter of immigration. The language has changed since his times, of course. In 1983 Beryl was writing about 'Asians' and 'Indians' interchangeably, but not 'British Asians'. The demographics of Bradford have been in flux for three or more generations, and at the last (2011) census twenty percent of the population was of Asian heritage, predominantly Pakistani. In some parts of the city it is closer to ninety percent. Jack would have been amazed to have walked with me the two miles from the centre of Bradford to his old street, and seen hardly anyone whose family wasn't originally from south Asia, and all the mosques, and the shops glittering with gold and silks (Jack, by the way, *loved* to shop), and the spices in the air, and the occasional Polish deli, and the extraordinary number of cars with women in hijabs, and other cars (or the same cars) vibrating with music from every continent.

But this also makes it sound more exciting than it is, because I think what would have struck Jack even harder than the arrival of so many Asians in this stolid northern town are the rows of broken and boarded-up shops, especially in the old centre. It is a Sunday, mind you, but all along Kirkgate and Market Street and Bank Street and Hustlergate, and throughout the magnificent but battered Victorian centre where Jack used to linger in his lunch hours, escaping the office for an hour (or three), there is almost nothing but closed and bankrupted shops. Waterstones is still here (and a beautiful branch it is), but the streets are empty and littered and if you stand at the junctions of Bank and Tyrrel streets all you'll see are 'To Let' and 'For Sale' signs and closed charity shops. The council has been putting money in – the paving is fresh and patterned and young street trees flutter on the sides of the roads – but everyone out today looks hard-pressed and the last few shops look on the verge of collapse.

Jack said he'd like to end his days running a stall at Kirkgate Market, selling old books and gossiping with the tobacco and hat sellers. The old market was ripped out in the 1970s and replaced with a characterless concrete box, so I think he'd struggle to raise any enthusiasm for what he'd find there today. There's a new shopping centre in town, The Broadway near Cheapside, and it seems to be draining the last of the life out of the surrounding streets, and maybe also the old/new Kirkgate Market. There's only so much money to go round and this is where it has apparently pooled, among the familiar signage of Next, Carphone Warehouse and H&M.

I wander over to 'Little Germany', as the area behind the cathedral is marketed by an anxious tourist board. When he was young, Jack was star-struck by the community that lived and worked here – musical, cultured, alien – they made Bradford 'at once one of the most provincial and yet one of the most cosmopolitan of English provincial cities'. The houses here are majestic and just waiting for an influx of eager residents or entrepreneurs or anyone who's going to make this area hum again. Perhaps they're on their way. But as Jack says, the city lost something when the German-Jews disappeared in the war, changing their names or going out of business or leaving for good. What he wrote in 1933 is horribly, upliftingly familiar today:

> I liked the city better as it was before, and most of my fellow-Bradfordians agree with me. It seems smaller and duller now. I am not suggesting that these German-Jews were better men than we are. The point is that they were different, and brought more to the city than bank drafts and lists of customers. They acted as a leaven, just as a colony of typical West Riding folk would act as a leaven in Munich or Moscow. Just lately, when we offered hospitality to some distinguished German-Jews who had been exiled by the Nazis, the leader-writers in the cheap Press began yelping again about Keeping the Foreigner Out. Apart from the miserable meanness of

the attitude itself – for the great England, the England admired throughout the world, is the England that keeps open house, the England of Mazzini, Marx, Lenin – history shows us that the countries that have opened their doors have gained, just as the countries that have driven out large numbers of its citizens, for racial, religious or political reasons, have always paid dearly … Bradford is really more provincial now than it was twenty years ago. But so, I suspect, is the whole world. It must be, when there is less and less tolerance in it, less free speech, less liberalism. Behind all the new movements of this age, nationalistic, fascistic, communistic, has been more than a suspicion of the mental attitude of a gang of small town louts ready to throw a brick at the nearest stranger.

Jack (being Bradford to his bones) blamed Londoners for the death of his city. The creepiest character in *Bright Day* is a chancer called Nixey, who is sent by London head office to reorganize a wool firm's local 'Bruddersford' branch. Nixey doesn't know much about wool or textiles, and doesn't care about anything other than his own advancement. As Gregory, the-character-who-is-really-Jack, writes, 'I never met a man who had an expert knowledge of things or the making of things who hadn't a decent and honest core to his character; and I never met a man who thought first of money and profits and cared nothing about the things he dealt in who seemed to me a satisfactory human being.' It is the lament of a Bradford man, who has watched his city and the hard, solid, useful, profitable work it once did upturned by a system that values the extraction of profit over the creation of goods. Years later, Jack/Gregory meets Nixey again, and he's now Lord Harndean, a hollowed out, successful man, and 'there was nothing about him, I decided, that you could lay a finger on and declare to be wrong, yet what he offered you, in his dapper and pleasant fashion, never added up to anything satisfying and right. He was never quite there on the spot with you.'

And if I am loitering in the pages of *Bright Day*, it is because Jack could not be more accurate, or insightful, about what has happened to his beloved Bradford and so much else. At some point the Nixeys of this world won the argument – or simply sidestepped it – and we all decided, or passively accepted, that it didn't really matter what a business or organization made or did, or where it was based, they could all be run to the same formula. And nor did it really matter who was doing the work, so long as they could be slotted in or pulled out with the minimum of fuss. Jack, a self-proclaimed romantic, and an old textiles hand, thought that was a miserable, soul-sapping proposition. And time has proved him right.

Beryl and Jack agree that the best thing about Bradford ('a city entirely without charm', grumbles Jack, misleadingly) is the moor that surrounds the city. It's so easy to get out there. Just one bus ride and you're in the hills with Heathcliff and some of the finest walks and pubs in Britain. They both headed for Hubberholme, with its ancient church and inn, and this is where you'll now find Jack, slumbering in the churchyard, not too far from the nearest pint. But I want to stay in Bradford a while longer, wandering the windblown streets. I visit the National Science and Media Museum, which has had its main collection removed to London, and spend a happy hour in the basement, looking at old Kodak cameras and images of a vanished world. Jack's world! And Beryl's. And mine … that model of Polaroid camera now looking awk- wardly analogue in the display case was once my pride and joy.

It is such a relief, halfway down another empty street, to come across the Sparrow bar. Just as I'm passing, the door opens and a fug of music and beer floods out – and I follow its irresistible path straight inside. 'Well, I hope he likes the banjo,' the young fair-haired woman on stage drawls at me, and everyone in the little packed bar (about forty of them) rumbles their sardonic West Riding welcome. Jack and Beryl loved live music, especially the kind where you could join in – and I think one of them must have led me here, at this moment, because the young woman is brilliant, with a voice that wraps the room in honey and hope, and everyone is uninhibitedly hanging on her words, and urging her on, humming or singing or thumping out the rhythm. I am squeezed in, with my back to the bar, and I've somehow managed to separate a young British Asian couple (whom I have to say I'm very pleased to see, having read far too many po-faced articles about the deep and irreversible schisms of Bradford), but they don't seem to care – in fact no one seems to care about anything that's happening outside the dripping windows, because the music and the beer is flowing and all is right with the world. Jack liked to pound away at the piano at these moments, although what he loved most was chamber music, and there's not so much of that in Bradford these days.

I sit outside after the music has stopped and smoke a cigarette (yes, I know, but that's my last) and when I stub it out in an empty ashtray, a hugely apologetic young woman hurries across the street and wonders if I've now finished with the butt. It's shocking. There was terrible poverty here when Jack and then Beryl visited. Beryl was told by a local reporter that 'at least fifty percent of the Asian community are unemployed, but it's difficult to get exact figures because they all deny it and some of them don't like signing on'. And Jack was heartbroken when he discovered that some of his old comrades from the trenches did not feel able to attend the reunion battalion dinner because they were so ashamed of their lack of funds.

> They ought to have known that they would have been
> welcome in the sorriest rags ... They were with us, swing-
> ing along, while the women and old men cheered ...when
> the crowds threw flowers, blessed us, cried over us ...
> and then they stood in the mud and water ... saw the sky
> darken and the earth open with red-hot steel ... came
> back as official heroes and also as young-old workmen ...
> and now, in 1933, they could not even join us in a tavern
> because they had not decent coats to their back.

People said Jack never wrote about what happened to him in the war, but that is just not true. He raged about it. And he despised those who were nostalgic for war, or thought another one would bring us together or solve anything at all. It is never war that is right, he said, it is the peace we have made that is wrong. The sight of the absolute poverty blighting parts of Bradford today would have felled him.

I wander up to Hanover Square, which Beryl visited with her TV crew in 1983. Back then it was derelict, but saved from demolition and transformation into something anodyne or ugly by the fact that many British Asian families had chosen to live here and would not move. It is now a charming little three-sided close, with honey-coloured houses backed by an old mill tower, and a strip of grass in the centre, behind iron railings, over half of which the residents have chosen to park their gleaming cars. I am admiring the square, and taking photos, when a man suddenly erupts out of one of the houses (which is a centre of some kind) and starts shouting, 'Where are you from?' He yells it over and over: 'Where are you from?' I mumble something about J. B. Priestley and Beryl Bainbridge, and that I'm looking for the places where they once roamed. 'I don't think so,' he shouts. 'I don't think so. I know who you are really looking for. I know!'

He's British Asian, not a very tall man, about forty years old, lushly bearded and wearing traditional Pakistani dress. He's also furious and standing too close and I turn quickly to leave the square. I have watched too many films and TV shows loaded with negative imagery (haven't we all?) and I am already thinking about violence and knives. Even though, as I've said before, 'Where are you from?' is the most human question in the world. We love to know the answer to that one – about others and ourselves – but at the same time 'Where are you from?' can be freighted with rejection. You're not from around here. You're not one of us. Perhaps you don't even know? In the mouths of Jack's small town louts it carries menace and threat.

I still feel sad that I hurried away. It is always better to try and connect. Maybe this obsessive, instinctive categorization of each other will run its course, undone by love, sex, music and market forces, leaving only 'unknown' or even 'not important' – although the need to be part of a community (and the associated suspicion of outsiders) runs deep. Anyway, if we don't categorize people, how can we root out discrimination? And (I go on) how awful when people feel they have to deny or subsume their identity. Bring back the Flemish-Welsh and their psychic sheep shoulder-blades! We all have multiple identities, of course we do, and they wax and wane, and they are there to be enjoyed, or rejected, or slipped between, even though I think we are right sometimes to be suspicious of the helpfulness of hyphens. Really, I don't think we know what we want, but it is surely a matter of hope that there are so many people and groups in Bradford doing so much to try and bring people together. Festivals and twinned schools. Sport, art and commerce.

These pompous half-thoughts (and more) are rattling in my head as I scuttle out of the square, but when I look back I see that the short, angry man is already screaming at some other hapless fool, for parking his car badly, and it strikes me, but too late: OK, he's just another local busybody. You get them everywhere. And so much of this hand-wringing is unnecessary. It is easy to get on. Isn't it? We could at least start by not jumping to conclusions about whole groups, communities, even nations, based on the behaviour of one random individual.

On his way back from a day on the moors Jack was dropped off on Market Street by his friends, who couldn't understand what he wanted to do all alone in Bradford city centre on a Sunday night. He drifted from pub to pub, with a light but flattening drizzle in the air, and that is exactly what I do – except Jack had many more pubs to choose from and wherever he went there were subdued young men and women sipping at their Sunday beer. He even came across a crowd of pipe-smoking men watching a Salvation Army band blasting out their tunes on a street corner, and Jack decided that if ever he were to become religious, he would join the Salvation Army. Or maybe become a Catholic. Both of them had a passion for what they preached. All I find is a couple of almost empty pubs, in which it is hard to linger. But still, this means that I end up earlier than expected in a curry house up the hill, which is glowing and packed and extraordinarily welcoming. Jack had a 'pitiful evening', he decided, 'a miserable, barbaric affair', and Beryl clearly couldn't wait to get out, but I've finished my time in Bradford in the right place, surrounded by a crowd of happy, well-fed, uncategorizable people, united in their enthusiasm for good cheap food. Although, with my soft southern palate, I can't help finding the meal teasingly over-spiced.

There is sunshine on the hills when I leave Bradford the next day. I am driving to Liverpool, the city that in 1983 Beryl still called 'home', even though she had left it for London in 1952, returned to get married and start a family, and then finished with it for good in 1963. She said that she went back at least six times a year, and would go to the barricades for the place if the call ever went out (which, in 1983, with Margaret Thatcher in full flow, she felt fairly sure it soon would).

As soon as Beryl had checked into the Adelphi Hotel (where Jack also stayed – he described it as 'hot from mingled shame and vexation' ever since the Atlantic passenger traffic was moved from Liverpool to Southampton), the first place Beryl visited was 22 Huskisson Street, the house in Toxteth that was her home for five years from June 1958. She lived there with Austin, her husband, and their two young children (the second, Jo Jo, was born soon after they moved into the house; the first, Aaron, had been born a year earlier). It doesn't sound like she was very happy there. Austin was preoccupied with establishing himself as an artist, and spent much of the time out working (and carrying on with other women); and then Austin decided to go to Paris to find himself and Beryl started an affair with a solicitor called Mick, who lived down the road; and in 1959 she turned on the gas cooker, lay down with her head near the oven, and waited to die: she was saved only by Austin coming home early with a few friends. Austin moved out in October that year, with Beryl filing for divorce almost immediately afterwards.

And yet, Beryl once wrote that 'nothing shall be as sweet as the Liverpool days', and some of those must have been during the time she lived in the house in Huskisson Street. It sits in the Liverpool 8 area, also known as Toxteth, and at the time it was a shabby, bohemian part of town, frequented by artists, actors and the down-at-heel. Beryl wrote here, and started painting, and in October 1959, just before Austin left, they held a party which was attended by members of the Liverpool Philharmonic and three of the Beatles, before there even was such a thing, and a drunk, sixteen-year-old George Harrison managed to offend the orchestra's principal flautist by demanding they find some Elvis records to play. Or so the legend goes ... and Liverpool does love its legends. When Beryl came back in 1983, accompanied by her TV crew, she found the house derelict and burnt, the balcony toppled into the street and one of her dining room chairs tossed into the rubble of the backyard (she had always meant to send for her possessions, she said, but had never had the money – and once she did, she no longer had the space). She got straight into a taxi and spent the rest of the day in her room at the Adelphi, mourning for everything that was lost.

The area around Huskisson Street is now known as the Georgian Quarter, on account of its beautiful Regency houses. Many of them are still flats, but just go to No. 22 today. There's no sign of any rubble or burnt balconies: it's a picture-perfect, creamy-white, large-pillared home with a rippling wave of black railings leading to a shiny green door and immaculate sash windows. It's more Jane Austen than Beryl Bainbridge – and anyway Beryl wouldn't have bothered with painting the outside and she kept a stuffed water buffalo in the hallway of her London home and her study/bedroom upstairs was a chaos of strange knick-knacks and unusual artefacts she could never throw away, because she liked to be able to touch tokens of her past, even if she was notoriously unreliable in her interpretation of it. If she's haunting No. 22 Huskisson Street, I think she'd soon be driven away by the stench of fresh paint and property developers.

A middle-aged man in a beanie hat shouts across the road, and I get ready to tell him that I don't have any cigarettes (Bradford is still hanging heavy), but all he wants to do is help. 'All right, mate, you lost?' He is eager – desperate – to make sure I know where I am going. Is that a Liverpool thing? I ask him the way to Hope Street, because I'm worried he might implode if I don't give him something, and he insists on leading all the way, even though there it is, in plain view, at the end of the street.

When Jack walked among these Georgian houses in 1933 he grumbled that 'the owners lived here no longer; the crew had taken possession'. They were all slum tenements, 'the buildings were rotting away, and some of the people were rotting with them. Faces that had shone for a season in brothels in Victoria's time now peered and mumbled at us.' I don't think that Jack – from across the Pennines – much cared for Liverpool. He kept calling it a 'great city', but he found it dark and unsettling, and it bothered him, and the docks and slums were depressing, and that comes out in an uncharacteristic and troubling rant about the many Irish who had settled here and done so much to build the place. 'From such glimpses as I have had', he sniffed, 'the Irish appear in general never even to have tried; they have settled in the nearest poor quarter and turned it into a slum.' He reckoned 'Liverpool would be glad to be rid of them now', except de Valera would never have them back: 'he believes in *Sinn Fein* for Ireland not England'. Beryl makes no mention of Jack's outburst, but it's a rare moment when his assumptions of what is acceptable are so obviously out of kilter with our own times. Before slapping him down, or walking away, we should probably see how the rest of us stand, ninety years from now.

By the way, not long after Beryl had completed her trip following Jack around England, she had 'a marvellous' lunch with him and his wife, Jacquetta Hawkes. By this time Jack was almost ninety years old, somewhat deaf ('which I took to be more of a convenience than an affliction') and still writing every morning. Beryl was nervous, as she wrote in *The Times*.

When we were alone for a few minutes, I said to him: 'It's confusing, isn't it … this television business?' He said, 'What?' a shade tetchily, and beckoned me to sit closer to him. 'What are you on about?'

I didn't want to shout, so I wrote on the back of my chequebook, 'I'm a bit in the dark, too' and showed it to him. He looked down at it, baffled, and at that moment people came back into the room, and I snatched the chequebook away. God knows what he made of it.

Beryl and Jack. They are both very easy to love.

When Beryl was here in 1983 she met David Sheppard, the Anglican Bishop of Liverpool, who had coined the phrase 'flickers of hope'. It was very soon after the 1981 riots and Liverpool was drained of funds and optimism and local control (the Thatcher government having decided the council couldn't be trusted with the money), and the pair of them went looking for 'flickers' in the infamous Netherley Estate. Beryl found it distressing – and I don't think she found the bishop very easy. 'Having been an actress', she wrote (and she was, for a while; she even had a small part in *Coronation Street*), 'I was a bit self-conscious about what I would say to a bishop.'

She was much happier on Hope Street. It is bookended by the two great Liverpool cathedrals, the Anglican to the south and the newer, Catholic cathedral in the north. Beryl had converted to Catholicism, having met a number of glamorous Catholics among the actors at the Playhouse, but she never reconciled herself to the Catholic cathedral, which she found 'so ugly that in a hundred years, if it hasn't collapsed due to faulty welding, it might conceivably become acceptable as an example of twentieth-century eccentricity'. Her main problem with it ('I know little of architecture') was that it had taken so long to build – and it is true that the Catholics of Liverpool spent decades scraping together the pennies to fund its construction, but in the end only the wondrous crypt was made according to Edwin Lutyens's original, overblown, 1930s plans, and the main building (which I found soothingly austere) now trembles like the tip of a small jagged iceberg on top of its own massive, vaulted, underground chambers.

Beryl may have converted to Catholicism (which irritated Austin), but I don't think she was anything more than occasionally enthusiastic about its practices and strictures. She certainly preferred the Anglican cathedral and its sunken graveyard where she once roamed with her father. And she found it exhilarating to stand on Hope Street, 'facing the river and the distant hills of Wales, the cathedral rising pink as a rose into the northern sky. The blackened city sails in an ocean of white cloud, perpetually racing before the wind.' It is not often that cathedrals generate a feeling of awe, or that's what I find, but the Anglican cathedral of Liverpool has power and purpose, the kind of certainty of spirit I had found in the tiny, living churches of Gerald's Wales. There's a large, swirling pink, hand-written neon statement floating over the western end: 'I Felt You and I Knew You Loved Me' (Tracey Emin, 2008). And that works, too. Even if the effect is slightly dampened by the lights of the over-eager shop and a clatter of cutlery coming from the café.

So, there is still a lot of hope on Hope Street. Even Beryl was happy, and she hated much of what had happened to Liverpool, especially since the riots. Here she goes again: 'Toxteth has been improved – that is to say vandalized – by the city planners and the architects. Terraces and churches, breweries and warehouses have been bulldozed into rubble.' Well, I wouldn't know (shifting baseline syndrome), but there's still plenty to admire. The Philharmonic Dining Rooms, the churches and chapels, the art college and the cafés. The walk from cathedral to cathedral in the sunny morning of the day is uplifting. Beryl points out that Alois, Adolf Hitler's half-brother, lived nearby on Stanhope Street with his Irish bride, Bridget Dowling. Their son was born there, William Patrick Hitler. Beryl was as preoccupied with the Second World War as the rest of her generation. She was seven when the war started and in 1947, aged fifteen, she started a love affair with an ex-German POW, a man called Harry Franz, whom she came across in the woods near her home. They met often, and when he went back to Germany they continued to send each other letters of love and longing, although in the end Beryl moved on more quickly than he did.

Beryl and Jack and I all spent some time in the docks. Jack had 'rarely seen anything more spectral and melancholy', as he wandered in the gloom, with his hands thrust deep in the pockets of his overcoat, past decaying warehouses, 'empty of everything but shadows'. By 1933 the Liverpool Docks had seen much better days. And of course, as Beryl says, those better days (for Liverpool and Britain, but most certainly not for everyone else) had involved sailing ships carrying cotton goods to Africa, refilling their holds with slaves, bearing them in misery to the West Indies, before returning in triumph to Liverpool 'loaded with sugar and rum'. And, she says, 'in the Gorée warehouses behind the offices of the Mersey Docks and Harbour Board, beneath the rusticated arcades supported on columns of cast iron, slaves were tethered (so they say) by long chains to the bulky rings projecting from the walls'.

I can't find the rings, but I may be looking in the wrong place. Even so, and despite Beryl's qualifying 'so they say', there's no doubt that African slaves were traded in Liverpool – bought and sold and kept in chains on the steps of Custom House. You can read about it in a book called *Liverpool and Slavery*, written in 1884 'by a Genuine "Dicky Sam"' – and a 'Dicky Sam', I now know, is another word for a Liverpudlian. He says the trade was still going on in 1766. Eighty years later, in October 1846 the escaped American slave, Frederick Douglass, was in Liverpool, speaking to a crowd of over 3,000 people, and he cursed the churches of the southern states of America:

> Ministers of religion defend slavery from the bible – ministers of religion own any number of slaves – bishops trade in human flesh – churches may be said to be literally built up in human skulls, and their very walls cemented with human blood …

What Douglass wanted more than anything was for British Christians to join him in denouncing the churches of America's south. In Scotland, the 'Free Church' had recently split from the established church and had raised some of its funds from American slave-owners. And so, when Douglass got to Paisley, just outside Glasgow, and spoke in the Exchange Rooms, he made this simple suggestion:

> We want to have the whole country surrounded with an anti-slavery wall, with the words legibly inscribed thereon, SEND BACK THE MONEY, SEND BACK THE MONEY.

Which has a certain timeless resonance.

The docks have been transformed, again, since Beryl was here in 1983, and they're now spruce with salmon-pink columns and clean empty walkways and a map of Britain floating perilously in the harbour, from which I'm told someone occasionally presents the weather. There are statues everywhere – Liverpool seems to have a fixation with large bronze memorials – and I get my photo taken in front of the Fab Four: vast, grinning, hurrying away from here and out to sea. Later, outside the Cavern, I will ask another tourist to snap me hanging on to the shapely bronze figure of Cilla.

The docks, though, don't feel right, despite the rolling revamps. Are we all (Jack, Beryl and I) picking up on the misery of ages? The slaves and the decay. Is it hanging in the air? Ploughed into the ground? 'This unspeakable development, this act of outrage', snarls Beryl. And, yes, the Liver Building looks disconsolate; the ships have gone; there's no one working here, other than the uni-formed staff at the galleries, hotels and museums. I drop into the Merseyside Maritime Museum where there's an exhibition about black sailors in the British Navy, and I think: here's yet another part of our history that needs digging up, turning over and hold-ing up to the light. About four percent of the British Navy was black at the time of Trafalgar, and some of them, presumably, were ex-slaves who were now seeking perilous refuge in British ships – and whose stolen forebears had left in chains from these very docks. One thing's for sure: we're going to need a lot more historians.

Beryl spent five days wandering around Liverpool. She was happy to find that the Nook pub in the Chinese quarter was still there, and still 'full of Chinamen speaking their own tongue'. The Nook used to be run by the grandfather of her editor, Anna Haycraft, who when Beryl first met her in the early 1950s was Anne Lindholm, and later wrote novels as Alice Thomas Ellis. They were great friends, although in later years that friendship was tested to destruction by Beryl's long-running affair with Anna's husband, Colin, who ran Duckworth, the publishing house for Beryl's novels and indeed her *English Journey*. If you want the full tangled details (of this and much more) you'll find it in Brendan King's biography, *Love by All Sorts of Means*. Beryl seemed to have a talent for confusion in her private life and absolute, heart-tugging clarity in her fiction.

Much of Beryl's life appears in her fiction, only tidied up, after a fashion. In *English Journey* she passes the Playhouse Theatre and tells us that 'I was fifteen when I joined the company as an assistant manager and character' (she was seventeen), and then remembers her time as a young actress and stagehand, when she understudied Cleopatra ('and every day I prayed for the continuing good health of the leading lady; I would have died rather than prance about the stage with nothing more substantial covering my bonny legs than a wisp of gauze'), and how she fell tumultuously in love with the designer, who was much older than her, and the actors talked Catholicism and sexual despair, and one of them 'placed me across his knee and beat me with a rolled up newspaper. I thought he didn't like me', and she ended up marrying an awkward but persistent young man from the Art School (Austin). This is basically the plot of *An Awfully Big Adventure*, one of her sweetest, saddest novels.

In the end, though, and just like Jack, Beryl was undone by Liverpool. 'I don't understand the malevolent force behind the destruction of this city,' she wrote, in pain. I like to think (but how can I know?) that she might be heartened by some of what has happened since. Certainly there is more obvious money around, prettifying the streets; and there's also a liveliness to this city – its shops and squares, restaurants and pubs – that made me happy. Perhaps I am still reeling from Bradford. But it was different for Beryl. Liverpool had been her home – she felt it still was – and so on the last day of her trip she stood for a long time at the window of her room in the Adelphi Hotel, staring down Church Street, and all she could see was what was no longer there.

All the landmarks I remembered, gone without trace. No Boosey and Hawkes … No gunsmith's … No ice-warehouse, no Bears Paw restaurant, no pet market … Gone … Obliterated … slung onto the refuse tips … I could blame the Conservatives for greed … the social-ists for naivety … But it hardly matters now. It's too late. Someone's murdered Liverpool and got away with it.

Maybe that's the message. Don't ever look back.

Charles Dickens & Wilkie Collins,
Cumberland to Doncaster, September 1857

EIGHT

'The Doncaster Unhappiness'

'Time would pass, old empires would fall and new
ones take their place, the relations of countries
and the relations of classes had to change, before I
discovered that it is not quality of goods and utility
which matter, but movement; not where you are
or what you have, but where you have come from,
where you are going and the rate at which you are
getting there.'

C. L. R. JAMES, *BEYOND A BOUNDARY*

And here comes Dickens. Racing up the country on the London express. Wheels spinning, engine roaring, throwing out steam and sparks and clouds of black smoke, battering through the stations, with horses and cattle (and even once a crowd of fear-stricken pigs) scattering across the fields in their wake. Dickens is riding high, first class, up front, on board with his friend Wilkie Collins, and even the voluble Wilkie must be temporarily stunned into silence in the presence of his employer, the Chief, the self-styled (half-mockingly, but with unassailable truth) 'Inimitable' Charles Dickens.

He is even more restless than usual. He had written to Wilkie only a few days earlier, pleading with him to come on a trip ('anywhere' would do), and had then dismissed Wilkie's suggestion ('Norfolk?') and announced instead they were going to Cumberland, inspired, he told his friend John Forster in yet another of his many letters, by the thought of some 'promising moors and bleak places' he had read about in a book. This was *The Beauties of England and Wales* (Vol. III) by John Britton and Edward Wedlake Brayley, written in 1802 – and the fact is he'd just snatched it up and plumped for any old place, so long as it was somewhere North and not too far from Doncaster, where an eighteen-year-old actress called Ellen Ternan was due to appear later that month, with her mother and sisters, at the Theatre Royal. Dickens was forty-five years old, married to Catherine, with ten children, and right now he was being tossed around in the jaws of an existential, exponential mid-life crisis. 'I want to escape from myself,' he had written to Wilkie. As if that were ever possible.

He must have thought Wilkie would make the ideal travelling companion. For one thing, they knew each other well (there was that jaunt to Italy with Augustus Egg in 1853), and they could also use the trip to generate some articles for the magazine he edited, *Household Words*. There was never any question that this would be a real holiday for Dickens (nothing ever was, for long), but for the purposes of the journey, or rather the journalism, fictional stories and book that would emerge from their collaboration, he suggested they adopt the personas of 'Two Idle Apprentices' on a 'Lazy Tour'. They called themselves Francis Goodchild (Dickens) and Thomas Idle (Wilkie) after Hogarth's series of ten prints, *Industry and Idleness*. Which is pretty odd when you consider that in Hogarth's version Francis Goodchild, a paragon of hard-working virtue, ends up Mayor of London while the shiftless Idle is hanged at Tyburn.

A joke, of sorts, runs through the book, *The Lazy Tour of Two Idle Apprentices*, in which Goodchild/Dickens is not really lazy at all, but Idle/Wilkie is catatonically so. It is telling, or perhaps sad, and also infuriating, that Dickens was pretending to be a much younger man than he was, with time on his hands, going wherever the mood or the weather took them. This really wasn't true. Dickens liked to plan ahead – and his and Wilkie's rooms in Doncaster, not to mention a carriage and driver, were booked as soon as he decided on the trip, to coincide with the week of the St Leger Stakes, and most especially the arrival of the (probably) unsuspecting Ellen Ternan. And that's the other great thing about Wilkie, Dickens must have thought: he was unmarried, and he had a mistress, a widow called Caroline Graves with a young child, so he was never going to give anyone a hard time about young actresses.

It is seven years since we left Wilkie in Cornwall and much has changed. Most obviously, he has allowed his inner bohemian to emerge, in his increasingly outspoken opinions, his fast-spreading beard and his flamboyant clothing (just like Dickens, he sports a florid waistcoat). He is now thirty-three years old. Since *Rambles Beyond Railways* appeared in early 1851, he has published five more successful and sensational works, including the novels *Basil*, *Hide and Seek* and – hot off the press – *The Dead Secret*. He is a contributor to *Household Words* and other magazines. His greatest fame is still ahead of him (*The Woman in White* in 1860 made him, briefly, the most sought-after man in London), but he is already a well-known literary figure. Being adopted by Dickens certainly helps. They have just co-written and starred in a play, *The Frozen Deep*, the preposterous plot suggested by Wilkie, which ran for four nights to vast applause at Dickens's home in Tavistock Square (he had hired Britain's greatest maritime painter to provide the scenery), before transferring to the professional stage in Manchester. And this is where Dickens had met the enchanting Ternan sisters and had given such an overwhelming performance in the character of Richard Wardour, the self-sacrificing sea captain who allows himself to freeze to death in order to save the life of his love rival (played by Wilkie), that Maria Ternan, Ellen's older sister, appearing as Clara, the woman Wardour loves, had wept tears of genuine grief on stage, in front of an audience of thousands, straight into his open and gasping mouth.

So the train steamed north. At one point they thundered between Liverpool and Manchester (hello, Jack and Beryl) and Dickens, in the guise of 'Francis Goodchild', presses his nose to the window as the engine, 'the greatest power in nature and art combined ... shrieked in hysterics', and 'the pastoral country darkened, became coaly, became smoky, became infernal, got better, got worse, improved again, grew rugged, turned romantic; was a wood, a stream, a chain of hills, a gorge, a moor, a cathedral town, a fortified place, a waste'. After a lot more of this, they arrived in Carlisle. It looked, wrote Dickens, 'congenially and delightfully idle'.

There is a bond, something umbilical, between Dickens and trains. He defined his age just as much as they did (and isn't that a surprising thought?). You could almost say they grew up together. The first commercially successful steam locomotive started running in 1812, the year of his birth; and he turned eighteen when the railways came of age with the opening of the Liverpool and Manchester Railway. 'The Age of the Railways' jostles with the 'Dickensian'. Of course, he was just a reporter to their all-conquering revolution, and filling his novels with their heat and fury, and no one can deny the way they transformed Britain and then the world, but even so, in his pomp, and on through the decades that followed, it was also Dickens who changed our language and our dreams. Readers in New York stormed the wharf when the final instalment of *The Old Curiosity Shop* was rumoured to be arriving by ship from London. 'Tell us about Nell', they screamed up at the sailors, 'does she live?' Printers' lads would tear the sheets hot from their presses to find out what was happening to Oliver, Fagin and the Artful Dodger, Pickwick, Scrooge, Squeers, Sykes, Smike, Copperfield, Micawber, Pip, Uriah Heep ... 'I'm a very 'umble person', 'What larks, Pirrip!', 'Barkis is willin'', 'It was the best of times …', 'I loved her against reason, against promise, against peace, against hope, against happiness …', 'Something will turn up', 'Fog everywhere', 'Wery good', 'A mist hung over the river', 'Please, sir, I want some more?', 'A Merry Christmas to us all; God bless us every one!' … 'Bah humbug!'

Dickens and trains. When *The Frozen Deep* was booked into the Free Trade Hall in Manchester, Dickens and the rest of the troupe, plus hangers-on, piled into the train in London, and he led them all the way to the North in a whooping celebration, passing jokes and riddles out of the windows at the ends of their umbrellas and into the next carriages (there was no corridor). And George Dolby, the theatre impresario, tells how Dickens taught him to dance the hornpipe while lurching along in a train. And in 1865, the train was derailed in which Dickens was travelling back from France with lovely Ellen Ternan (Nelly to him by now), along with her mother, Frances, and it crashed off a broken bridge just outside Staplehurst in Kent. Dickens and the Ternans were in the first-class carriage, just behind the engine, and it remained attached, hanging almost vertically over the river. They weren't badly hurt, just battered and pitched into a corner, and Dickens, grabbing his brandy and notebook, bundled the women away (there was still the risk of scandal) and scrambled down to the river, where he tended the wounded and the dying, and handed around his brandy and radiated limitless gigawatts of goodwill.

Before he and Wilkie left for Cumberland and then Doncaster in September 1857, Dickens had given his first ever public readings – of *A Christmas Carol* at St Martin's Hall in Covent Garden – and 2,000 people had turned up to weep and scream and bellow their approval. It is not surprising it turned his head. Against the advice of his great friend John Forster, who thought public speaking was no way for a gentleman-novelist to behave, he spent the rest of his life being shunted across the country by train, express wherever possible, and into Ireland, rattling from city to city, drawing huge, insatiable crowds to see and hear him act out the highlights from his most popular works. It killed him in the end, only thirteen years after he'd given his first reading, struck dumb and then dead by a stroke (not his first) at his home in Gad's Hill, near Rochester in Kent. He was only fifty-eight. His body was taken for burial by special train to Poets' Corner in Westminster Abbey, against his clearly stated wishes for a simple, local ceremony. A special train. Laid on for what was left of the Inimitable, whether he liked it or not.

Anyway. He's not dead yet. He paces around Carlisle, finding it dull (although it perks up on market day) and then he chivvies Wilkie towards 'a certain black old Cumberland hill or mountain, called Carrock, or Carrock Fell', because he felt it 'would be the culminating triumph of Idleness to ascend the same'. This is the hill he must have read about in his book *The Beauties of England and Wales*, which describes it as 'a singular eminence … 520 yards above the surrounding meadows'. No one has since been able to work out why Dickens and Wilkie chose this particular hill in the Lake District to climb – they travelled close to Skiddaw after all – because there's nothing especially exciting about Carrock Fell, certainly not compared to most of the rest of the area, but perhaps that helps explain why Dickens dismisses the whole Lake Country as having 'vaunted himself a great deal more than his merits deserve'. So much for Wordsworth. Wilkie tagged along, although he was not keen on the idea of the climb. He said he was missing London already. And as for me, I've just been up a proper mountain, Snowdon, with Edith and Martin, so I am happy not to join them. As an 'umble tribute to the theme of 'Idleness', obviously.

In the event, their climb ended in disaster. They sat in the nearest inn, drinking whisky and eating oatcakes (rather like Edith and Martin), until a guide failed to appear and the innkeeper volunteered himself to lead them to the top. Dickens bounded ahead, outstripping the innkeeper (much to his delight), with Wilkie, who writes this part of the narrative, trailing behind. They got to the top in choking fog, and then got lost on the way down. Dickens is being insufferable with his new compass, which Wilkie is quietly pleased to see him drop and break, and the innkeeper keeps urging them to go 'round' the mountain in the hopes of reaching 'a certain point', before they can begin their descent. Wilkie is adamant that 'when three men want to get to the bottom of a mountain, their business is to walk down it … and he put this view of the case, not only with emphasis, but even with some irritability'. He is overruled. He then falls behind in the fog, for the fifteenth time, slips on a rock in a stream, in his tiny little shoes, and tears his ankle ligaments. In the book, Dickens and the innkeeper have to help Wilkie in agony down the slopes and to safety; but in Dickens's letter to his sister-in-law, Georgina Hogarth, he makes out that he had to carry Wilkie like a baby, his big head bumping against his shoulder. There was always an edge of competitiveness to Dickens. People had to know who was boss. It would be depressing to think that the cliché is true and this is the way of most male friendships, but consider how Edith and Martin cared for each other all the way up and down Snowdon, even if they were cursing the days they were born.

It is a long time before Wilkie is able to walk again, and even then he is hobbling around with sticks, and this propels Dickens into an even higher pitch of activity. He moves them from hotel to hotel; he berates poor Wilkie for his idleness (he won't even read, he scoffs – he just wants to dream and drivel about the perils of physical activity); and Dickens walks everywhere: twelve miles for the morning post, he crows, fairly *astonishing* their landlord. All under the guise of 'Goodchild' and 'Idle', of course, but away from these adopted characters Dickens is becoming irritated with Wilkie's extreme slovenliness (Wilkie was chaotic, except in his choice of waistcoats) and his penny-pinching griping about the bills.

Hidden in plain sight in the pages of *The Lazy Tour* is a record of Dickens's rising infatuation with Ellen Ternan. He knows it – he knows himself very well – but he can't stop it. He wants to shout about it. His letters to friends and family are laden with unsubtle hints. He sighs and calls himself a 'young lover'. 'Goodchild' is described as a young man who's always in love, often with more than one woman at a time. He includes a short creepy story, about an evil old man who kills his young, 'fair, flaxen-haired, large-eyed' wife through willpower alone. 'Die!' he says to her, over and over, 'Die!' The name of this beautiful young bride is Ellen. You could say he is conflicted … He laughs at himself, and lets Thomas Idle say (because by this stage Dickens is writing almost every word in their collaborative book): 'You can't play. You don't know what it is. You make work of everything. If you were to go up in a balloon, you'd make for Heaven.' And he announces, as though it has just occurred to him, that they are off to the races at Doncaster.

It is where everyone else is heading. The train is packed with racegoers, with only one name on their lips, the mysterious John Scott, champion jockey, or 'Joon Scott' as Dickens sometimes transcribes him in broad Yorkshire, with all 't'harses … fly horses and omnibus horses of Doncaster and parts adjacent, rampant, rearing, backing, plunging, shying'. Dickens cannot shake the idea that he has wandered into a 'Lunatic Asylum', and peering out from his (pre-booked) hotel bedroom every morning, he 'saw the Lunatics, horse-mad, betting-mad, drunken-mad, vice-mad' and – he could have added – 'love-mad', or 'Ellen-mad', or 'driven mad by a sudden, all-consuming horror of ageing and loss and missed promise'.

But how could Dickens, of all people, ever think that his life was not successful enough, or full enough, or rich enough? He only had thirteen years left to live. Did he sense it? He was ageing, fast – he looked older than his forty-five years – and while he was happy to be gadding around with Wilkie, he was also feeling hemmed and crushed by his responsibilities. He'd never had a childhood of his own (his father in prison for debt, young Charles sent out to work in the blacking factory), and now here he was, beset on every side: his useless, impoverished, importuning brothers, a wife he no longer loved, their ten children (his limp, hopeless sons, the daughters to marry off), an ageing, dependent mother, a new country house in Kent – the home of his child-hood dreams – to rebuild and furnish, and his London home to maintain, magazines to edit, new books and articles to write, money (more and more money) to be made to keep the whole boiling afloat, and charities to run, societies to promote, reading tours to organize, letters, friends and theatricals, contracts to negotiate, copyright to protect – and so many stories to tell and teeming multitudes needing his help. And now an eighteen-year-old actress to persuade to become his lover – or not. What about the core message in all his books? Protect the innocent. Think of Little Nell. (Although, why is he now calling this childlike actress 'Nelly' of all things? With her big blue eyes and flaxen hair.) But this is Dickens and it doesn't matter how high he has flown, or how far he has come, he still wants MORE (please, sir) and he is straining and raging against the bounds, even though he knows that the spectacle of a middle-aged man losing his head over a teenage girl is a joke and the morality, with his power and fame, is unpleasant and undeniably wrong. Even in 1857. Thanks in part to his own campaigning efforts.

Predictably, as far as the actual racing was concerned, Dickens spent his week in Doncaster winning, and boasting about it. I am here, too. It is my first proper race outing, if I don't count the handful of point-to-points I went to with my family in deepest, rural Sussex, all the way back in the sixties and seventies. The first I remember through the pursuing fog was when my father handed my brother and me 50p each or even (yes) ten shillings apiece, and told us to go and spend it on the horses, because 'it would be a useful lesson in the futility of gambling'. We wandered about, entirely unsupervised (can this be true?), placing bets on random horses with red-faced tweedy men, who were happy to take money from a six- and an eight-year-old. I think we rather liked the Number Nine and a horse called Mossy Face, and we returned to my father with a great booty of winnings, the coins spilling from our clammy little hands, and were sent to spend it all on chocolate and sweets. It is a wonder I didn't descend into a lifetime of gambling, but ever since I have always known, with unquenchable certainty, that when I do finally choose to resume my betting career, I cannot possibly lose.

If you filter your expectations through Dickens's writings, then you are always going to be disappointed. Everything is slightly less exciting than it should be: tamed, and rinsed through with a light grey wash. Not by much, but no reality can compete with Sam Weller and Mr Pickwick and the technicolour spatter-bomb of Dickens's London streets. It's still a glorious day at Doncaster Racecourse. Ladies Day, no less ('naturally there will be an abundance of the finest fillies out in force', the website blethers), and it is hot in the stands and blue in the sky. There's a large crowd hosing itself down with an unwavering flow of lager and white wine. Mostly lager, and mostly men, but there are still plenty of women who have heeded the call to come and compete for the 'Best Dressed Lady' crown. Many are wearing hats, huge, flyaway confections, and I haven't seen this many trilbies and flat caps since the newsreel footage of 1958.

I am absolutely thrilled to be here. I am packed into the roiling stands, even though Dickens preferred the turn behind the brow of the hill, or sometimes the start, or the 'coming-in', where he can see the Grand Stand:

> rising against the sky with its vast tiers of little white dots of faces, and its last high rows and corners of people, looking like pins stuck into an enormous pin-cushion … When the race is nearly run out, it is as good as the race … to see the flutter among the pins, and the change in them from dark to light, as hats are taken off and waved.

Dickens could get up close, and he could see the big picture, although here, at Doncaster Races, what he really longed to do was freeze time, at the exact point when the St Leger was about to run (but now never would), leaving him to stand for ever at the side of the girl in 'little lilac gloves and a winning little bonnet', a 'dear unknown [ha!] wearer with golden hair'.

Just let me off this train, please, if only for a while.

The races do run, today and in 1857. Dickens collects his winnings and courts Ellen (Nelly) Ternan, taking her for rides in his carriage, but always we think under the watchful eye of her mother. And I lean forward from the stands and assess the horses with a lagerish eye and decide that Number Seven is the glossiest, most vibrant and tightly muscled horse I have ever seen, and anyway I always must back Number Seven if I can, because that's the horse that's winning the race on the cover of my copy of *Totopoly* ('The Great Race Game by the Manufacturers of Monopoly') so how can it possibly lose? Which of course it does, repeatedly (new Number Sevens, different races), until finally the message burrows through to the darkest, most stubborn recesses of my ancestral brain, that there is more to horse racing than a glossy coat and an old board game, but not before the red-faced tweedy men have recouped their losses, with enormous interest, from their disastrous day at the Sussex point-to-point so many years earlier.

I may be getting poorer, along with almost everyone else, but that has done nothing to dampen the rollicking atmosphere. There's a large man stuffed into a pinstripe suit standing just in front of me, in amongst a posse of elaborately hatted, bare-backed young women, all of them waving racecards and lager, and he oozes confidence at the start of every new race. 'I say it's a kind race to me', he confides to the woman on his left, just as the 3.35 begins, 'and I can't do wrong by it.' And sure enough, as the horses gallop up the hill and around the final bend, and the crowd thickens and sways in the stands, and the row in front of me chants in rising ecstasy, 'Come on son … come on son … *come on son* …', the man's horse pounds to the front, right at the end, 'By half a length and seven hands,' he exults, and the women yell, 'Get the drinks in, Dad!' and he drains his pint and barrels down the concrete steps, but not before he has turned to his daughters (and can they really *all* be his daughters, these women of many shapes and shades?) and he says, 'Oh sure, he never whipped it, like, he just pushed it home, hands and heels.'

Dickens was never a great sportsman, despite the walking, but he did enjoy his cricket. Nelly, too – it is said she once played a vigorous game with a couple of Dickens's young sons, although his daughter Katey thought it was improper for a lady to be rolling around on the grass with such abandon. Dickens used to organize games for his local team in the grounds of his home at Gad's Hill and would spend a happy day scoring, sitting (or pacing) in the pavilion he had raised on the boundary for the occasion. He must have played sometimes when he was a younger man and I have read he turned out at least once in his later years, bowling with an underarm action, even though the rules had already changed to allow the ball to be released from above the shoulder. When Dickens cancelled a reading tour of Australia in 1861, the disappointed entrepreneurs, William Spiers and Christopher Pond, owners of the Café de Paris in Melbourne, booked an English cricket team as a substitute. It was the first time an English team had ever visited Australia, and so a long tradition was born out of Charles Dickens's reluctance to travel so far (despite the very generous terms), perhaps because he could not bring himself to leave Nelly Ternan alone for too long.

Wilkie had no interest in playing games or sport of any kind. The way he tells it in *The Lazy Tour*, it was one of the great lessons of his life: attempts at active exertion only ever end in disaster and illness. He writes how 'shortly after leaving school, he [Thomas Idle] accompanied a party of friends to a cricket-field, in his natural and appropriate character of spectator only'. But the team needed another player, Wilkie was enrolled, and the next thing he knew he was being 'roused from peaceful slumber in a dry ditch, and placed before three wickets with a bat in his hand'. The bowler (usually the 'meekest and mildest of human beings') flung a ball straight at him and it was only through a supreme act of athleticism that Wilkie was able to save his shins and dive out of the way, leaving 'the full force of the deadly missile to strike his wicket instead of his leg'. Wilkie then caught a chill while fielding, certainly not the ball, and had to take to his bed for several weeks with a nasty fever. I don't suppose Dickens was impressed.

The love of cricket runs deep in this part of the world, here and on the other side of the Pennines. The Trinidadian writer, C. L. R. James, was living in the town of Nelson in 1932 (round about when Jack Priestley drifted by), not far north of Burnley, drawn by his friend Learie Constantine, who had been hired to play Lancashire League cricket for the local team. As James puts it in *Beyond a Boundary*, his beautiful book about cricket, socialism, West Indian culture and colonialism (and really, you don't have to like cricket to love it): 'I was singularly fortunate in that my first introduction to England was to the working people of the North, and not to the overheated atmosphere of London.'

Constantine had arrived in 1928 with his wife Norma, making them, James says, the only two black people in Nelson. When James became their lodger, that made it three, by which time 'Constantine, by his cricket, by the demeanour of himself and his wife in what all could realise was no easy situation ... had created an enormous interest in the West Indies and West Indians.' He and Constantine went on to make dozens of speeches at countless halls, preaching West Indian self-government (the islands were still British colonies), and equal opportunity, and the absurdity of racial discrimination, all of it wrapped in the comforting blanket of cricket. 'There might have been something of an edge to me', James writes, possibly with understatement, 'particularly at the beginning. As far as I could see no one ever resented it. If they did there was always Constantine's reassuring presence and a few pleasant and graceful words at the end.'

The local people adored Learie Constantine. He was a brilliant cricketer, but there was so much more to it than that. When he and Norma finally decided to go back to Trinidad, the locals begged him to stay. 'That story', writes James, 'is sufficiently known. What is not known is that the Nelson people conquered him.' And so he lingered, through the war, right up to 1954, because, as he said, 'he had earned his living in England and when the country was in trouble he was not going to run out.' In the end, after a few years in Trinidad, he returned to Britain, by now a lawyer

and a politician, and became the country's first black peer: Baron
Constantine of Maraval in Trinidad and Nelson in the County
Palatine of Lancaster.

James loved the books of Charles Dickens. He adored all the
nineteenth-century British writers. Growing up in Trinidad, in
a poor, middle-class black family, living on the edge of the local
cricket pitch, he devoured Keats and Shelley, Arnold and Austen,
Collins, Dickens and Thackeray (especially him; *Vanity Fair* was his
bible, he read it dozens of times, and he was still amazed, despite
his underlying realism, to arrive in England for the first time in
1932 and find everything not quite as expected). 'People educated
as I had been', he wrote, 'could move rapidly from uncritical
admiration of abstractions to an equally uncritical hostility to
the complex reality.'

It was cricket that shaped his politics, although he didn't realize
it at the time. In the 1920s there was blatant racism at home in
Trinidad, dictating who could play for which club, and this was
what had driven Constantine, a dark-skinned man, away from
the islands to play in the Lancashire League. James just wanted
to watch him bat – or field in the covers, where he transformed
our idea of what is possible. He was also a penetrating fast bowler,
and was the first West Indian to take a wicket in a Test match
against England.

And it was cricket, not politics, that got James his first job in
Britain. He saw the incomparable Sydney Barnes playing in the
League in 1932, already nearly sixty years old, and he interviewed
him and sent the article to the *Guardian*. Their cricket correspond-
ent, Neville Cardus, hired him on the spot. And so round it goes:
my father, born in 1912, used to rave about Sydney Barnes's
off- and leg-cutters: 'He tore them from the sky', he would say
to me, 'he tore them down from the sky.' And he would hold the
cricket ball in his large hand, fingers either side of the seam, and

demonstrate how Barnes had got the ball to fizz and spit from the pitch. Learie Constantine reckoned the finest innings of his career was played against the sixty-year-old Sydney Barnes. 'To score', wrote James, 'he had to get the leg-break away through two short-legs and force the off-break through two gulleys. Against the break all the time. I did not see the innings, but I can visualise the billiard-like precision and concentration with which it was done.' That was against overarm bowling, of course, something Dickens never mastered … and we do need to get back to him, tempting as it is to linger with James and Constantine in the long-ago summers of the Lancashire League.

What, I wonder, did Nelly Ternan make of Dickens's attentions? She was only eighteen. She had two older sisters, whom Dickens was helping, and would continue to help, in their acting careers. Her mother was on hand and was not about to let her throw herself at a middle-aged married novelist, even though discrepancies in age were not so remarkable then; but the pre-existing *marriage* was rather more to the point. Dickens burned thousands of his letters in a huge fire one day in September 1860 at his home in Gad's Hill. Nelly destroyed her letters from Dickens before she died. And ever since biographers have argued about Nelly and Dickens, and many refuse to believe that they ever had a sexual relationship, but the facts are these: she gave up acting, moved to France for a while (where he visited her frequently), was put up by Dickens in a country cottage near Slough (where he visited her frequently) and, according to Claire Tomalin in what feels like the definitive account, she probably had a baby in France, who died when he was only a few months old. She was on her way back to England when her train went off the rails at Staplehurst. Six years after Dickens died she married George Wharton Robinson, and had two children.

After 'the Doncaster unhappiness', as he called it to Wilkie, Dickens went back to London aflame with an unrequited obsession with Nelly – and set about tearing his own and other people's lives apart. He treated Catherine viciously, forcing her to call on the Ternans, apparently to prove that his relationship with Nelly was innocent, and accusing her of 'not understanding' him (when Dickens had a mid-life crisis, he raced through all the clichés and then multiplied them by ten). He pressed for divorce and moved Catherine out of their home. He cut anyone dead who didn't back him. He blocked Catherine from their daughter's wedding. He gave up his charities, lost many friends, and left *Household Words* to set up a new weekly magazine, *All the Year Round*, because he'd fallen out with the publishers. He sold the house in London and launched his career of public readings, feasting on the rapturous crowds. He wrote some of his best books, even as the darkness spread. But we know all this. He was still incomparably the best.

'A man writes much better than he lives', wrote Samuel Johnson, one hundred years earlier, although we should not 'wonder that most fail, amidst tumult, and snares, and danger'. And welcome back, Enid. But Dickens tried, hard, to live up to what he knew to be right and true, and his novels, it is good to remember, are full of moments of redemption and forgiveness.

Here's a song he knew and loved and must have sung many times.

> Believe me, if all those endearing young charms,
> Which I gaze on so fondly to-day,
> Were to change by to-morrow, and flee from my arms
> Like fairy-gifts, fading away!
> Thou wouldst still be ador'd as this moment thou art,
> Let thy loveliness fade as it will …

And who was on his mind as he sang? Not Catherine, not by the time he left Doncaster. He couldn't even bring himself to write to her. And Nelly? They must have stayed close, even if they never married nor acknowledged any kind of relationship. It was in truth Dickens who was fading, although that's an absurd word to use about him. He fought every inch of the way and blazed through every minute of every hour of the thirteen years he had left. But even so, from our perspective, looking back at this moment from the improbable future, it is quite clear that it is Dickens who is faltering, who is no longer so easily, so abundantly certain about the best way forward.

We will see him in Kent. But now here is Sam Johnson, riding the coach north from London, heading for Scotland in the year 1773, passing by Doncaster, just three years before the first St Leger Stakes was run. And what larks it all is, Pip, *what larks!*

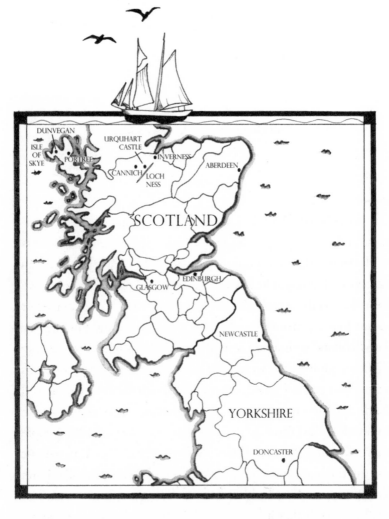

Samuel Johnson & James Boswell,
Edinburgh to Skye and back, August to November 1773

NINE

A Wilderness

'All change is of itself an evil.'

SAMUEL JOHNSON

To the North! And the wild lands beyond the wall. Ice mountains and savage peoples loom and gnaw at the troubled dreams of the south, although I think by now we can safely agree that any dread of what might lie beyond the border should rightfully have been flowing the other way. Even so, when Celia Fiennes made her Great Journey around England in 1698, she would not venture into Scotland without an armed guard. 'Their miles are soe long in these countrys', she wrote, and she had heard there are no towns where you can get a bed, other than Edinburgh, Aberdeen and Kerk, and most travellers have to 'go from one Nobleman's house to another' and those houses are mostly castles and the people there 'live in so nasty a way … one has little stomach to eate or use anything as I have been told by some that has travell'd there; and I am sure I met with a sample of it enough to discourage my progress farther in Scotland'. The problem was the people – idle for the most part, she decided – but as she skirted tentatively along the border (on the Scottish side, rather bravely) she did come across the finest French claret she'd 'dranck this seven year'.

Seventy-five turbulent years after Celia had reined back at the border, Samuel Johnson and James Boswell made their own celebrated journey to the Highlands and Islands. Boswell, a Scot, had been trying for years to persuade his friend to come on a tour with him, but Johnson was always too busy (or so he liked to think), and sometimes too depressed, or he was short of money, and anyway ever since 1745, when Bonnie Prince Charlie and his alarmingly (romantically) feral Highlanders had marched into England, all the way to Derby, and even threatened London, before sloping back to Scotland to be butchered like cattle at the Battle of Culloden, ever since then it had been hard to choose a good time to head into the unknown. Especially since Johnson was known to be a Jacobite sympathizer. But in 1773 Johnson decided that it was probably now or never. The Highlands were being sanitized, stripped of their customs and emptied of their people. He was sixty-three years old. And although he might have preferred to hang around in Streatham with his beautiful young friend Hester Thrale (whom he loved, even though she was married to Henry, a brewer), she urged him to make the trip. So to everyone's surprise he fired off a message to Boswell in Edinburgh and told him to start planning their route. No doubt he hoped to impress Hester with a flow of gripping and insightful letters, but he was also genuinely excited about the prospect of encountering the last of Britain's untamed wilderness.

One last awkward fact: Johnson was presumed to hate the Scots and Scotland. There were his famous sayings (best read out loud, slowly, as he spoke, with thunder on the mountain): 'Sir, the noblest prospect that a Scotchman ever sees, is the high road that leads him to London.' AND 'Knowledge was divided among the Scots, like bread in a besieged town, to every man a mouthful, to no man a bellyful.' Johnson, like Jack Priestley, was a tease, but much more than Jack, what he really liked to do was argue. When his friend and sparring partner Gilbert Walmesley died, a 'Whig of great malevolence', Johnson wrote that 'after his death I felt my Toryism much abated'. Johnson became morose if he didn't have someone to argue with – to 'toss and gore' – and depressed if he spent too long alone. But it didn't always mean very much. Most of the time he just enjoyed holding a contrary view and wrestling an adversary to the ground. Sometimes literally. He was a big man and he liked to show it.

So: he was easily bored, restlessly clever, he had to talk – and he loved the idea that someone was taking notes. Before Boswell, it was (among others) his great friend and one of the only pupils in his hopeless school, the actor David Garrick. After Johnson's school near Lichfield had failed, burning through his wife's inheritance, he left for London with Garrick, both of them hoping to make their fortunes. Johnson was twenty-six, Garrick twenty. They remained life-long friends, tinged (at least on Johnson's side) with a whisper of jealousy. Garrick is full of gossipy tales, including the time when Johnson told him that life's greatest pleasures were (and remember – out loud, with a s-l-o-w rumble): 'Fucking, [Sir], and the second is drinking.' 'And he wondered why there were not more drunkards, "for all could drink though not all could fuck."' He must have been some schoolteacher.

Both Johnson and Boswell published accounts of their journey, Johnson in 1775 (he needed the money, and Boswell was always going to defer to the great man), and Boswell in 1785, one year after Johnson's death. Put them together and you have the authentic Johnson, the man who shocked Lady MacLeod at dinner in her castle in Skye by telling her that men and women had no more natural goodness than wolves, but who also delighted almost everyone he met with his kindness and deep interest in their affairs.

In Inverness Johnson held forth about the benefits of conquest. The Romans, he wrote, had spread civilization to England, and Oliver Cromwell's soldiers had brought shoes to the Scots (as well, it seems, as a recipe for cooking kale). Most importantly, the Acts

of Union between England and Scotland in 1706 and 1707 had
been a wonderful thing for the untamed and under-civilized North:

> Till the Union made them acquainted with English
> manners, the culture of their lands was unskilful, and
> their domestick life unformed; their tables were coarse
> as the feasts of Esquimaux, and their houses filthy as
> the cottages of Hottentots.

Raw colonialism, you see. And yet Johnson hated what was being
done at that time to the Native Americans, some of it perpetrated
by Highlanders fleeing the depredations of the English and their
own feudal lords, and he was also unflinching in his denunciations
of slavery. His servant, Frank Barber, was a freed slave, originally
from Jamaica, who had been with Johnson since the age of eleven,
given (yes, *given*) to him in 1752 by a friend, Richard Bathurst, who
thought Johnson needed cheering up after the death of his wife,
Tetty. It would do him good to look after someone, his friends
felt. And so he did: when Johnson died it was found that he had
left everything he owned to Frank Barber, a fact that outraged
some, in particular Sir John Hawkins, the fussy and unimaginative
man who was Johnson's first biographer and also in charge of his
funeral, which he seems to have skimped on in sulky protest. But
it suited Boswell, who got on well with Barber and was able to
persuade him to part with, or sometimes sell, Johnson's journals,
letters and other effects, all of which ended up in his monumental
Life of Johnson. Barber wasn't on the trip because Johnson was
trying to save money; but Boswell's servant, a tall Bohemian man
called Joseph Ritter, came along, as well as two Highlander guides.
   Johnson liked to joke and shock, but only in person. His writing,
as displayed in *Journey to the Western Isles*, is weighty, sometimes
hobbled by a desire to deliver the definitive aphorism, but packed

with observations. There's a tension between his innate conservatism, his distrust of change, his dislike of Whigs and their endless improvements, and his delight in happy anarchy. You can see it in his monumental *Dictionary of the English Language*, which took him nine soul-sapping years to complete. He wanted to fix every word in its place – and everything else – but he was too thoughtful and melancholic not to know that he would always be undone by the essential slipperiness of language and life.

Johnson also had a terror of going mad. People say that is why he was always trying to clamp order onto what could not be contained, including himself. He did *appear* mad. When the artist William Hogarth first met him, taking tea at Samuel Richardson's house, he assumed that the large man in the corner, who was grinning and gurning and rolling about, and stamping his feet, and puffing and snorting, was 'an ideot' who had been taken under the care of the kindly Mr Richardson. Until, that is, Johnson spoke and 'displayed such a power of eloquence, that Hogarth looked at him with astonishment, and actually imagined that this ideot had been at the moment inspired'. This was Sam Johnson, whose appearance in 1773 is best described, of course, by Boswell:

> His person was large, robust, I may say approaching the
> gigantick, and grown unwieldy from corpulence. His
> countenance ... was somewhat disfigured by scars ... His
> sight had always been somewhat weak. His head, and
> sometimes also his body, shook with a kind of motion
> like the effect of a palsy; he appeared to be frequently
> disturbed by cramps, or convulsive contractions ...

He also had a weird habit of thrumming his feet up and down when he was seated, and although his friend, the artist Joshua Reynolds, thought that he was quite capable of restraining himself,

Boswell was not so sure. 'He was', adds Boswell, slyly, 'somewhat susceptible of flattery'.

Boswell was waiting for Johnson in Edinburgh. He had married four years earlier and was now living in the city, making frequent trips to London. When he was younger, he had spent a couple of years in Edinburgh studying to be a lawyer, before he had managed to persuade his father to send him to London to join the army. Not that he had any intention of becoming a soldier; he just wanted an allowance and to get away from his father, an overbearing Presbyterian judge. If you read his journals of the time, they are full of a young man's longing for sex and approbation (sometimes the two combined: 'I picked up a girl in the Strand; went into a court with intention to enjoy her in armour [a condom]. She wondered at my size, and said if I ever took a girl's maidenhead, I would make her squeak'). And so on. The journals are extraordinarily frank and self-knowing. When he was only twenty-one he wrote this: 'I have discovered that we may be in some degree whatever character we choose.'

The character Boswell had chosen to pursue was that of literary superstar. He was still only thirty-two years old in 1773 and was the author of the well-received *Tour to Corsica*. Once again, the best person to describe how he was in those days is Boswell himself: 'He had travelled a good deal ... He had thought more than any body supposed ... He had all Dr Johnson's principles, with some degree of relaxation. He had rather too little, than too much prudence, and, his imagination being lively, he often said things of which the effect was very different from the intention.' He was clever and bumptious and underestimated by most of Johnson's friends.

Boswell had first managed to meet Johnson on 16 May 1763, ten years before their Scottish tour, at Davies's in Russell Street, where he was drinking coffee when Johnson walked in. 'Don't tell him where I come from,' he shouted at Davies, but too late. '"Mr Johnson," said I, "indeed I come from Scotland, but I cannot help it." "Sir," replied he, "that, I find, is what a very great many of your countrymen cannot help".' And how the company laughed. Once he had Johnson's attention, Boswell didn't ever let go, following him around, feeding him lines, writing down whatever came back out. On this trip around the Highlands (which was the longest time they ever spent together) he worried that he was running out of topics. As for Johnson, he was thrilled that someone was on hand to write him into posterity (he must have known he couldn't do it himself), even if at times Boswell's eager attentions proved too much. There's a telling moment in Skye when Johnson sends Boswell to his room to spend more time polishing his journal ('my *Journal* is really a task of much time and labour, and he forbids me to contract it'). It sounds like a parent sending his children out into the garden to count the leaves.

Johnson arrived in Edinburgh on 14 August 1773 and immediately got into a row with a waiter, who had dropped some sugar into his lemonade 'with greasy fingers' and Johnson, in a rage, had flung it out of the window. He would have liked to have knocked the waiter down, but Boswell scooped him up and they walked, arm in arm, up the high street towards Boswell's home, only for some homeowner, leaning out from one of those high Edinburgh houses, to tip 'the evening effluvia' over them both. They arrived in disarray ('I smell you in the dark!' growled Johnson), and Mrs Boswell served tea to this huge, twitching, sodden and reeking stranger, where 'his conversation soon charmed her into a forgetfulness of his external appearance'. And the smell of human sewage.

We could linger for days in their company. Like Boswell, I spent a few foggy years as a student in Edinburgh (the fog was mostly mine), and I am amazed how little it has changed – the dark streets, the glowing pubs – but Johnson will not be denied:

'On the eighteenth of August we left Edinburgh, a city too well known to admit description.' Boswell counted his blessings. Like a dog jealously guarding a bone, he now had Johnson all to himself, and he said goodbye to his wife, who 'did not seem quite easy when we left her; but away we went!'

I am standing on the ruined walls of Urquhart Castle, on the northern banks of Loch Ness. It is mid-November, late in the short day, and the sun is hanging low over the loch in a sky the colour of last year's blackbird eggs. A chill, lazy wind is probing from the far-off mountains. Closer, the hills are purple and black, and – where the shoreline greets the steel-blue waters of the loch, and as the sun slips down the horizon – all of a sudden the lower slopes flare with a golden, tawny fire. I have whisky on my mind, naturally enough, but it's larch trees, I presume, and the last of their needle-leaves, breaking out into an autumn display, before the long Scottish winter claws them clean.

There are several tourists here, even at this time of the year. Almost 250 years ago, when Johnson and Boswell rode along the side of the loch, there were none: just them, their guides, some soldiers, and the remnants of a local population that had mostly decided, despite the trauma of upheaval, to leave. (Dr J, growling: 'No man willingly left his native country.') A boat called *The Jacobite* (I think – it is darkening by the minute) is picking up an orderly row of tourists from the green in front of the castle and taking them off to the next stop on their Highland tour. People have come from all around the globe to drink deep of the romance of wild, untamed Scotland: there are only about twenty of us left in the castle, but as I pass little groups I hear Chinese, Italian, Spanish and (I guess) Urdu being spoken. North American too, of course, because that's where so many of the Highlanders ended up – and now their descendants are back, bags stuffed with shortbread and tartan tam-o'-shanters from the gift shop, marvelling at the barren beauty of the place their ancestors were forced to leave. Johnson thought they would retain their customs in their new, fertile, alien land. But he thought many things, and despite his imperial proclamations he felt a deep pain that the clans were being disbanded: 'their military ardour is extinguished, their dignity of independence is depressed, their contempt of government subdued' and their 'language attacked on every side'. He needn't have worried about the Scots' contempt for government, but the Erse language was indeed almost entirely eviscerated, the local children forced into schools where only English was spoken, and that, at another time, contrary dog that he was, Johnson deemed a fine thing: 'It is the rude speech of a barbarous people, who had few thoughts to express.' It's a wonder no one tossed the old monster into the loch.

It is strange to think of Johnson and Boswell on horseback, especially Johnson, whom we tend to imagine rolling and lurching along the London streets, but apparently he was a confident horseman. Only once, descending a steep incline just north of here, did the guides have to seize the reins. But he was not as secure as he seemed. Soon afterwards, he threw an absolute hissy fit and threatened to turn for home when Boswell announced that he was going to ride ahead to prepare their evening reception. It took all of Boswell's skills to soothe him into continuing their journey.

Like any Highland visitor today, Johnson and Boswell were looking for wild landscapes and wilderness, but more importantly (certainly for Johnson), they wanted to meet with people whose customs, language and traditions were different to their own. They knew that time was running out. Between 1763 and 1775 twenty thousand Highlanders and Islanders emigrated, four thousand from Skye in just one year. In future, Johnson writes, 'a longer journey than to the Highlands must be taken by him whose curiosity pants for savage virtues and barbarous grandeur'. And then he roars: 'To hinder insurrection, by driving away the people, and to govern peaceably, by having no subjects, is an expedient that argues no great profundity of politicks ... It affords a legislator little self-applause to consider, that where there was formerly an insurrection, there is now a wilderness.'

Johnson may have thought that the Highlanders' lives were being improved with the rule of law, and the building of roads and schools, and the disarming of the clans, but he was disgusted by the human cost. He was just in time to witness colonialism this close to home – more than once he compares the Highlanders to Native Americans. And so, if you ever do find yourself marvelling at the scoured beauty of the Scottish landscape, consider Dr Johnson. In the end, he is cynical: 'They are now acquainted with money, and the possibility of gain will by degrees make them industrious.' As for Boswell, we can assume that he was more interested in showing off his famous and eccentric friend to his contacts in the Scottish nobility than fretting about emigration.

I think Johnson's despair about Scotland's battered and drained land is one reason why he spends so much time complaining about the remarkable lack of trees on their route. According to Boswell, this got him into trouble with the Scots, and Boswell smooths over the matter by explaining that there are indeed very few trees in the *east* of the country, which is where they travelled first from Edinburgh, via St Andrews, Aberdeen and Inverness, but the *west* is very different. In any case, it becomes an obsession with Johnson and the subject crops up throughout *Journey to the Western Isles*. 'From the bank of the Tweed to St Andrews I had never seen a single tree, which I did not believe to have grown up far within the present century … [slow rumble.] A tree might be a show in Scotland as a horse in Venice.'

He was quick to point out that the lack of trees and forests was not Scotland's natural state. Everywhere they rode through the deforested land they saw the stumps and roots of ancient trees. For many years, people have taken this as confirmation that up until the early eighteenth century much of Scotland was covered in trees. Now, we are not so sure. The stumps Johnson was seeing may well have emerged, hundreds of years old but perfectly preserved, from a peat bog. What we can say is that the Great Caledonian Forest had at one time covered most of the land north of the River Clyde and west of the River Tay, or so said Pliny the Elder, with a shiver of Roman disdain, and in the early eighteenth century it still spread over a much larger area than it does today. But it is also likely that most of it had been destroyed long before, through grazing and the never-ending incursions of humanity.

Even so, after the Battle of Culloden in 1746, some of the English victors, and their Scottish allies, seem to have enjoyed a stampede for the last of Scotland's timber. No attempt was made to manage or stagger the destruction, or to replace what was being taken out with new plantings. Forests of pine and oak were floated down the lochs and shipped off to England. If, today, you are looking for truly ancient forest in Scotland, it has to appear in the records before the year 1750. That date, just four years after Culloden, is significant. In England and Wales it is the year 1600. Before then, in all three countries, no one seems to have felt the need to plant new woods. But if a wood in Scotland can be traced back to before the year 1750, it has probably been flourishing since the last Ice Age.

As they plodded along the shores of Loch Ness, Johnson gazed at the 'limpid waters', the 'high and steep rocks shaded with birch' and the rocks 'towering in horrid nakedness'. He's clearly itching for a fight, because he picks one with Boethius, the sixth-century philosopher, who had written that Loch Ness was twelve miles across. It's not, Johnson harrumphed. Boswell was enjoying himself, the scene 'as agreeably wild as could be desired'.

They stopped at the hut of 'an old looking woman' (says Boswell, who thought Johnson might find it amusing to pay her a visit). The hut was primitive ('a wretched little hovel of earth only'), its only window closed up with a slab of turf. Johnson found that smoke from the fire escaped from a hole in the roof, but 'not directly over the fire, lest the rain should extinguish it'. The woman may have looked old, but she had five young children (the eldest was thirteen) and an eighty-year-old husband out working in the hills. She gave them whisky and Johnson mused on 'the old laws of hospitality' that had not yet broken down in this remote place. He probably thought he was back in the days of Homer. Boswell, meanwhile, got into the woman's bedroom, ignoring her protests, and found that there was a 'kind of bedstead of wood with heath upon it by way of bed'. They gave the woman money, and then they left, chuckling over her 'ludicrous coquetry' (Boswell), ribbing each other over who might have alarmed her more. As others have said, she must have been terrified: an English officer had committed murder and rape in this same hut a few years earlier. I presume she waved her visitors off with relief, shouting prayers, in Erse, at their departing backs.

I head further north the next morning. I am childishly thrilled to see Highland cattle and then, around a misty bend, mooching in a corner of a field, Shetland ponies. More heather and bog. Dark plantations of pine. Sheep drifting idiotically on the empty road. The beauty – and the dizzying air – dances through the open car windows. It is something other than alpine, although that is the only reference I have. I wish, not for the first time on this trip, that I had someone to share it with. Everyone I am following did, except for Jack Priestley, and he had many people to meet, and if he didn't he would become maudlin or start lashing out at the ugliness of unfamiliar cities and the grotesque unfairness of everything. Boswell or Johnson would never have come this far alone.

Still, I am travelling to meet Mick from the organization Trees for Life. He has said he'll be waiting for me in his van in the car park at Cannich. We are going to be driving up to areas they've been planting on Forestry Commission land in Glen Affric, and the pockmarked road is no place for my cossetted city car.

Trees for Life was founded in 1989 by a man called Alan Watson Featherstone, who has dedicated his life (until very recently – he is now photographing monkey puzzle trees in Chile or something) and given all he can to bringing back the butchered and almost extinct Great Caledonian Forest. He wants to restore the wilderness to Scotland. We all have a lot to thank him for, as well as the thousands of volunteers who have turned out over the past thirty years to work on fencing, to remove non-native trees and to plant Scots pine, birch, holly, rowan, alder and other indigenous species. Where they think they can, they just let nature go her own way – although that is not always as easy as you might imagine, in a deer-ravaged landscape with no wolves to keep them at bay.

I have broken my own rule and briefly left Johnson and Boswell riding further to the west, but I think Johnson would allow me the detour, given his new-found obsession with trees. Boswell will do as he's told. Mick has three others with him waiting in the van, Roy and Howard (who have been volunteering for years) and Fitch, a tall young Chinese man from Guangzhou. There is anticipation in the air. 'Have you ever been to Glen Affric?' someone asks and when I say 'no', there's a collective 'ah …' (although not from Fitch, who is also on his first trip) and looks are exchanged that say, well, just get ready, because what you are about to see is something beyond the ordinary. Howard puts an anxious hand on my shoulder. 'You're not going to write about this place, are you?' And I say, 'Don't worry', laughing, 'I hardly think what I write will change a thing,' which of course is true, but I can't help feeling later (here, now) that even so I should just shut up, or lie, and pretend that there's not a lot that's special about Glen Affric (just move along, nothing to see here, Loch Ness is the place – you'll find tea shops), but I have also come to believe that we cannot fence off our last few remaining places of wild beauty and hope that they will remain hidden or ignored or immune to the spread of human need and the accelerating churn of consumption. They may, of course. In Sam Johnson's short fable *Rasselas*, a prince and his companions are suffocating in a glut of perfection, their every need anticipated and fulfilled, and so they escape from their Happy Valley. 'I have already enjoyed too much', says the prince; 'give me something to *desire*.' All they find is misery and so they go back and pull up the drawbridge. But that's not an option for us – and anyway the real message from Johnson, the man who claimed to hate change, is right here: 'Do not suffer life to stagnate; it will grow muddy for want of motion: commit yourself again to the current of the world.'

Almost every conservationist will now say that the only way to ensure any wilderness survives is to expose as many people as possible, especially the young, to its wonders. Why else would anyone care? Or rouse themselves to fight? Which is all very well in theory (and I agree – or I want to), but imagine ranks of coaches drawn up, here, by the pines and the birch, the fallen rocks and the heather, the ice-sparkle of the peat-dark rivers, and on these lonely one-track roads, among the waterfalls and the eagles.

So, what else can I say? Glen Affric is one of the most beautiful places I have ever visited. Our van meanders and thumps over the potholes towards the Trees for Life bothy, where we are going to stay the night, and every few yards someone gives a shout and Mick stops the van and Howard or Roy leaps out and decapitates a rogue lodgepole pine (an unwelcome, non-native species, spread here from one of the Forestry Commission plantations – it grows fast and in the early years can quickly overwhelm the slower-growing, native Scots pines). At one point we haul up by the side of the road and spread out across the valley. I have been given gloves and some loppers and told to hunt down any lodgepoles, but to everyone's relief there are very few here. Anyway, it is easy to become distracted by the ancient Scots pines and ragged clumps of juniper and the reindeer moss and heathers (the ground is the colour of faded tartan), and the onrush of young downy birch, bristling with hope, shielded behind fencing from the ravages of the insatiable deer. In one heart-stopping moment a family of partridges crosses my path in single file. The other side of the valley is devoid of trees (Sam Johnson is growling), the soil bare to the rock, but here on these slopes we are walking among groves of Scots pines, and single veteran survivors of the Caledonian Forest, especially where the ground tumbles steeply, but also, spreading back to where the van is parked, there are dozens, perhaps thousands, of young trees, no more than knee- or ankle-high, almost all self-seeded, a miniature forest of the future.

I haven't found a single lodgepole pine, but they are hard to differentiate from Scots pines when young (you can snap their less fibrous needles – or is it the other way round?) and anyway I was told earlier how one of the Trees for Life volunteers had one year proudly destroyed several Scots pines before anyone was able to stop him and I don't want to be added to their annals of shame

as the Man Who Killed All The Trees. The others are nowhere
to be seen. That's one of the reasons we are here, of course – to
get away from other people. In the distance I see a great shaking
in a grove and a thirty-foot lodgepole pine comes crashing to the
ground. Roy emerges with needles in his woolly hat and beard
and a look of joy on his face.

We are at the outer reaches of the western range of the
Scots pine, which is not exclusively Scottish at all, but spreads
all the way across northern Eurasia. To the west of here it is too
damp for the pines and (or so the books tell us) what you should
find instead are birch and then oak forests. In reality, it's mostly
bare mountains and moors and planted blocks of Sitka spruce
and lodgepole pine. For some years now, Forestry Commission
Scotland has been working with Trees for Life – and on its own –
to re-establish native species, and open up its woods to the rest of
us, so it does seem as though things are changing for the better.
It's just that, at this rate, it's going to take many long centuries to
reforest the Scottish Highlands, unless there's an unprecedented
surge of rewilding. Also, someone is going to have to do something about the deer. And especially the grouse moors, which are
kept free from trees (they are burned) so that the birds can thrive
in sufficient numbers to give passing pleasure to the men with
guns. What do we want with this land? And who should decide?
Unless I happen to be addressing one of the very few aristocrats,
charities or traceless overseas companies who own the vast bulk
of Scotland's Highlands, I'm afraid it's not you.

A single prop plane putters overhead. *The Thirty-Nine Steps*!
We are in an empty place, a John Buchan land of fugitives and
pheasant shoots, musty tweed and the prince across the water,
eagles clasping crags with crooked hands, the Monarch of the
Glen, and Queen Victoria strolling along a brook with her kilted
Mr Brown at the ready. Empty, though. The last wolf in Scotland

was shot not long before Johnson and Boswell got here – rumours
of lone wolves lingered on – and the brown bear and the lynx were
exterminated much earlier. Here's Johnson: 'All the beasts of the
chase would have been lost long ago in countries well inhabited,
had they not been preserved by laws for the pleasure of the rich.'
So maybe we don't need access for all; and it doesn't matter if
we enthuse future generations to love and cherish someone else's
land; and perhaps it's the rich in their fenced Happy Valleys who
are the best or indeed the only hope for preserving and restoring
the glories of the Scottish wild. They certainly seem to think so.
There's a hunting lodge nearby, looking trim and well-tended. And
there are a few landowners in Scotland who are working hard to
bring back the forest, and fill it with lynx, beaver and boar. Even
wolves, some of them, if they ever get permission from a nervous
government. Should we just let them seal themselves off (assuming
we even have the choice), and leave them to their schemes? Who's
to know what they or their successors might do next? Scotland's
private land is concentrated in fewer hands than anywhere else
in the developed world. Wouldn't it be wiser to let more people
have a say? And where does this leave the extraordinary work of
the volunteers for Trees for Life?

One thing I do know: the idea of the rich and powerful being
the best stewards of the land would make me feel less queasy if we
weren't looking down the valley towards the ruined remnants of
yet another abandoned hamlet. People lived here once. Perhaps
they still did, when Johnson and Boswell were riding to the south.
It cannot have been easy, but they fished in the river, and worked
their land, and drove their cattle, and managed the trees for timber,
and then, like so many others, they were dispossessed by bailiffs or
troops, poverty and rampaging rents. It is a beautiful place, Glen
Affric, and full of wonder and hope, but it makes for an easier
time if you keep your mind fixed in the present.

The bothy sits at the head of the valley with a distant backdrop of snow-capped mountains and, closer by, a flourishing thirty-year-old copse of birch and Scots pine. It's the first ever Trees for Life planting. There's a generator for electricity and water is drawn from the ice-cold burn. The nights are long this far north and we sit down to eat early, around a small table, with a wood fire burning, and candlelight, and a chill wind drawing us close.

Mick tells us about deer stalking. They employ a stalker on their Dundreggan estate, over the mountain, along with a couple of locals to help out, one of them ex-Army, but it's not easy. The deer are nervous, and whole days can be lost in the fog. Without any wolves, what is to keep the deer in check? There's a portrait of a wolf on the wall, following me with feral eyes. Everyone here has seen the short film of what happened in Yellowstone Park when wolves were reintroduced. How the deer were kept on the move. The wildflowers and the trees and the butterflies flared into life, the river changed course and the fish flowed back. Could that happen here? Do we owe the wolf that? And the boar, beaver, lynx and all the other creatures we have driven from this land. What have we lost? Mick is just back from the National Parks of North America, where people crowd the lay-bys and jostle for a view of a grizzly or a wolf pack. The parks are too busy, where once they were not busy enough – or that's what someone in the US government decided and they launched an advertising campaign and now look: you cannot escape the tailbacks of cars and motorhomes. I hear that to the east of here there are many eastern Europeans working in the supermarkets' organic carrot fields – and we've just picked up a packet in the local shop for only £1. Just think what people were paid, all along the chain, to get that onto our table. Mick says he wants to see what it's like, working in those fields, being towed in a trailer behind a tractor, leaning over the back, five of you, in a row, weeding the

carrots, up and down the fields, all day long – and here they are,
£1 per bag. What is the value of things? This is a plate of *food*.
Surely it's worth more than a few seconds' worth of bollocky
talk from some management consultant? Let them try pulling
carrots, or stalking deer. And so back to the wolves. The lynx
and the pine marten. Don't we need them in our lives again?
And the raptors – the hen harrier and the golden eagle – they
are being poisoned and shot (or so it is said) by the men who
work on the grouse moors, and so are the beautiful mountain
hares, in their hundreds, just to keep the moors free and the food
bountiful for the game birds. It's subsidized slaughter. But the
landowning lobby is strong. I'd be hitting the whisky by now if I'd
remembered to bring any. At least my smoking days are behind
me. What is wrong with people? And the Forestry Commission,
which hosed millions in public funds over these hills, planting
trees that no one could ever use (there are no roads to get them
out), and no one ever wanted, spending even more getting rid of
them. Exasperation, strangely affectionate, settles on the table. We
have all been here before. Except for Fitch, who smiles and now
tells us he studied fashion design in Guangzhou, and has been
working for a year with autistic children in Ireland, and soon he
is heading back to China, where his Scottish girlfriend will teach
English and he – what? – he doesn't know. In our little hut in
the wilderness we offer up advice by candlelight. The wonder
of it. But soon we are back on national parks, Scottish this time,
and destructive road schemes which make almost no allowance
for wildlife, and housing developers who buy up land in the
parks (which surely should be protected) and who never give up
on their plans, because even if they don't get approval the first
time, they just poison the land, or plough it up, or let it rot, and
then they come back again. They'll get there in the end. They
almost always do. The pressure is all one way. 'But', someone

says, with pain in their voice, someone who would really like an answer, 'but', I say, with surprising naivety, 'they know what they are doing is wrong, destroying irreplaceable ancient forests and driving rare species to extinction, when they could just as easily be building somewhere else. And still they press on. Why?!' But there is of course no answer, or no good answer, although we all know that something has to change, and we have to find a way to put a value on things that are currently regarded as worthless, or taken for granted, because value is not a question of money, and what really matters in life (our human community, food, clean air, water, shelter, friendship, love – just say it: the impossible but undeniable interconnectedness of every living thing, and perhaps even more than that, the rocks and rivers and mountains and stars), none of that counts for anything in a company balance sheet. We just don't care enough about any of the important stuff until we need it. And it's only at times like this, away, finally away from the daily clatter, that we catch hold of what we are missing (although it is slippery) and that in fact is what someone – Howard? Roy? – is saying right now, that people, the volunteers and the staff, they all come here for the warmth of the community. And isn't that something? Even troubling? We come here, to the wilderness, far from everything and everyone we know, to find friendship and simple human connection. Why is it so hard to find at home? And I wonder if the people who want to be part of this – all of us, and countless others – will manage to make their way here, or some place just like it, one way or another. Is that what a community is? A nation? It is always and ever the idea that matters. Even if, as Norman MacCaig once said, with his Edinburgh purr, and I hope we can all agree, 'I hate a man who calls his country his.'

Anyway, I don't suppose Boswell would have bothered to lift up his pen, but at least I was on hand.

'I'll have a large Talisker, please.' The barman pours, and winks, and whisky slurps merrily over the measure and into the glass. I have found my way to a snug bar in the port of Portree in the east of the Isle of Skye. Johnson and Boswell had been brought here in a large boat, with eight oars, conveyed by Lord Raasay from his own island of Raasay, along with Mr Malcolm McCleod, Mr Donald McQueen, Dr Macleod 'and some others'. They had 'a most pleasant sail between Rasay and Skye and passed by a cave', Boswell tells us, 'where Martin says fowls were caught by lighting fire to the mouth of it. Malcolm remembers this. But it is not now practised, as few fowls come into it.' And who can blame them? Johnson talked 'of death', of course. 'There is no rational principle by which a man can die contented, but a trust in the mercy of God, through the merits of Jesus Christ.' Everyone listened to this Sunday sermon on the calm flat waters of the channel with great satisfaction.

They had travelled up from Fort Augustus on Loch Ness, via Glensheal and the west coast at Glenelg, and so across to Skye, over to Raasay, and back again. There had been a fair bit of bickering and pontificating. Great God! Look at that *immense* mountain, said Boswell. 'No: it is no more than a considerable protuberance', replies Johnson. 'But look at *that* mountain, shaped like a cone,' says Boswell. 'No, sir ... it is indeed pointed at the top, but one side is larger than the other.' And so on. They were both in clover.

When they arrived at the harbour in Portree, Johnson found that 'a ship lay waiting to dispeople Sky, by carrying the natives away to America'. It was the *Nestor* and Johnson refused to go on board, but Boswell had a good look round and found a little library and a cabin for the captain that was 'commodious, and even elegant'. There is no mention of the sleeping quarters of the emigrants. Boswell was told that only last year most people had so hated the idea of leaving that 'they tore the grass with their teeth', but now 'there was not a tear shed ... This indifference is a mortal sign for the country.' Johnson rumbled through the reasons (skyrocketing rents, oppression, poverty, the dismantling of the Highlanders' culture and traditions), but he still thought 'a man of any intellectual enjoyment will not easily go and immerse himself and his posterity for ages in barbarism'.

Skye and the Highlands weren't just emptied by emigration: in their turn these colonized peoples provided a turbo-boost to the British Empire. Here's the historian A. M. Mackenzie: 'In the forty years after 1797, *Skye alone* gave the British Army 21 Lieutenant-Generals and Major-Generals, 48 Lieutenant-Colonels, 600 Majors, Captains and Subalterns, and 10,000 private soldiers.' You would not think there had ever been enough people living on Skye to supply such an extraordinary glut of soldiery, but reading Johnson and Boswell's accounts you can see that despite their tales of emigration, the islands were full and *busy* – and so much more so than they are today. Even in 1841 there were almost 50,000 people living on Skye, Islay and Mull. Today Skye has a population of just over 10,000. The migrations that so distressed Boswell and Johnson intensified in the century after their visit.

Population is on my mind as I sip Talisker in the Portree pub. It (or rather the perils of depopulation) obsessed Johnson as much as the absence of trees. Both were signs of a damaged land. Most developed nations have the same worries today. South Korea, Japan, Russia, Italy ... their governments agonize over falling birth rates and ageing populations. Johnson would understand, but he came from a time when a nation's wealth was measured by the number of its people, and the size of its army, and the workers in its fields. I'm just happy to be watching Champions

League football in a drowsy bar with a couple of Frenchmen (it's Lyon against Manchester City tonight), pleased not to be in London (I'm tired of it – whatever Dr Johnson may say), and far away from the self-proclaimed centre of things. By the time my third overpoured Talisker has arrived, I have decided that a falling population is a good thing. Bring on the AI. Wasn't that the point? To set us free. Let the robots weed the carrots. Give a warm welcome to the migrants (emigrants and immigrants, us and them) fleeing uninhabitable lands. The remaining humans will drink whisky and watch football and – because this is the real point – stop defiling the planet and slaughtering its creatures. We need to take up less room.

By this stage of the night Johnson would have been in full voice (on one occasion with a local lassie bouncing on his knee), joining in with a song or declaiming aphorisms to the bewildered islanders. He wasn't a drinker, although he had been when younger and he well knew he couldn't go there again. Boswell, though, liked to drink. Two weeks after landing in Portree he got into 'a riot' with some lads and crept into his bed at five. Johnson was in the room the next morning. '"Sir," said I, "they kept me up." He answered, "No, you kept them up, you drunken dog."' Kingsley would be interested to hear that Boswell's host poured him a tumbler of brandy, 'which I found an effectual cure for my head-ach'.

From Portree, Boswell and Johnson headed around Skye. Johnson even slept the night in the bed that Bonnie Prince Charlie had used when he was fleeing the English soldiers, although he claimed not to have been impressed. Perhaps he was still hiding his Jacobite sympathies. They met Flora MacDonald, the young woman who had led the prince to safety by dressing him as her maid. They moved into Dunvegan Castle, with Lady Macleod, and Johnson decided the comfort and company was much more to his taste. But after two weeks, he suddenly wanted to get home

('I want to be on the main land, and go on with existence. This is a waste of life'). But the September, and then the October, weather was against them, and they had to wait for the sea passage to be safe.

Skye can be bleak, it is true. There are still very few trees, even though Trees for Life and Forestry Commission Scotland have both been here, but the island holds an ancient, raw beauty, changing its colour and shape by the hour. The morning after my night in the Portree pub it is brown and waterlogged (perhaps its natural state), with heather feathering the low flat hills. They look like they've had their tops removed, conical even, although Johnson would no doubt beg to differ. I am driving down the west coast of the island, tracking my quarry. They stopped in Ullinish, so I follow them there, my car rocking and bucking in a tormented wind, hoping to drink coffee in a place they once loitered, but the small, eighteenth-century Country Lodge seems to have closed for the season, if not for ever.

I decide to walk towards the sea. There is a tiny island here that is accessible only at low tide and I want to stand on its furthest point and look out, all the way to America, but the wind is now so strong that it is almost impossible to make headway. I struggle alone, head down, across a sedgy plain. There's a wooden sign: 'Dogs will be shot'. 'What! Is it you, you dogs?' roared Johnson out of the window of his home late one night, in his nightclothes, when two of his friends turned up, reeling drunk, unable to let the evening end. 'I'll have a frisk with you.' And out and on they went, long ago, into the dark London night.

A great green sea is piling onto the beaches to my left. I hide behind some gorse bushes and watch the tops of molehills being whipped off and the black earth flung to the west. There is a slather of human detritus – plastic bottles, bags and sheets, buoys, nets, orange ropes – smeared all over the high tide mark, with the heavy waves straining to reach further, beyond, almost airborne in the driving wind. The ground behind the gorse bushes feels like it is losing its shape.

Is this wild enough? To the north and the west there are low islands in a racing, turquoise sea, like the farthest reaches of a fabled land. At the headland, the tide is high, and I cannot walk onto the island. I don't mind. It is sheltered here, lying on my back in the soft brown grass, out of the wind, looking up to torn clouds, a falling gull, an innocent blue sky. Have I come far enough? It doesn't matter. The route has turned south and towards home.

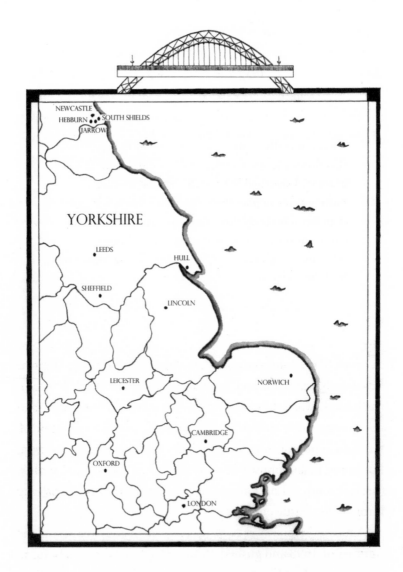

J. B. Priestley & Beryl Bainbridge,
Tyneside to Lincoln and London, 1933 and 1983

TEN

Fog on the Tyne

'I was not really completing the journey but suddenly
abandoning it, giving it up as a bad job. In the original
itinerary I sketched for myself – in that first idiotic
flush, when you plan things for a self that is not you
at all but somebody three times as strong, energetic,
conscientious, determined – there were hopeful
references to places like Newmarket, Cambridge, Bury
St. Edmunds, Ipswich, Colchester ...'

J. B. PRIESTLEY, *ENGLISH JOURNEY*

From Skye, Johnson and Boswell made their way back to
Edinburgh, via Mull and Iona and Boswell's father's house in
Auchinleck, where Johnson and the Whiggish old judge managed
not to argue for at least three days, until there was an eruption of
Krakatoan proportions, which left Boswell shaken and Johnson,
I presume, frisky. Johnson left Boswell in Edinburgh and caught a
carriage south to London and his beloved Hester Thrale, passing
through Newcastle en route.

Almost everyone loves Newcastle. Celia Fiennes was here in the
summer of 1698 and gushed: 'It's a noble town tho' in a bottom,
it most resembles London of any place in England, its buildings
lofty and large of brick mostly or stone.' She stood on a hill on the
outskirts and watched 'an abundance' of little carriages, drawn
by pairs of horses and oxen, taking coal down to barges on the
Tyne. The coal, she said, was 'black and shineing', which showed
its goodness, and 'this country all about is full of this Coale the

sulpher of it taints the aire and it smells strongly to strangers'. The land was covered with coal pits in every direction, the wealth of the city on show.

Celia lingered in the market in the heat of the day and picked up some bargains. 'I saw one buy a quarter of lamb for 8 pence and 2 pence a piece good large poultry.' There were leather, woollen and linen garments for sale, 'and all sorts of stands for baubles'. But she thought the cheese indifferent ('black on the outside … soft sower things'). She went to the Barber Surgeons' Hall, where she examined two skeletons. The flesh had been boiled from the bones of one of them, which had then been patched together with what was left of the dried ligaments. She was also able to view the skin of a man that had been stripped from his body (after he was dead, she clarifies) and stuffed, although she doesn't say with what. 'It look'd and felt,' she wrote, 'like a sort of parchment.' She lived in days when barbers – of which Newcastle still has a superfluity – doubled up as surgeons. They must have had strong stomachs, our ancestors, with death so present and visible.

Beryl Bainbridge was here, three hundred years later, also enjoying herself. 'There's a very festive atmosphere in Newcastle. I'm beginning to think I like it better than Liverpool,' she wrote. She went shopping in the Eldon Square centre and watched as thousands and thousands of young people loaded up with hats, shoes, trousers, jackets, boots 'and shiny belts and handbags'. She roamed through the 'miracle parlours of Top Shop' (she loved a good Top Shop) and she couldn't understand why, in 1983, when the region was being mauled by recession and unemployment was brutalizing local families, there was so much money about. People were rushing the shops with wads of fivers in their hands.

This question also bothered Jack Priestley, who was here in 1933, when there was an even more ferocious recession scouring the city and its shipyards. The centre looked 'busy and quite prosperous', he found. But Jack was also running a fever for the week he was here, and was drenching himself with a patent medicine, concocted by his doctor, mainly featuring Belladonna (from the deadly nightshade plant), which we now know should be taken sparingly, and certainly not with alcohol (Jack …), and this 'more than usually disgusting bit of autobiography' explains why things 'looked very queer indeed and were a little larger and wilder' than usual. Basically, Jack was tripping the entire time he was on Tyneside. He was also, being Jack, grumpily irritated by the Geordie accent ('the most barbarous, monotonous and irritating twang … The constant "Ay-ee, yer b—" of the men's talk and the never-ending "hinnying" of the women …'). Jack liked local accents, in theory, but he drew a line around the north-east, and that – along with the cold and the drugs – clouded his experiences. But it's also true that once he'd seen what he'd come to see, and visited Gateshead and North and South Shields, and Jarrow and Hebburn, he never once felt sorry for himself again. Not because of the poverty – or not just – but because there is 'something bracing about the Tyne'.

The Tyne and Wear Metro system was opened by the Queen in 1981 (it was Britain's first light railway system), but Beryl almost didn't take it because there was no smoking allowed on the trains and not even – the horror – on the platforms. If it's so efficient and modern, she moaned, why couldn't they afford to put in some ashtrays and air filters? My days of addiction are once again safely behind me (I may have mentioned), so I'm taking the short journey on a half-full and sparkling train from Newcastle central station to Jarrow. We skirt Gateshead ('the whole town appeared to have been carefully planned by an enemy of the human race,' Jack bleared, to vast and enduring controversy once his book was published) and trundle through Felling and Hebburn. I am surprised to see (and I blame Jack for this, as do many others) that

Hebburn in particular looks rather fetching on this fine December morning. There are horses browsing in fields, red berries gleaming on the trees and in the hedgerows, and conservatories glittering in trim back gardens under a low, bleached-yellow sun. We pass banks of allotments, vegetables thriving in the mud, Irish, English and even US flags flying from the tops of countless little sheds. No Unionists here. There's a sign in their midst: 'Under New Management'. Over and beyond, down by the Tyne, the cranes are leaning into another working day.

Jack was in Jarrow only three years before the Jarrow March (or 'Crusade' as it was once known), when 200 local men set off to walk to London in October 1936, carrying 11,000 signatures pleading for help from the government. At the time, unemployment in the area was running at seventy percent. The only employer in town, Palmers Shipyard, had closed in 1934. Jack arrived just in time to see it lying idle, the surrounding area derelict. 'Jarrow is dead', wrote Jack, and 'the whole town looked as though it had entered a perpetual penniless bleak Sabbath.' It was, he said, 'even at its best, when everybody was working, a mean little conglomeration of narrow monotonous streets of stunted and ugly houses'. At the end of October 1936, when the marchers reached London after a month on the road, their local Labour MP, Ellen Wilkinson, said that the town wasn't just dead, it had been 'murdered' by bosses and government ministers. The petition was ignored, of course, but things did happen. After the Second World War, the Welfare State was born, its conception influenced, some said, by newsreel images of the Jarrow Crusaders. And almost forty years after that, Beryl found the town transformed, its shabby buildings razed to the ground, 'wiping away buildings and traditions and values in the twinkling of an eye'. But who would have thought, she wondered, that after decades of upheaval, nothing would really have changed at all, amounting 'in the end to no more than a modern version of that earlier, bleak Sabbath of a hole, with a shopping precinct and a dole-office called by another name … the grandchildren of its penniless generation supported by the state'.

Well, Jack really must have seen Jarrow at its grim worst – and anyway he could blame his fever drugs – but I'm not sure what to say about Beryl. Jarrow today is a compact place of low-rise housing, big skies, plenty of space, solar panels on the roofs, business parks, warehouses and vans. There's almost nothing dating back to the 1930s, other than the Town Hall, a huddle of larger houses near the centre of town and an old red-brick rectory, opposite a large car park that services the cut-price shops. Even if the rubble has gone, there's not much money around, just a few people out shopping. When Jack was here, 'there were men hanging about, not scores of them but hundreds and thousands'.

I wander about and meet a postman, who shouts a cheery 'good morning', before pushing through a low white wicket gate and striding up a well-mown front garden with a handful of letters. There's no one else to talk to. Unemployment levels are still higher here than the national average, but nothing like the catastrophic levels of the 1930s. Even so, I don't know where everyone is. It's just me and the seagulls as I wander around, checking out the Christmas decorations in the windows and the occasional statue in the gardens. All too soon, I'm at the edge of town, in a patchwork of streets named after the great poets: Shakespeare, Milton, Spenser.

> Sleep after Toil, Port after stormy Seas,
> Ease after War, Death after Life, does greatly please.

It is true. The place feels numb. Hollowed out. Slowed down. At rest after the storm. But what do I know? The streets are eerie and there's no one to talk to.

Jarrow is looped by a larger road, enfolding a 20mph residential zone. In the east the street names become ecclesiastical (Priory Road, Canon Grove, Hope Street), reflecting the proximity of Jarrow Hall and the ruins of the monastery that was once the home of the Venerable Bede, the seventh-century monk, theologian and historian. So, because I'm starting to feel like a fraud, traipsing around Jarrow for an hour or three and expecting to find someone to interview or something of note to say, dropping in and breezing out like some pie-eyed day tripper, I walk to the Hall, following a trail of very small polished silver crosses in the pavement, and settle into the café where I lunch on curried parsnip soup and a sublime cheese scone in surroundings of elegant simplicity. Jarrow, eh? It is nothing like anything you would expect.

It is said that Bede invented the footnote.* He was also the first person to describe the English people as a nation. I am very aware, sitting at my ease in this sumptuous café, in a house that would be more suited to a Jane Austen serialization, staring out of the windows at the Medieval Herb Garden, that I may have abandoned my tour of Jarrow town centre rather too quickly. Jack was attacked for his descriptions of Jarrow (and Gateshead, Hebburn, South Shields …), as was Beryl. The fact that they had both travelled from London to hand down their criticisms fuelled the resentment, even if Jack was from Bradford and Beryl a reluctant Liverpudlian. (And I am originally from the wooded badlands of the Kent–Sussex borders.) But I'm as certain as I can be that they described what they saw. Jarrow was scorched by Depression and Recession, and then abandoned. There was no Cadbury here: Charles Palmer seems to have had no thought or

---

* This is a joke I found on a sign near Jarrow Hall. Bede invented the footnote, we are told in a footnote. OK, it's a rather niche joke, but it resonates merrily with the title of this book.

concern for the workers who built his ships. The housing was the cheapest that could be got away with. The only amenities were those the people provided for themselves. Jack didn't think for a minute that the men and women of Jarrow were responsible for the hellhole they found themselves in. 'A stranger from a distant civilization ... would never believe us if we told him that in theory this town was as good as any other and that its inhabitants were not criminals but citizens with votes.' Beryl blamed Mrs Thatcher for the sorry mess. And Jack reserved his fury for London – the City and Westminster and Fleet Street – where people traded in luxury, and had no idea where their money came from, or what it was like outside their few gilded square miles. And he raged at those who were urging a return to:

> sturdy Victorian individualism ... I felt like calling back a few of these sturdy individualists simply to rub their noses in the nasty mess they had made. Who gave them leave to turn this island into their ashpit? They may or may not have left us their money, but they have certainly left us their muck.

The three-mile walk from Jarrow to South Shields should be pleasant, once they stop hammering at the roads and pavements and rebuilding the underpasses. There's a mix of new industry, or activity of some kind, and the mouldering detritus of the old. Early in my walk I pass tiny Jarrow Bridge, visible from the side of its newer replacement. It was built in the early eighteenth century and used by Johnson, perhaps, on his way back to London, and widened a hundred years later to accommodate the burgeoning industrial traffic. This was just after the opening ceremony for the Jarrow Colliery, when a crowd of 10,000 had watched an artillery display and the colliery's owner had laid the foundation stones for a hospital, a school, a seminary for young girls and a 'fever-house'. There must have been so much hope floating up into the clean air. The dark sluggish ooze I am now looking down at is the River Don. It is flowing quietly, I'm happy to report, perhaps enjoying a moment of pastoral bliss before it emerges into the chemical soup of the Tyne basin and off into our harried seas.

The skies look huge in this southern loop of the Tyne, as it curves round to the mouth of the estuary. I roam across a dual carriageway, and then back again, looking for a pavement. The traffic is constant, set-faced men and women, alone in their cars. I am excited to see I have wandered into 'Catherine Cookson Country', or so it says on a decorative oval plaque, behind a wooden fence, just to the side of the blustery road, next to a low iron bridge, alone in a small island of litter and brambles and lacklustre pine trees. She was born nearby in 1906 – younger than Jack – and headed south to marry a Sussex schoolteacher, but most of her novels are set in the area, although (and I'm no expert) I have a feeling that any of her many avid fans, looking to recreate the northern world she conjured, would be bewildered by what they find here today, what with the lines of dirty orange traffic cones and temporary iron fencing and the rumble and wail of the lorries and the torn plastic bags clinging to the sides of the street lights. Later in the day I find myself reading her short poem, 'Another Face of My Land', with its evocation of the North's 'hidden valleys', 'deep lakes', 'mountain shadows' and the 'sheer clear light' of the infinite skies, and I can understand why she left Sussex after a few years and returned home.*

---

* I could get used to these footnotes.

I just thought I should add, for clarity, because of course some people are inclined to *sneer* at any author with *vast* sales, that I *like* this poem, even if her use of 'homesteads' is undeniably hokey.

This short interlude on a grey dual carriageway brings me to
South Shields, and things start to look up again. I'm in another
area of low modern housing, with familiar displays of well-
trimmed front lawns, but there's more money here than in Jarrow.
It feels like the edge of countryside, even though the port is just
around the corner. I pass a string of young planted saplings, decorated with Christmas lights. There are dog walkers, hedgerows
(and more deep red berries), a low winter sun and long shadows.
A mother walks by, singing to her baby. There are gulls in the
silvery blue air and, at the far end of a strip of grass, two magpies
(joy!) hopping in unison down a narrow path towards a small park.
And then more, even newer houses, prettily done (if only they'd
thought to add some solar panels to the roofs), and before long I'm
in the centre of South Shields on its busy but rumpled high street.

I never make it to the beach and famous seaside resort, as I had
planned (and it was huge in Jack's day, maybe not so much in
Beryl's), because I become distracted by the South Shields Museum
& Art Gallery. You'll find it in an early Victorian building on the
high street and on the day I visited (once I had torn myself away
from the stuffed baby alligator and lion and monkey, and the old
scale models of sailing ships, and the actual gibbet in which the
wrong man was tarred and hanged, and the history of the local
collieries – and the boats that served them – and pipes and bottles
and toys and spoons and fossils and cases of joyous tat), I found,
on the first floor, an exhibition about South Shields in the wars
and in particular the role of women in the First World War.

I can sympathize with Beryl ('at the mention of the phrase "art
gallery" my heart had sunk. I am sick to death of art'), even though
she ended up having a marvellous time in the Jarrow museum
and art gallery. Local museums are the best. And also, as Beryl
said, there's something very disturbing about photographs from
the past. It is unsettling to see whole lives, entire eras, reduced to

displays in a glass cabinet case (or a book, I'm starting to think). But the women on show here, in photographs, letters and mementoes, working in the factories and the fields, come bursting to life. There's also a photo of Ferdinand Foch, the French general, talking to a large crowd in 1919, under a stone cross, when he said, with awful prescience: 'This is not a peace. It is an armistice for twenty years.' Jack would have read it and wept.

I do wonder about our obsession with the wars of the first half of the twentieth century. If anything, it seems to be growing. I know we've recently had the centenary of the end of the First, but it won't be long before the next cause for memorial comes along. I was born almost twenty years after the end of the Second World War, and yet my childhood was steeped in its imagery. Films, books, comics, jokes about Germans, television and radio, political speeches, churchyards and cenotaphs, fly-pasts, marches, burnished medals and moth-eaten uniforms. Somewhere in Britain there must have been people talking about it *all the time* – how to sell it, mostly, or plan the next shindig. Anyone who had actually been there was mute, as a rule. At least, that was the case with my own family.

My father had been in the retreat from Burma (and never talked about it, or rather he did just once, although he did find me watching *The Bridge on the River Kwai* at Christmas one year – about halfway through – and he immediately stormed out of the room at the sight of all those well-fed, chirpy prisoners of war, whistling along the road. I tried to tell him that Alec Guinness had done a deal with the Jap commander and that earlier in the film the prisoners had all been malnourished, but he was too upset to hear. 'It wasn't like that', is all he would say. 'It wasn't like that.' I was thirteen and thought he didn't understand Great Art). My uncle was one of those POWs – not working on the bridge, but in a camp in Palembang – and came home weighing six stone and never said a word. Another uncle was shot down over France and spent the war as a prisoner of the Germans (and returned emptier). My mother's boyfriend was killed flying a Hurricane. So there is something good, I suppose, about the way our cultural lives are still filled with these wars, although once again it is all of *us* doing the talking, and not anyone who was actually there, fighting to survive.

My grandfather was an army chaplain in Jack's war, the first one, and preached at the Somme. In the second war he lived in a rectory in a tiny village in Rutland and tried to keep pace with the burials from the nearby RAF camp. Jack, meanwhile, had a starring role, broadcasting a series of *Postscripts*, his famous BBC radio speeches to which one-third of all British adults listened. He'd been brought in as an antidote to the German (Irish) propagandist, Lord Haw-Haw, whose broadcasts from Berlin were proving surprisingly popular with the British people, who were probably bored, or enjoying his absurd accent, but also eager for news of any kind at all. The government wanted someone who would pull in the crowds and Jack was a raging success, with his soothing Yorkshire style and robust patriotism and misty-eyed visits to the enemy-plane spotters in the Downs or his favourite old pie shop in Bradford (bombed, but still defiantly serving its famous pies).

Jack was so popular that there's a rumour Churchill became jealous, although I think more likely he bridled at Jack's socialism (Jack had even managed to slip an approving mention of the *Communist Manifesto* into his 6 October 1940 broadcast). 'Mr Priestley's war aims are not my war aims,' Churchill is said to have growled, and someone in his Cabinet took him at his word and got Jack pulled from the airwaves. There was an outcry, and Jack came back briefly, before he disappeared once again two months later, comparing Conservative Central Office to the Gestapo. In truth, Jack had already had enough, but it also seems to show, I'm sorry to say, that even then, when fighting a national war for survival against a brutal and murderous foreign enemy, a war that united the country in a way it had never been united before (and has never been since), even then our leaders were preoccupied with their other war: the eternal, shape-shifting, one-sided, unmentionable war between the people who own things and the people who have nothing. They were already looking ahead to what would come next, once the war was over, even before they knew it could be won, and they didn't want it to be someone like Jack who provided the answers.

Well, maybe. Except in 1933, and I'm pretty sure for the rest of his life, even with his wild talk about the Gestapo, that's not entirely the way Jack saw it. He had made a friend in Gateshead, a local communist called Bob, who took him on a tour of the town, and although Jack shared his rage at the destitution and the awful waste, he was never one to join a party: 'The world he [Bob] lives in is not the sad muddle that most of us have begun to recognise, but is a mysterious and melodramatic place of vast sinister conspiracies, in which capitalists and bosses and officials plot together to trick him and his mates.' It's the old question, still unanswered. Conspiracy? Or cock-up? Jack left it hanging. 'I shall not join Bob's party yet; but I wish I had a party fit for him to join.'

Crossing the Tyne on the ferry, from South to North Shields. It is beautiful on deck in the last of the December light. The river on the turn. Midnight blue and black velvet brushed with orange. Arc lights on the banks. The glow of Newcastle upriver. Cranes swaying in the twilight. There's half a moon in a spangled sky. I love the smell and slow thrum of ferries.

When Beryl went downriver in a police launch, she mourned 'all those boundaries and symbols and monuments pulverised into dust. Nothing left of the yards or the mills or the factories but heaps of bricks and broken timbers'. She bore witness to a landscape of loss. And what Jack wanted to know ('chilled and aching', fighting his fever) was whether the centuries of industry, the millions of tons of coal, and the great ships and the enormous fortunes, and the intolerable housing and the lost brutalized lives and the ineradicable black scars that befoul this once beautiful green estuary … what Jack wanted to know was whether any of it had been worth it. What had been the point of it all?

> What great work, I asked myself, owes its existence to those vast profits? What sciences and arts had they nourished? What new graces had they added to English life in return for what they had taken away from here? The ramshackle telephone exchange, at the back of my mind, put the call through, and I heard the bell ring and ring: but there was no reply.

He has a powerful voice, does Jack, and it's hard not to be swept along. I have struggled to shake off every one of my fellow travellers. But the Tyne has not stood still. And I am here in different times. Maybe it's the soft close comfort of the night, and the purposeful, forward plunge of the ferry, but as we head cross-river in the dark I am happy to let Jack's heroic grumbling recede in our wake. I am instead alert to a sense of promise.

Slipping down the east side of England. Jack and Beryl and I are all eager to get home – and that's my excuse for cutting this journey short. Lincoln is the final stop and we all check into the White Hart Hotel at the top of the hill. Beryl has a very nice room with a balcony overlooking the street, and I have a view of the cathedral. We can leave Jack warming himself by the fire in the lounge.

Lincoln is a very relaxed city. There are people sitting in the pubs in the middle of the afternoon who look as though they are actually enjoying themselves. Tourists or students, probably, but I cannot be sure. The medieval city sits at the top of the hill, with its castle and cathedral, bookshops and pubs, but down the steep hill there is a twenty-first-century high street. It is late afternoon by the time I step gingerly down the narrow way to the bottom, and I am taken aback by all the lights and action. M&S! Pizza Express! Boots and Poundland! Beryl and Jack would not have noticed much of a change at the top of the hill, but I am sure that down here the Christmas lights and the young men dragging carts of illuminated balloons would have held their attention, not to mention Wham!'s 'Last Christmas' carousing from every street corner and some really very keen deals to be had for 'buttock sculpting'.

The Edinburgh Woollen Mill is closing down ('Everything Must Go'). The craft beer shops look glossy and well stocked. The second-hand bookshops are mouldering under the dust of ages. Changing times. Lincoln is lovely, of course it is, but I have recently arrived from some very different high streets and I cannot shake the feeling that everything here is very precarious. There is a veneer that is easily scraped away. It is a cold evening, and there are many rough sleepers in the doorways, even here in Lincoln.

I head to the cathedral, seeking some solidity. Parts of it have been here since 1092 and John Ruskin thought it was the greatest piece of architecture in the British Isles. Gerald (hello again!) lived in Lincoln later in his life, writing and studying, when his efforts to win the St David's bishopric were all but over. I hug this bit of information to myself. Evensong is about to start, and I hang about shyly on the fringes, wondering whether to go in (it is being

held among the choir, but I'm not sure if anyone can join them).
A woman priest sees me and waves me through. 'Of course!' she
says. 'But I'm afraid we're a bit thin on the ground tonight. The
cold is keeping people away.' I am shown to one side. 'The seats at
the back are the most comfortable,' I am told by another woman
priest. I am the only person in my row, although across the aisle
there are twelve other congregants, all of them at least eighty years
old, staring rheumily in my direction. I feel – and I don't know if
this is the right word to convey my awkward isolation – but I feel
Londonish – and lost.

The service starts and the choir fills the vast hall with a chant
of absolute purity, even if one of them looks distractingly like
Graham Linehan, the Irish comedy writer. Maybe it's him? I guess
not, although I seem to remember an episode of *Father Ted* when
he was dressed as a Catholic priest and this could easily be him,
now, in his ecclesiastical robes, just twenty years later. But my
unease is slipping away. I'm here. The exquisite woodcarvings
in the pews and the soaring stone vaults, the pulse of the music,
chants and organ and the strong, high voice of the priest. I'm
back here with Gerald. And Beryl, who tried to climb the tower,
'up to the actual bells, but I had to give up half way because of
smoking so much. I thought I was going to die in church'.

They turn to Psalm 137: 'How shall we sing the Lord's song
in a strange land?' and I think I might be about to cry. Psalm
138: 'I will praise thee with my whole heart: before the gods
will I sing praise unto thee.' The angelic voices spiral upwards.
I am clutching the seat of my pew and all of a sudden I realize
I might be about to come rushing back to the faith I abandoned
over thirty-five years ago. Or it slipped away when I was looking
elsewhere. There's a sermon, about greed, and the shops of the
lower town, and then we are asked to pray for the library advisory
committee and for Philippa its chair and also for someone who

died in 1542 and I can see that Graham Linehan is picking his nose and then the service is over and I'm back outside in the cold.

There is a family walking home with two Labrador dogs. One of the children looks back at the cathedral. 'What a scary building,' he says – and maybe that's what churches now mean to most people. Dark, forbidding places, only seen in frightening films. It is true that a cold mist has gathered around the black medieval walls, but when I look back from the street, with the cathedral lit up in saffron and gold, I am staggered by its beauty.

I spend the evening in one of the many full and busy pubs. Everyone is smiling widely and looks like they should be in an episode of *Emmerdale* – although what's with all the kilts? And then at exactly ten o'clock, with the bells ringing out across the freezing streets, I walk back to the front of the cathedral for one last look. There's a man stumbling around, all alone, obviously very drunk, and he is trying to light a cigarette while also looking up at the sumptuous, golden façade, with its twin towers and extraordinary stone carvings, and you really will struggle to find anything more beautiful across this land, but as he leans back for an even better look (perhaps straining to see the famous tower clock) he trips and stumbles over a low wall and flounders backwards, in complete silence, before cartwheeling back into the ground and lying there as though he has been shot. The human comedy. It has been playing here for a thousand years.

Everyone. Somewhere. Sometime.

ELEVEN

Last Supper

'We sat down, jammed together, in a dining-room that can never have held more people in all its existence. It was not full, it was bursting. We could hardly lift the roast beef and apple tart to our mouths. Under the coloured-paper decorations, we sweated like bulls. The ale went down sizzling.'

J. B. PRIESTLEY, *ENGLISH JOURNEY*

Here's a question. Who would you ask to dinner, if you could choose from anyone in history? Jesus often gets a look-in. As do Dorothy Parker, Albert Einstein, Oscar Wilde, Frida Kahlo, Leonardo da Vinci, Cleopatra, Malcolm X, Mae West, Confucius … Which is all well and good, but this is my hard-to-beat selection: Enid Blyton, Wilkie Collins, Ithell Colquhoun, Celia Fiennes, Gerald of Wales, Edith Somerville, Violet 'Martin' Ross, J. B. Priestley, Beryl Bainbridge, Charles Dickens, James Boswell, Samuel Johnson.

We are going to need a round table. Charles Dickens would sulk and leave early if he found he hadn't been placed at the head, and he's unlikely to be the only one. I imagine an old-style room above a pub (anything too modern would be distracting). There'd be wide, mellow, antique pine floorboards (creaking and somewhat off-kilter), a Persian rug or two, a chandelier, that large round table (bare oak, guttering candles, gleaming silver cutlery, small bunches of wildflowers in vases, fresh linen napkins, several crystal glasses each), prints on the panelled walls (maybe some of Ithell's, to get the conversation rolling), more candles on the walls and mantelpiece and a log fire ablaze in the hearth (it is winter outside). I realize it all sounds very Dickensian, but that'll please the man himself – and our guests would recoil from any attempt at minimalism.

The menu is as follows, with something for everyone, except vegetarians:

Fresh Cornish oysters.
Soups – one cold (clear consommé); one hot and spicy
    (mulligatawny).
Fish – smelts fried in parsley butter.
Shellfish – broiled lobster.
Game – roast quail.
Entrée – roast beef. Vegetables.
Pudding – spotted dick, with custard.
Sorbet – orange.
Cheeses – British.
Fresh Fruit – strawberries, peaches, apricots, grapes …
Coffee or Tea.

Guests will be greeted with a bowl of hot gin punch (made by Dickens). Fresh lemonade is available throughout. The wines are French. The ale is British. Port will be served with the cheese. Brandy to finish. Coffee (with tea for Dr J). The ladies will *not* be leaving the table, whatever Dr Johnson may say (and nor will any of them be expected to sit on his knee and sing, although Beryl may get the urge).

Anyway, just the ten courses. They don't have to be large. We'll let Dickens carve (there's no stopping him, so we might as well submit with good humour). Gerald will find it all very surprising, but then again he probably ate lark and swan in his day. He will not be thanked for giving any sermons (on gluttony, for example), but he will be asked to say a short Latin grace at the start of the meal. If he doesn't, Sam Johnson will put him straight. I don't think we need any music during the meal – we can save it for later. Smoking is permitted. The windows will be flung wide to help with the fug and the acoustics (there are some very powerful voices here), although there is nothing to see outside but the black empty night.

I have thought hard about the seating plan. Some of it was easy. Beryl should sit next to Dr Johnson. She wrote a book about him, after all, but I am also certain that he'd enjoy her extravagant stories (so long as she doesn't slide under the table too early in the evening). Enid should sit next to Dickens. She will be thrilled to see some of his magic tricks, and he'll enjoy the Whoopee cushion she has brought with her. They can also compare notes about public readings, cruelty to animals and corporal punishment. I think we need to separate Wilkie from Dickens, and Boswell from Johnson (although the last two need to be kept close enough so Boswell cannot fret about missing some choice saying or other). Edith will be very happy chatting to Dickens, and he will be further energized by her beauty and wild laughter (and kept in line by her patrician manner). They can talk about hunting, dogs, servants, Home Rule and women's rights. Also easy is putting J. B. Priestley on the other side of Beryl (so many notes to compare), with a vast ashtray between them – and also next to Edith (I don't think they ever met, but they both loved Ireland and are easily roused to delight and indignation). Gerald should of course sit next to Enid (religion) and Martin (politics), while Martin and Boswell would have a scream: gossip, Tory politics, more gossip. I've placed Celia on the other side of Boswell because she may remind him not to get overexcited or drunk; then again, because we don't in fact know too much about her (other than that she was brave and enjoyed French claret and beer and a stormy coastline), we may find they leave together at the end of the night. Dr Johnson will keep an eye on them from the other side of the table. Wilkie, Celia and Ithell, meanwhile, can talk about Cornwall and ghosts and art, all of which are subjects on which Dr Johnson will want to expand (although what isn't?). If Johnson feels the need to argue with someone, and he will, he has eleven opinionated opponents to choose from.

At the end of the meal Gerald will say grace again and Dickens will shoot his sleeves and astonish the company with a little bit of magic. Jack, Edith and Martin will perform some music (piano, cello and violin) – and perhaps Celia will be persuaded to sing (who knows what musical talents may lurk?). If she won't, Enid most certainly will. Edith, Enid, Jack and Wilkie will organize the charades. And Dr Johnson will demonstrate his celebrated impersonation of a kangaroo (to the absolute astonishment of Gerald and Celia), by bundling up his tailcoat at the front to resemble a pouch, and bounding around the room with great, floorboard-shattering leaps. Martin will join in with her imitation of a howling fox terrier (it is extremely loud and life-like). Jack will massage Beryl's toes. Sometime later, Wilkie will introduce Ithell and Gerald to laudanum ('let me tell you about beavers', Gerald begins) and Boswell (very drunk, rebuffed by Celia) will take Dickens to one side and suggest they see if there's any action to be had outside on the street.

My seating plan is below and the age of the guests is given in brackets.

Charles Dickens (41)

Edith Somerville (28)

Enid Blyton (44)

J. B. Priestley (38)

Gerald of Wales (60)

Beryl Bainbridge (40)

Violet 'Martin' Ross (36)

Dr Samuel Johnson (63)

James Boswell (26)

Ithell Colquhoun (50)

Celia Fiennes (35)

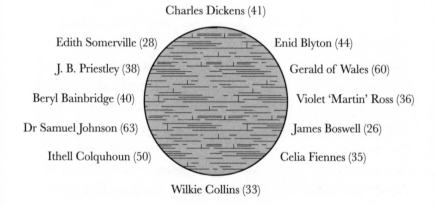

Wilkie Collins (33)

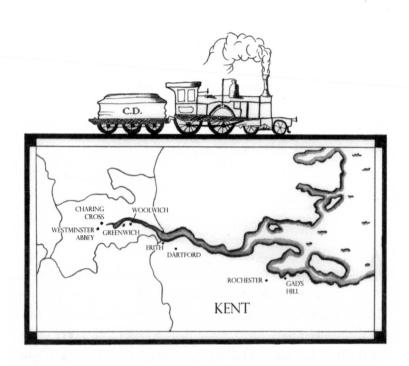

Charles Dickens,
Gad's Hill to Westminster Abbey, 14 June 1870

TWELVE

Larger Than Life

'Barkis is willin'.'

CHARLES DICKENS,
DAVID COPPERFIELD

And here, once more, comes Dickens. The Inimitable. Lying on his back, on a sofa, in the dining room of his home, Gad's Hill, in Higham, near Rochester, Kent. The house on the hill. He had walked past it with his father, when he was a very small child. His father had said that if he worked really hard he might one day come to own it. A ridiculous dream. He has lived here for thirteen years. His immense success. Riding the train between Higham and London. One time, walking through the night, thirty miles from Tavistock Square to Gad's Hill. And now ... it is 9 June 1870 and his doctor, Frank Beard, is here, and his sister-in-law, Georgina, and two of his daughters, Katey and Mamie, and his beloved, hopeless, first-born son, Charley. And Nelly, too. She has been sent for, from her home in Peckham. All here, watching him die. He is, or he was, fifty-eight years old.

Were *they* also here, at the end? Scrooge and Micawber, Quilp and Miss Havisham, Sikes, Bumble and Pip? There is a famous picture of Dickens by Robert Buss called *Dickens's Dream*, which hangs at his old home in Doughty Street, and in it Dickens is drowsing in a chair, pushed back from his desk (although his eyes are half-open), and dozens of his characters are gathering around him, in miniature, some of them pressing in, a tiny

Little Nell on his knee, begging his attention, but also in bed, dying, and there's David Copperfield, and Krook and Poor Jo, and Marley's Ghost, and all the Nicklebys (Mrs Nickleby, Kate and Ralph) and the boys of Dotheboys Hall, and the Dombeys and Jenny Wren and the Dedlocks and Skimpole and Betsey Trotwood and Uriah Heep, of course, and Mr Pickwick, and Oliver, Fagin and the Artful Dodger and – there are so many of them, mostly minding their own business, some of them fading away, but others crowding around their creator, with his wild hair and beard, and immaculate white collar, and his pen drooping in his hand. He looks lined, thoughtful, unusually quiet, worn, perhaps sad. He looks like he would be happy for it all to end.

Dickens's readers loved a good death scene and he always gave them what they wanted. 'Dead, your Majesty. Dead, my lords and gentlemen. Dead, right reverends and wrong reverends of every order. Dead, men and women, born with heavenly compassion in your hearts …' 'It is a far, far better thing that I do, than I have ever done; it is a far, far better rest that I go to than I have ever known.' 'No sleep so beautiful and calm, so free from trace of pain, so fair to look upon.'

No one quite agrees on his last words, but they are unlikely to have been the ones reported in *The Times* just after his death: 'Be natural my children. For the writer that is natural has fulfilled all the rules of art.' Surely he couldn't have composed these perfectly formed words, not as the stroke claimed him. He wouldn't even have agreed. What seems to have happened is that he wandered into dinner after a day's writing, rambled (at times incoherently) to his sister-in-law, Georgina, stood up, swaying, and she said to him: 'Come and lie down,' and he replied, 'Yes, on the ground,' and he did – just set himself down on the floor and someone fetched a sofa and put him on it and he lay there, mumbling, until he ran out of breath twenty-four hours later. 'And, it being low water, he went out with the tide.'

The house in Gad's Hill is still here, although at the moment it is a small private school and is only occasionally open to visitors. It is set back from the road, approached by a curve of carriage sweep, and the sight of it – so like its photos, in which Dickens poses with family or friends on its front steps – makes me quite breathless. Well, it's either that, or the brisk twenty-minute walk from Higham station. How Dickens would have scoffed. The house stands on the main Rochester to Gravesend road and in his last book, *The Mystery of Edwin Drood*, Dickens wrote that the days of the coach and the high road were now almost over, replaced by the all-conquering railways. And here we are. There are so many lorries and cars and builders' vans screeching past that it takes me five minutes to find a way to sprint across to the school.

I creep furtively around the boundary hedges (probably, on reflection, not the best way to behave around a school), wondering whether to stride up to the front door and tell them – what? That I love *Great Expectations*? 'Please let me in.' Dickens would have, I suppose, but the place looks peaceful and also forbidding. Hardly changed. Apparently Katey's art is still there, on the banisters. A teacher ambles past, notebooks and files under her arm. Hans Christian Andersen, the Swedish fairy tale writer, a lugubrious man with very little English, came to stay at Gad's Hill for two weeks and ended up staying for five, driving Dickens to distraction. Wilkie was there, too, and Andersen thought it was funny to decorate his wide-brimmed hat with daisy chains, secretly, and watch him wander off into the village, not that Wilkie would have cared. There are no daisies today on the well-trimmed lawns. It is a cold day in early January.

Perhaps it is right that Gad's Hill is now a school. I remember reading *Nicholas Nickleby* aged ten, all of us helped through it by the headmaster's wife over the course of one term. We thrilled to the jolting power of the descriptions, and the agony when Nicholas had to leave his family, and we sniggered at the strange, powdered, foreign milliner ('demmit'), but most of all I remember the terrifying headmaster, Wackford Squeers, and his awful wife, and young Wackford his son, and their beating of Smike and the other desperate boys (all of this resonating painfully in my own life) and then that moment of pure joy, that surging rush, when Nicholas seizes the cane at last and thrashes them all, rescuing Smike, the boys cheering, and fleeing for London, the nightmarish Wackford Squeers and his brutish son bellowing in pain and thwarted rage. That was Dickens. He was on our side. No wonder crowds of thousands turned out to pay their respects at Westminster Abbey, as soon as they heard, even if he had been very clear that he didn't want any pomp or fuss and he wanted to be buried as close to Gad's Hill as was possible. Rochester Cathedral was as far as he was prepared to be taken.

But Dickens was no longer in charge of his own life (Queen Victoria intervened, even though he couldn't have cared less about meeting her thirteen years earlier) and on 14 June 1870 his body in its oak coffin was taken through Higham village by carriage, accompanied by his family. And so off we go.

The tiny village of Higham slumbered in deep country in Dickens's day. Now, a much larger village, it lies in a battered strip of green belt, on the uneasy eastern fringes of London. Thirty miles to Tavistock Square. The Thames Estuary close by, just to the north. The walk from Gad's Hill to the station is downhill, past streets of bungalows, a block of housing ('Dickens Court'), high winter hedges punctured with narrow unfriendly driveways ('Private', 'Neighbourhood Watch', 'Beware. Dangerous Dogs'), a Shetland pony in a field, ignoring a huddle of sheep, the Gardeners

Arms pub (perhaps old enough to have seen Dickens's body carried by), the chip shop and the mini market ('Get Your Dream Ticket Today'), oast houses on the horizon, and pylons, orchards, more pylons, cows, 4 x 4s racing up the lane … the mashed edgelands of merry England. A woman in a van nearly reverses over me and gives a cheery thumbs-up.

My train is heading to Luton. Dickens was taken in his special train straight to Charing Cross, and then three horse-drawn carriages proceeded to the abbey, but I have to change at London Bridge. There is no one else on the platform, not even in the train when we lurch into life. Dickens left in sunshine. There are fields with cows, hedges and banks of brambles, tall bare poplars by the line, a farm, patches of scrub, the low dip of the Kentish hills, bound with pylons, a sewage depot and warehouses, a gasworks with the cylinders down low, a vast graveyard for rusting trains, marshland over towards the estuary (steady, Pip), the first uncertain graffiti, green ivy, terraces of housing, some of it, just maybe, already here when Dickens rolled past, and cars parked by the thousands, alone in the streets or herded together in their tarmac parks.

There are some dramatic chalk cliffs at Gravesend. An old quarry perhaps. Carved and left to rot. A lake. We pass through cuttings, thick with more dark ivy, under a damp sky. Car parks and Northfleet station, pylons everywhere, dead brown flowers hanging from the buddleia, wind turbines and warehouses – so many warehouses – and all the while the same grey spiked fence running at our side. Industry, now. Tall chimneys – dormant – huge cranes, the Thames basin coming into view (the sweet, oily Thames; Dickens's Thames), tower blocks in the distance, the train inching into Swanscombe – grey platform, grey railings, a grey shelter from the grey rain – but Dickens's train doesn't stop. Our doors squeal and beep. Into a tunnel, to the sound of another automated announcement: 'The next station will be Greenhithe, for Bluewater Shopping Centre.'

And here it is. 'Greenhithe for Bluewater' say the station signs. Shopping. All the riches of the earth. And the desolation. Supermarkets and warehouses. Gravel and sand mounded high for more building. Pylons. The last of the countryside vanished behind us. Gone. Beaten. This is bleak. I am fighting – and losing – a battle against a longing to return to another time, another place. My head is full of *David Copperfield*. Barkis flicking at his horse as the cart makes its way, so slowly, along the dusty empty lanes, past the dog roses and the wild marshes, the scent of honeysuckle, and Peggotty emerging from a hedge, shaking off the pollen, the butterflies rising in clouds, Peggotty drawing sandwiches and cakes from her floury apron. And here too, of course, is Enid. Always Enid. In her little village under a lovely, clear blue sky. The jolly policeman calling out good day. The angler, dozing with his cider-filled basket by the bulrush-fringed pond. The ancient oak on the green. Wading through golden meadows, with cornflowers and poppies, foxgloves and scabious, the buttercups and the daisies, tansy and clover and the warm, sunlit aroma of wild thyme. Skylarks on high, the boom of the bittern. What is this? Where does it all come from? Why would anyone pretend that this is what we still have? All those nature writers, all that filtered, blinkered, soft-focus maundering on TV. The timeless customs. The pigs and their pannage, rooting for acorns; the falcons wheeling in the sky; the eternal, unchanging, rolling of the seasons. Who are we trying to kid? Our land is tormented. Poisoned. Dying. None of this is any longer there, at least not in untroubled isolation. It probably never was. Not like that. But always there's Enid. Inescapable. With her beady-eyed robins and jolly little car. The endless disapproval. Children sent to their rooms. The beatings. The ration books and home-made jams. The suspicious foreigners and thieving, brown, bearded outsiders. Her insane pogonophobia. Please, for the love of God, just fuck off, Enid, and leave us all alone.

I may have nodded off. I'd dropped into the Sir John Falstaff pub earlier, for a pint of Cornish pale ale. It is opposite Dickens's old home and he used to go there sometimes to cash his cheques. He'd called in on the morning of 8 June, the penultimate day of his life, to exchange a cheque with the owner for £22. Life was going on, so far as he was concerned. The pub is reassuringly old school, by which I mean 1970s psychedelic carpets and listless curtains and not Dickensian at all: no log fires or brass bonhomie. I join three old men swapping familiar stories, and order salt and vinegar crisps (no lunch on a Monday). The beer is good. There are prints of Mr Pickwick and Charles Dickens on the walls, and foggy London streets, and in the corner the fruit machine is aglow. No doubt Dickens would have rung up the jackpot. We are all very happy, although I have a train to catch.

I come awake, emerging from a long tunnel. The train is still empty, but the bleached image of a Victorian woman, with crinoline skirts and a wide hat, and a small pale child, is fading from the seat opposite. What a terrible journey it must have been, on this train, with Dickens dead in his coffin, moving inexorably towards London. He spent his life journeying to and from the city and he made his characters do the same. There are more warehouses and housing out of the window. How big can London grow? There's almost nothing Dickens would recognize. New houses. Marketing suites. Portakabins all along the route. Bales of rubbish for recycling. Deserted caravans (looking curiously Dickensian). There's a school playground, where the children are running about, leaping over tyres, skipping, shoving, screaming, giggling. Up they rise. They were here when Dickens passed, his family – too few and too small – staring from the carriage windows.

And now we're through Abbey Wood and the housing is growing taller. There are timber yards and more supermarkets. Allotments, looking loved. Solar panels, satellite dishes and flags on the roofs. Where is the squalor that Dickens wrote about? It's not here. Not the kind he knew. At Charlton someone has scrawled 'Call in Sick' in huge letters just outside the station, something Dickens never did. More tunnels. More houses. There is no end or beginning to London. Just streets and bridges and level cross-ings, playing fields, gum trees and proliferating spasms of graffiti.

The spiked grey fence is still tracking us, now covered in thick effusions of the wild clematis known as old man's beard. Wilkie! He will be waiting at the abbey. The woods around Gad's Hill are full of old man's beard, where Dickens loved to walk, alone or with his guests. They are empty, on a Monday in January, and the only people I pass are builders working in the wide fore-courts of the large detached homes. The woods are quiet, and hard to reach, what with all the signs saying 'Private' and 'Keep Out'. The A2 is over the hill, a background howl and moan, people on the move. 'Danger of Death', I am reminded by a bright yellow sign on a telegraph pole. And down at Crabbles Bottom, a scrap of ancient woodland just next to the A2 that the local council is doing its best to nurture, someone has torn down the fencing and sprayed the ground with black bags of litter, most of them burst open, a sodden toy giraffe smeared into the mud. At the end of his working life Dickens had lost almost all humour and hope, until only the rage was left. But we don't have to follow down that path, or remember him that way. Although sometimes it is hard.

We ride into London and its death-dealing air. In a great vista of new housing, stretching down to the Thames and away to the south, it is only the old pubs and churches, and sometimes the warehouses that survive. I wonder if Dickens is still with us, or if he too is fading from our lives. At Greenwich station there is an upsurge of energy on the platform, of the kind Dickens needed and fed upon, and a noisy group of schoolchildren swaggers onto the train. Deptford Creek slops muddily down below, hiding Fagin's treasures. More, taller towers. The streets start to narrow and crowd. At last this is something that Dickens would recognize: tight little lanes, pubs, dark buildings, black railway arches, a firestorm of graffiti ('ACAB' written in letters eight feet tall), the tip of the gherkin ('saucy!' yells Nancy), and here we are, clanking into London Bridge, and on for Charing Cross, never mind the gap.

At last, the Thames, 'stretching away to the great ocean, Death'. We have not left anyone behind. Not even Enid. The London Eye and a cider lodge and the train crossing the river, and to either side there are people strolling in the short January afternoon over the elegant new footbridge. The train comes to a halt by the side of the Playhouse Theatre, opened twelve years after Dickens's death. It is what it is. And these are the times we live in.

There were perhaps fourteen people in Westminster Abbey to see Dickens's coffin lowered into the ground, as well as a few idle (or even startled) sightseers. At least they had listened to him to that extent, and kept the moment as private as possible. Perhaps Nelly was lurking, although no one says that she was. Wilkie was there, of course, along with his droopy brother Charles, an artist, who ten years earlier had married Katey Dickens, much to her father's irritation. She left for her honeymoon wearing funereal black, even though, so far as we know, no one had died.

There are hundreds of people in the abbey today, many of them milling and bumping around 'Poets' Corner', trampling over Dickens and his peers. He really didn't want to be here. Perhaps he's happy to be this close to Sam Johnson, although they would surely annoy one another after a while. Or maybe not. The place has a strange atmosphere, with tour groups drifting by, pausing at Kipling 'the writer of *The Jungle Book* and the poem "If" and, next to him, Charles Dickens, buried here against his wishes. You probably know him best from *Oliver*'. When the news of Dickens's death reached his friend, the poet Longfellow, in Boston, he refused to believe it: Dickens 'was so full of life', he wrote, 'it did not seem possible he could die'. Longfellow has a bust, erected by his 'British friends', but many of the other poets, writers and dramatists memorialized here are not in fact buried in the abbey. One exception is Sam Johnson – interred in 'the cheapest manner', as Sir John Hawkins fumed that Sam had left everything to his old servant and friend, the freed slave Francis Barber.

Wilkie lingered for a while. He probably chatted to his brother Charles, then waved him off with Katey. He may have talked to John Forster, although they were never close. Forster thought Wilkie a bad influence. He was more likely to have spent time with Frank Beard, who was his doctor as well as Dickens's, and a good friend. Maybe his gout was troubling him. In any case, he will have stayed, I am sure, to see the ground closed over Dickens (although he did not live long enough to know the extraordinary radiance with which the brass letters shine from the worn black stone of Dickens's grave). And then he will have left, his thoughts turning to his new mistress and the next calming draught of laudanum. Straightening his waistcoat. And limping off into the night.

The Company
of Great Writers

Dame Beryl Margaret Bainbridge
21 November 1932–2 July 2010

Novelist, playwright, journalist, TV presenter, actor and artist. Shortlisted for the Booker Prize a record five times. Born in Allerton, Liverpool, grew up in Formby, her father a failed businessman, her mother a housewife, one older brother. Worked at the Liverpool Playhouse Theatre from the age of seventeen, where she met Austin (married in 1954, two children, divorced in 1959). Moved to London for good in 1963. Had one further child with the author Alan Sharp. Died in London.

Gerald de Barry
(*aka* Giraldus Cambrensis, Gerald of Wales)
c.1146–c.1223

The youngest son of the Norman knight William de Barry and his Norman-Welsh wife, Angharad. Always destined to join the Church (he built sand cathedrals, not castles, on the beach near his childhood home), but spent his adult years vainly longing and fruitlessly plotting to become the Bishop of St David's. Found time to write many books, including *Topography of Ireland*, *Journey through Wales* and *Description of Wales*. Died in Hereford, or maybe Lincoln, sometime between 1220 and 1223.

Enid Mary Blyton
11 August 1897–28 November 1968

Born in East Dulwich, London. The daughter of Thomas, a salesman, and Theresa, a housewife. Two younger brothers. Left home at eighteen to become a teacher. The author of at least 750 books, with worldwide sales of over eight gazillion, translated into every possible language. Founder of numerous clubs. Married Hugh Alexander Pollock in 1924, two children, divorced in 1943, married Kenneth Darrell Waters the same year. Unofficially banned by the BBC. Keen gardener.

James Boswell, Ninth Laird of Auchinleck
29 October 1740–19 May 1795

Born in Edinburgh and destined to become the Ninth Laird of Auchinleck. Two younger brothers. Father a judge. Studied Law at Edinburgh University from the age of thirteen, but with no enthusiasm. Moved to London to mingle with 'the great, the gay, and the ingenious', brought back to Edinburgh by his father, escaped again to London where he met Samuel Johnson soon afterwards and never let go. Married Margaret in 1769 with whom he had five children. Author of the world's greatest biography, the *Life of Johnson*.

(William) Wilkie Collins
8 January 1824–23 September 1889

Lived in London all his life. Wrote many sensational novels, as well as numerous short stories and plays. Author of *The Moonstone* and *The Woman in White*. Son of William, a conventional artist, and the charming hostess Harriet. One brother. Friends with

Charles Dickens. Had long-running (overlapping) relationships with Caroline Graves from 1856 and with Martha Rudd from 1864 (with whom he had three children). Occasional champion of women's rights.

(Margaret) Ithell Colquhoun
9 October 1906–11 April 1988

Surrealist artist and visionary author, born in Assam, educated in England. Divided her time between Hampstead and her beloved Lamorna Valley in south Cornwall. Author of *Goose of Hermogenes* and *The Living Stones*. Married the Belgian surrealist Toni del Renzio in 1943, divorced in 1947. Died in Lamorna Valley.

Charles John Huffam Dickens
7 February 1812–9 June 1870

The Chief. The Inimitable. Son of John and Elizabeth Dickens. Sent to work in a blacking factory from the age of twelve. Journalist and then serial novelist. Author of fifteen novels, plus plays, journalism and short stories. Married to Catherine in 1836, ten children, unhappily broke with her in 1858. Campaigner, philanthropist, actor, magician, public performer, entertainer. Defined an atmosphere, an era, a city, a nation … Dickensian.

Celia Fiennes
7 June 1662–10 April 1741

Travelled through every English county, most of them many times, when the roads could not have been worse. Kept a detailed journal, finally published in 1888. From a family of religious Nonconformists. Daughter of Colonel Nathaniel Fiennes, an unsuccessful soldier on Parliament's side in the Civil War, and Frances. Never married. Died in Hackney, East London.

Samuel Johnson
18 September 1709–13 December 1784

Born in Lichfield to a spendthrift bookseller, Michael, and his wife Sarah. Afflicted with scrofula, probably also Tourette's syndrome, and taken when a small boy to be 'touched' by Queen Anne, who was the last British monarch to perform this 'cure' (it didn't work with Sam). Married Elizabeth 'Tetty' Porter in 1735. Spent her money on running a failed school. Moved to London in 1737. Journalist, biographer and poet. Author of the parable *Rasselas*. Took nine years to compile the English language's first major dictionary. Lover of clubs and conversation. The subject of Boswell's ur-biography. Quotable.

Violet Florence Martin (*pseud.* Martin Ross)
11 June 1862–21 December 1915

One half of the writing duo that produced *The Real Charlotte*, the Irish R.M. stories and twenty-nine other books (sixteen of them after her death). Born in Connemara, County Galway, into the Anglo-Irish Ascendancy, the youngest of sixteen children of James and Anna Martin. Met Edith Somerville in 1886 and wrote together (and lived together when they could) until her death in a nursing home at Cork. Keen fox hunter.

John Boynton Priestley
13 September 1894–14 August 1984

Born in Bradford. Father, Jonathan, a teacher; mother, Emma, probably a millworker, died when he was two. Fought in the First World War, wounded and gassed three times. Prolific author of novels, plays (including *An Inspector Calls* and *Time and the Conways*) and reams of journalism and non-fiction. Hugely popular broadcaster. Inadvertently started the Campaign for Nuclear Disarmament with an article for the *New Statesman* in 1957. Married three times: Emily 'Pat' Tempest (1921–1925); Jane Wyndham-Lewis (1926–1953); and Jacquetta Hawkes (from 1953). Five children. Died at home near Stratford-upon-Avon.

Edith Anna Œnone Somerville
2 May 1858–8 October 1949

One half of the writing duo that produced *The Real Charlotte*, the Irish R.M. stories and twenty-nine other books (sixteen of them after the death of her writing partner, 'Martin Ross'). Born in Corfu (into the Anglo-Irish Ascendancy), eldest of ten children to Thomas and Adelaide. Trained as an artist in Paris. Met Violet Martin in 1886 and wrote together (and lived together when they could) until Martin's death in 1915. Fox hunter and Irish nationalist. Died in Castletownshend, County Cork.

Acknowledgements

Love and thanks to Anna, who set me on the path to Enid Blyton, and walked some of the way, and made all of this possible; also Natalie, Alex and Esme for the comments and encouragement. Thank you, once again, Sam Carter of Oneworld Publications, for the pitch-perfect support and thoughtful editing (and the C. L. R. James books); Jonathan Bentley-Smith, also of Oneworld; Kathleen McCully, for the sharp copy-editing; to Alice Carter, for the glorious maps; Josie Sommer of Seven Stories, the National Centre for Children's Books; Louisa Price, Curator, Charles Dickens Museum; Miranda Kaufmann, for her research help, and also Michael Obajanu; Martin Fiennes for letting me loose on Celia Fiennes' journal; Nathaniel and Mariette Fiennes; Ivor Fiennes; my brother, Toby Fiennes, especially for the family tree; Aunt Biddy; wordsmith Ruth Jarvis, for the title!; Andrew 'Rudi' White; Tom Holland; Nick Marston; Conor McCutcheon; Felicity Lawrence; Simon Rohde, Judith Hawley and Philip Horne, for many suggestions; Gill Morgan; Angharad Penrhyn Jones; Kevin Ebbutt, for introducing me to Ithell Colquhoun; Mick Drury of Trees for Life, and my bothy-buddies Howard, Roy and Fitch; Nick from the Wirral; Brendan King, for getting me started with Beryl Bainbridge; Caroline Knox of the Boswell Trust; Geoff Metzger, for the Seven Ages; Ben Tippet; and last but very much not least, my enormously helpful agent Rebecca Winfield (david-luxtonassociates.co.uk).

Permissions

I have quoted from many writers and poets in these pages and am extremely grateful to all the copyright holders who allowed me to use their words. I made strenuous efforts to secure permissions (reluctantly jettisoning some favourites) and apologise if there are any omissions or mistakes. Please get in touch if so! You'll find most of the sources in the Select Bibliography, but I would also like to acknowledge the following:

Lines from 'Praise of a Man' © 1990 Norman MacCaig, from *Collected Poems*, published by Chatto & Windus. Reproduced by permission of the estate of Norman MacCaig.

Extract from *Cat's Eye* by Margaret Atwood, Copyright © 1988 by O. W. Toad, Ltd. Used in the UK and Commonwealth, excluding Canada, by permission of Bloomsbury Publishing Plc. Used in the United States by permission of Doubleday, an imprint of the Knopf Doubleday Publishing Group, a division of Penguin Random House LLC. All rights reserved. Reprinted in Canada by permission of Emblem/McClelland & Stewart, a division of Penguin Random House Canada Limited. All rights reserved.

Extracts from Enid Blyton reproduced by permission of Hodder Children's Books, an imprint of Hachette Children's Books, Carmelite House, 50 Victoria Embankment, London, EC4Y 0DZ.

Extracts from *The Living Stones* by Ithell Colquhoun, 1957, reproduced by permission of Peter Owen Publishers, UK.

Select Bibliography

This could go on a while, except I won't let it. Instead, here are all the books mentioned in the text, plus a handful of others that were especially engrossing when I was researching and writing *Footnotes*. I've put the primary texts for each journey first.

GENERAL

AA, *Illustrated Guide to Britain* (Drive Publications, 1971)

Anderson, Sarah, *Anderson's Travel Companion: A Guide to the Best Non-fiction and Fiction for Travelling* (Scholar Press, 1995)

Briggs, Katharine M., *British Folk Tales and Legends: A Sampler* (Routledge and Kegan Paul, 1977)

Chaudhuri, Nirad C., *A Passage to England* (Macmillan, 1959)

Crane, Nicholas, *Great British Journeys* (Weidenfeld & Nicolson, 2017)

Davidson, Peter, *The Idea of North* (Reaktion Books, 2005)

Drabble, Margaret, *A Writer's Britain* (Thames & Hudson, 2009)

Grigson, Geoffrey, *The Shell Country Alphabet: The Classic Guide to the British Countryside* (Penguin Books, 1966)

Hibbert, Christopher, *The English: A Social History 1066–1945* (Guild Publishing, 1987)

Holmes, Richard, *Footsteps: Adventures of a Romantic Biographer* (Penguin Books, 1985). I started here.

Ingrams, Richard (Ed.), *England: An Anthology* (Collins, 1990)

Ishiguro, Kazuo, *The Buried Giant* (Faber & Faber, 2015)

Kaufmann, Miranda, *Black Tudors: The Untold Story* (Oneworld Publications, 2017)

Klein, Naomi, *This Changes Everything* (Penguin Books, 2014)

Legget, Jane, *Local Heroines: A Travel Guidebook to Women's History in Great Britain* (Pandora, 1988)

Macfarlane, Robert, *The Old Ways: A Journey on Foot* (Penguin Books, 2013)

McGarvey, Darren, *Poverty Safari: Understanding the Anger of Britain's Underclass* (Luath Press, 2017)

Minshull, Duncan (Ed.), *While Wandering: A Walking Companion* (Vintage Books, 2014)

Monbiot, George, *Feral: Rewilding the Land, Sea and Human Life* (Allen Lane, 2013)

Montgomery, Charles, *Happy City: Transforming Our Lives through Urban Design* (Penguin Books, 2013)

Morley, Paul, *The North (and Almost Everything In It)* (Bloomsbury, 2013)

Morton, H. V., *I Saw Two Englands* (Methuen & Co., 1942)

Morton, H. V., *In Search of England* (Methuen & Co., 1927)

Morton, H. V., *The Call of England* (Methuen & Co., 1928)

Orwell, George, *Inside the Whale and Other Essays* (Penguin Books, 1957)

Orwell, George, *The Road to Wigan Pier* (Victor Gollancz, 1937)

Overy, Richard, *The Morbid Age: Britain Between the Wars* (Penguin Books, 2009)

Paxman, Jeremy, *The English: A Portrait of a People* (Penguin Group, 1998)

Priestley, J. B., *The English* (William Heinemann, 1973)

Roberts, Alice, *The Celts: Search for a Civilisation* (Heron Books, 2015)

Rutherford, Adam, *A Brief History of Everyone Who Ever Lived: The Stories in Our Genes* (Weidenfeld & Nicolson, 2016)

Schama, Simon, *A History of Britain Vols. I–III* (BBC Books, 2000–2002)

Schama, Simon, *Landscape & Memory* (HarperCollins, 1995)

Sheers, Owen, *A Poet's Guide to Britain* (Penguin Books, 2010)

Stringer, Chris, *Homo Britannicus: The Incredible Story of Human Life in Britain* (Penguin Books, 2006)

Thomas, R. S., *Collected Poems 1945–1990* (Weidenfeld & Nicolson, 2000)

Tombs, Robert, *The English & Their History* (Penguin Books, 2014)

Westwood, Jennifer and Simpson, Jacqueline, *The Lore of the Land: A Guide to England's Legends, from Spring-Heeled Jack to the Witches of Warboys* (Penguin Books, 2005)

Wilson, A. N., *The Victorians* (Arrow Books, 2003)

Winder, Robert, *The Last Wolf: The Hidden Springs of Englishness* (Little, Brown, 2017)

ENID BLYTON & DORSET

Enid Blyton wrote over 750 books. There's as complete a list as you'd think possible at the Enid Blyton Society website (enidblytonsociety.co.uk) in the 'Cave of Books', which also includes a list of her journalism and poetry. My favourite has always been *Five Go Adventuring Again*.

Blyton, Enid, *The Story of My Life* (Pitkins, 1952)

Baverstock, Gillian, *Enid Blyton* (Evans Brothers, 1997)

Howard, Nesta and Underwood, Spencer, *The Penguin Guide to Wilts and Dorset* (Penguin Books, 1949)

Norman, Dr Andrew, *Enid Blyton and Her Enchantment with Dorset* (Halsgrove, 2005)

Pitt-Rivers, Michael, *A Shell Guide to Dorset* (Faber & Faber, 1935)

Pollock, Ida, *Starlight: A Memoir* (Authors Online, 2009)

Smallwood, Imogen, *A Childhood at Green Hedges: A Fragment of Autobiography by Enid Blyton's Daughter* (Methuen Children's Books, 1989)

Stoney, Barbara, *Enid Blyton: The Biography* (Hodder & Stoughton, 1974; Tempus Publishing, 2006)

Also, the film drama *Enid* (BBC, 2009)

WILKIE COLLINS, ITHELL COLQUHOUN & CORNWALL

Wilkie was prolific – the best places to start are *The Moonstone* and *The Woman in White*. There are books in print by Ithell Colquhoun at peterowen.com and psupress.org.

Collins, Wilkie, *Rambles Beyond Railways* (out of print; first published 1851)

Colquhoun, Ithell, *The Living Stones* (Peter Owen, 1957)

Ackroyd, Peter, *Wilkie Collins* (Vintage, 2013)

Betjeman, John, *A Shell Guide to Cornwall* (Faber & Faber, 1964)

Carey, Peter, *The Chemistry of Tears* (Faber & Faber, 2012)

Clarke, William M., *The Secret Life of Wilkie Collins* (Allison & Busby, 1988)

Gasson, Andrew, *Wilkie Collins: An Illustrated Guide* (Oxford University Press, 1998)

Jenkins, Elizabeth, *The Mystery of King Arthur* (Michael Joseph, 1975)

Lycett, Andrew, *Wilkie Collins: A Life of Sensation* (Windmill Books, 2014)

Peters, Catherine, *The King of Inventors: A Life of Wilkie Collins* (Secker & Warburg, 1991).

Smith, Laura, Tassi, Enrico and Bennett, Eloise, *Virginia Woolf Exhibition Book* (Tate Publishing, 2018)

Time Out Guide to Devon & Cornwall (Time Out Guides, 2012)

White, Paul, *Druids in the South-West?* (Bossiney Books, 2017)

White, Rupert, *The Re-enchanted Landscape: Earth Mysteries, Paganism & Art in Cornwall 1950–2000* (Antenna Publications, 2017)

CELIA FIENNES & THE WEST COUNTRY

Fiennes, Celia, *The Journeys of Celia Fiennes* (Ed. Christopher Morris, Cresset Press, 1949)

Douglass, Frederick, *My Bondage and My Freedom* (Penguin Books, 2003)

Douglass, Frederick, *The Portable Frederick Douglass* (Penguin Books, 2016)

Fiennes, Celia and Morris, Christopher, *The Illustrated Journeys of Celia Fiennes* (Michael Joseph, 1988)

GERALD OF WALES, EDITH SOMERVILLE, MARTIN ROSS & WALES

Gerald of Wales, *The Journey Through Wales / The Description of Wales* (Trans. by Lewis Thorpe, Penguin Books, 1978)

Somerville, E. Œ. and Ross, Martin, *Beggars on Horseback: A Riding Tour in North Wales* (out of print; William Blackwood & Sons, 1895)

Collis, Maurice, *Somerville & Ross: A Biography* (Faber & Faber, 1968)

Davies, John, *A History of Wales* (Penguin Books, 2007)

Griffith, Wyn, *The Welsh* (Penguin Books, 1950)

Jones, Gwyn and Ffowc Elis, Islwyn, *Classic Welsh Short Stories* (Oxford University Press, 1971)

Kightly, Charles, *A Mirror of Medieval Wales: Gerald of Wales and His Journey of 1188* (Cadw: Welsh Historic Monuments, 1988)

Lewis, Gifford, *Somerville and Ross: The World of the Irish R.M.* (Viking, 1985)

Lewis, Gifford (Ed.), *The Selected Letters of Somerville and Ross* (Faber & Faber, 1989)

Rhys, John and Brynmor-Jones, David, *The Welsh People* (T. Fisher Unwin, 1906)

Somerville, E. Œ. and Ross, Martin, *The Irish R.M. Complete* (Faber & Faber, 1928)

Somerville, E. Œ. and Ross, Martin, *The Real Charlotte* (Capuchin Classics, 2011)

Somerville, E. Œ. and Ross, Martin, *Wheel-Tracks* (Longmans, Green & Co., 1923)

Williams, Gwyn A., *When Was Wales? A History of the Welsh* (Penguin Books, 1991)

J. B. PRIESTLEY & BERYL BAINBRIDGE, THE MIDLANDS, THE NORTH & LINCOLN

Bainbridge, Beryl, *An Awfully Big Adventure* (Duckworth, 1989)

Bainbridge, Beryl, *English Journey or The Road to Milton Keynes* (Duckworth/BBC, 1984)

Priestley, J. B., *Bright Day* (Penguin Books, 1946)

Priestley, J. B., *English Journey* (William Heinemann, 1934)

Cook, Judith, *Priestley* (Bloomsbury, 1997)

Dicky Sam, *Liverpool and Slavery: An Historical Account of the Liverpool–Africa Slave Trade* (A. Bowker & Son, 1884)

Gray, Dulcie, *J. B. Priestley* (Sutton Publishing, 2000)

Hughes, Psiche, *Beryl Bainbridge: Artist, Writer, Friend* (Thames & Hudson, 2012)

King, Brendan, *Beryl Bainbridge: Love by All Sorts of Means* (Bloomsbury, 2016)

Priestley, J. B., *Delight* (William Heinemann, 1949; Great Northern Books, 2018)

Priestley, J. B., *Outcries and Asides* (William Heinemann, 1974). Mustn't grumble …

Priestley, J. B., *Rain Upon Gadshill* (William Heinemann, 1941)

Priestley, J. B., *The Priestley Companion* (Penguin Books, 1951)

Scott, Walter Dixon, *Liverpool 1907* (A. & C. Black, 1907)

CHARLES DICKENS & WILKIE COLLINS, THE LAKE DISTRICT & THE NORTH

If you don't know Dickens, I would start with *Great Expectations*. Or maybe *Oliver Twist*, *David Copperfield* or *Nicholas Nickleby*. Probably not *Pickwick Papers*. Certainly not *Our Mutual Friend*. *Bleak House* is also a good introduction, although Esther is irritating and the tone is undeniably … bleak. If the size of the novels is daunting, perhaps try a ghost story. *The Signalman*, for instance, has some classic Dickensian railway action.

Collins, Wilkie and Dickens, Charles, *The Lazy Tour of Two Idle Apprentices* (out of print; first published 1858)

Ackroyd, Peter, *Dickens* (Vintage, 2002)

Britton, John and Wedlake Brayley, Edward, *The Beauties of England and Wales; or Delineations, Topographical, Historical, and Descriptive, of Each County, Vol. III* (out of print; first published 1802)

James, C. L. R., *Beyond a Boundary* (Stanley Paul & Co., 1963; Serpent's Tail, 1994)

James, C. L. R., *Cricket* (Allison & Busby, 1986)

Nayder, Lillian, *Unequal Partners: Charles Dickens, Wilkie Collins, and Victorian Authorship* (Cornell University Press, 2002)

Slater, Michael, *Charles Dickens* (Yale University Press, 2011)

Tomalin, Claire, *Charles Dickens: A Life* (Viking, 2011). Near definitive.

Tomalin, Claire, *The Invisible Woman: The Story of Nelly Ternan and Charles Dickens* (Viking, 1990)

SAMUEL JOHNSON & JAMES BOSWELL, SCOTLAND

All you really need is Boswell's *Life of Johnson*.

Boswell, James, *The Journal of a Tour to the Hebrides*
Johnson, Samuel, *A Journal to the Western Islands of Scotland* (Penguin Books, 1984)

Bainbridge, Beryl, *According to Queeney* (Little, Brown, 2001)
Bone, Stephen, *A Shell Guide to the West Coast of Scotland: Skye to Oban* (B. T. Batsford, 1938)
Boswell, James, *Everybody's Boswell: Being the Life of Samuel Johnson* (G. Bell & Sons, 1935)
Boswell, James, *The Journals of James Boswell 1762–1795* (Yale University Press, 1991)
Boswell, James, *The London Journal 1762–1763* (William Heinemann, 1950)
Delaney, Frank, *A Walk to the Western Isles: After Boswell & Johnson* (HarperCollins, 1994)
Dunn, Douglas, *Scotland: An Anthology* (HarperCollins, 1991)
Johnson, Samuel, *The History of Rasselas, Prince of Abyssinia* (Nonsuch Publishing, 2007)
Morton, H. V., *In Search of Scotland* (Methuen, 1929)
Nokes, David, *Samuel Johnson, A Life* (Faber & Faber, 2009)
Picard, Liza, *Dr. Johnson's London* (Weidenfeld & Nicolson, 2000)

RESOURCES

GENERAL

Oxford Dictionary of National Biography (oxforddnb.com): the first stop for any biographical enquiry.

Trees for Life (treesforlife.org.uk): support them!

Vision of Britain (visionofbritain.org.uk): holds the full texts of numerous journeys, including those of James Boswell, Celia Fiennes, Gerald of Wales and Samuel Johnson.

Wikipedia (en.wikipedia.org): I would have been lost without it.

BERYL BAINBRIDGE

Someone should set up a Beryl Bainbridge Society.

ENID BLYTON

Enid Blyton (enidblyton.co.uk): the official website, run by Hachette, her publisher.

Enid Blyton Society (enidblytonsociety.co.uk): everything you ever needed to know. Run by super-fans (and questions answered by Barney the dog …).

Seven Stories: National Centre for Children's Books (sevenstories. org.uk): based in Gateshead. Visit to view a collection of Enid's diaries, letters, first editions and more.

JAMES BOSWELL

Boswell Book Festival (boswellbookfestival.co.uk): a festival of biography in Ayrshire, run by the Boswell Trust.

Boswell Society (theboswellsociety.wordpress.com).

The Journal of a Tour to the Hebrides with Samuel Johnson (visionofbritain. org.uk/travellers/Boswell): the full text is available here.

WILKIE COLLINS

Wilkie Collins Society (wilkiecollinssociety.org): this was founded in 1980.

ITHELL COLQUHOUN

Ithell Colquhoun (ithellcolquhoun.co.uk): an all-encompassing site managed by Richard Shillitoe.

CHARLES DICKENS

Charles Dickens Museum (dickensmuseum.com): visit to soak up the atmosphere, or to consult the superb archive.

Dickens Fellowship (dickensfellowship.org): a worldwide fellowship of Dickens fans, founded in 1902.

Dickens Society (dickenssociety.org): dedicated to spreading the word of the great man.

CELIA FIENNES

Through England on a Side Saddle in the Time of William and Mary (visionofbritain.org.uk/travellers/Fiennes): Celia's journeys online.

Broughton Castle (broughtoncastle.com): home, once upon a time, to Celia's scheming grandfather.

SAMUEL JOHNSON

A Journey to the Western Isles of Scotland (visionofbritain.org.uk/travellers/Johnson): the full text is available here.

Johnson Society (johnsonnew.wordpress.com): founded in 1910.

Johnson Society of London (johnsonsocietyoflondon.org): founded in 1928.

Dr Johnson's House (drjohnsonshouse.org): visit Dr Johnson's London home, much tidier than it once was.

J. B. PRIESTLEY

J. B. Priestley Society (jbpriestley.co.uk): founded in 1997.

University of Bradford Library J. B. Priestley Archive (https:// bradford.ac.uk/library/special-collections/collections/j-b-priestley-archive): Jack opened this library in 1975, and here is its collection devoted to the great man.

MARTIN ROSS & EDITH SOMERVILLE

Somerville and Ross Manuscript Collection (https://archiveshub. jisc.ac.uk/data/gb752-srmc): a vast selection of diaries, letters and memorabilia held at Queen's University, Belfast.

Drishane House (drishane.com): visit the Somerville home in south-west Ireland. Admire Edith's art and taste in wallpaper. Stay in a cottage. Loiter at the graves of Somerville and Ross.

GERALD OF WALES

The Itinerary of Archbishop Baldwin through Wales (visionofbritain.org. uk/travellers/Cambrensis_Tour): the full text is available here.

The Description of Wales (http://www.gutenberg.org/ebooks/1092): the full text is available here.